Richard M. Hunt.
Studio. Newport. 1884.

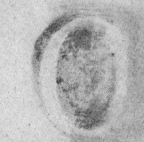

The Gilded Life of Richard Morris Hunt

ARCHITECTURE & ART FOR AN AMERICAN CIVILIZATION

Sam Watters

LIBRARY LIBRARY OF CONGRESS

Ah, silent multitudes,
ye are a part
Of the wise architect's
supreme and glorious art!

Richard Watson Gilder
on the Chicago World's Columbian Exposition, 1893

Library of Congress
101 Independence Avenue SE
Washington, DC 20540-4980, USA

First published in 2024 by GILES
An imprint of D Giles Limited
66 High Street
Lewes, BN7 1XG, UK
gilesltd.com

Library of Congress Cataloging-in-
Publication Data
Names: Watters, Sam, 1954- author.
Title: The gilded life of Richard Morris
Hunt : architecture & art for an American
civilization / Sam Watters.
Description: Washington, DC :
D Giles Limited in association with the
Library of Congress, 2024. |
Includes bibliographical references
and index.
Identifiers: LCCN 2024006447 | ISBN
9781913875817 (cloth)
Subjects: LCSH: Hunt, Richard Morris,
1827-1895. | Architects--United
States--Biography. | Architecture and
society--United States--History--
19th century.
Classification: LCC NA737.H86 W38
2024 | DDC 720.92 [R]--dc23/
eng/20240314
LC record available at https://lccn.loc.
gov/2024006447

ISBN: 978-1-913875-81-7

MIX
Paper | Supporting
responsible forestry
FSC® C118234
www.fsc.org

Publication of *The Gilded Life of Richard
Morris Hunt* was made possible with
generous support from Marc Appleton,
Edward P. Bass, the Library of Congress
James Madison Council, and the American
Institute of Architects/American
Architectural Foundation Gift Fund.

For the Library of Congress:
Director of Publishing:
Becky Brasington Clark
Project Editor: Susan Reyburn

New photography by Michael Froio
New floorplans by James B. Garrison

For D Giles Limited:
Copyedited and proofread by
Jenny Wilson
Designed by Alfonso Iacurci
Printed and bound in Europe

Front cover: *Richard Morris Hunt*, at 24
in Paris, Thomas Couture, oil on canvas,
1852, formerly in the collection of
Richard M. Hunt

Back cover: *Mother and Child*, William
Morris Hunt, 1864–65, Boston Museum
of Fine Arts; Administration Building,
Chicago, Hunt office, ca. 1892; boy in hat,
Richard Morris Hunt Sketchbook, 1874

Endpapers: Richard Morris Hunt
bookplates, ca. 1850 (front); created
for the Library of Richard Morris Hunt,
ca. 1900 (back)

Frontispiece: An American cultural
eminence at Hill-Top Cottage, his country
home; "Richard M. Hunt, Studio, Newport
1884, JH [Jane M. Hunt]."

Page 4: World's Columbian Exposition,
view to Hunt's domed Administration
Building (1893), Chicago; Thomas
Moran, 1894

Page 7: Anna and John Ward house and
studio final elevation; Hunt office, ca. 1869

Contents

9   Foreword by Carla D. Hayden

12   The Players

16   Introduction

22   Chapter 1
     No Small Potatoes

54   Chapter 2
     Soldier of the Crayon

92   Sketchbook Portfolio

96   Chapter 3
     **A Robust and Vivacious
     Temperament**

146 Chapter 4
     **Desirable Elements
     for Wealth**

194 Scrapbook Portfolio

198 Chapter 5
     Les Palais Hunt

262 Afterword

275 Acknowledgments

277 Sources and Abbreviations

278 Notes

302 Image Credits

306 Index

Foreword

Richard Morris Hunt, America's premier architect in the nineteenth century, and the Library of Congress—the largest library in the world—were first under the same roof in 1857, when Hunt worked as an architectural assistant at the US Capitol building, then home to the congressional book collections. He and the Library were reunited in 2010 when the American Institute of Architects, of which Hunt was a founder, and the American Architectural Foundation donated a trove of material to the Library. Hunt's parents were also acquainted with the Library: his mother copied bird illustrations from a recently published John James Audubon volume she found there, and his father served as a US congressman, representing Vermont.

The first American to study at the renowned École des Beaux-Arts in Paris, Hunt was classically trained, developing a reverence for the Western canon, which he expressed with cutting-edge technologies. Best known for his opulent Gilded Age mansions, he operated on a large scale in all facets of his life, from designing major private, commercial, and civic works to developing an intricately webbed transatlantic network of Fifth Avenue mansion dwellers, aristocrats, artists, collectors, industrialists, university presidents, museum trustees, and government officials. With these powerful and interconnected friends and partners, Hunt set out to fashion a society that valued education and celebrated the arts.

The Gilded Life of Richard Morris Hunt is the story of how he came to play an outsize role in shaping the contours and content of American architecture. Historian Sam Watters guides readers through an era of opportunity and oppression, when the wealthy felt a moral obligation to instruct the populace in what was brilliant, beautiful, and good. Following Hunt from a New England childhood through his worldly European education and his return to the United States determined to bring art to American architecture, Watters traces his subject's unparalleled rise in a field that was not yet professional, not yet American, but became so through his sheer force of will and constant activity. Not only would he join his clients and cohorts to define a model of cultured society, but, as their architect of choice, he would also lead the way in giving physical form to their ideas of a better, prosperous America.

Hunt was a collector—of friends, collaborators, clients, ideas—and he relentlessly acquired books, artworks, photographs, plaster casts, and other objects that he meticulously organized for reference in building his vision of America. Like Hunt, the Library of Congress is a collector, acquiring more than a million items annually through copyright deposit, curated donations, and select purchases. These items tell the story of humanity's ability to

Patriotic banner (detail), likely for
Metropolitan Fair annex, New York City;
Richard M. Hunt, 1863 sketchbook

create and to transform knowledge, a notion that was fundamental to Hunt's work and world view. Thus, the Richard Morris Hunt Collection, part of the American Institute of Architects/American Architectural Foundation Collection in the Prints and Photographs Division, fits as perfectly as a dovetail joint within the Library's holdings. It includes sketches and presentation drawings, notebooks and scrapbooks, and Catharine Howland Hunt's unpublished biography of her husband. In mining this archive and other primary sources, Sam Watters made new discoveries and unrealized connections that imbue this wholly original and insightful story of the "dean of American architecture."

The Library of Congress serves not only the legislative branch of the US government, but as America's national library, it serves the public as well. Those with an interest in architecture will find invaluable resources here, including works by major figures such as Benjamin Latrobe, Cass Gilbert, and Frank Lloyd Wright. I invite you to visit in person or online at www.loc.gov to see more of our remarkable collections.

Carla D. Hayden
Librarian of Congress

View from Jane and John Griswold's library to their dining room (1864) in Newport, Rhode Island; Michael Froio, 2019

The Players

Richard Morris Hunt was the protagonist in a grand, novelistic life, with a cast of interrelated characters. Here are some of the influential performers in his story. Portraits below are numbered P.1, P.2, etc; portraits in chapters are referenced by figure numbers, e.g., 1.2, 1.3, etc.

FAMILY

William H. Aspinwall (1807-1875), New York shipping tycoon, early art collector, museum trustee, cousin of Samuel S. Howland and guardian of his daughter, Catharine C.H. Hunt (P.1)

Henry C. Chauncey (1825-1915), New York-based investor with William H. Aspinwall, married to Catharine Hunt's sister Emily Howland

Joseph Howland (1834-1886), Civil War brigadier general, philanthropist, brother of Catharine Hunt, married to war memoirist Eliza N.W. Howland (3.23), builders of Tioronda house, Matteawan, New York

Samuel S. Howland (1789-1853), shipping magnate, he and his wife Joanna E. Hone (1799-1848), niece of New York City diarist and mayor Philip Hone, were the parents of Catharine Hunt

Catharine C.H. Hunt (1841-1909), heiress, philanthropist, collector, daughter of Samuel and Joanna Howland, wife of Richard M. Hunt, mother of Richard H., Joseph H., Catharine H., known as Kitty, Esther M., and Herbert L. (3.11)

Jane M.L. Hunt (1801-1877), Connecticut-born, daughter of a judge, granddaughter of a merchant and landowner, married to Jonathan Hunt, Jr., mother of Jane, William M., Jonathan, Richard M., and Leavitt Hunt (P.2, 1.2, 1.4)

Jane M. Hunt (1822-1907), known as Jennie or Jenney, watercolorist, family diarist, only sister of Richard M. Hunt (P.3, 1.3, 1.4)

Jonathan Hunt (1738-1823), land-rich, lieutenant governor of Vermont, father of Jonathan Hunt, Jr., grandfather of Richard M. Hunt

Jonathan Hunt Jr. (1787-1832), banker, US Congressman from Vermont, husband of Jane M.L. Hunt, father of Richard M. Hunt

Jonathan Hunt (1826-1875), known as John or Jack, doctor in Paris, brother of Richard M. Hunt (1.4)

Joseph H. Hunt (1870-1924), known as Dody or Joe, son of Catharine and Richard M. Hunt, partner with his brother Richard H. in the architecture firm Hunt & Hunt (SK.9)

Leavitt Hunt (1830-1907), born Henry L., known as Leav, early photographer, scholar of ancient civilizations, attorney, youngest brother of Richard M. Hunt, married heiress Katherine L. Jarvis, their sons were sculptor Clyde du Vernet Hunt and architect Jarvis Hunt (1.3, 1.4)

Richard H. Hunt (1862-1931), known as Dickie or Dick, son of Catharine and Richard M. Hunt, partner in Hunt & Hunt with his brother Joseph (3.11, 5.33)

William M. Hunt (1824-1879), known as Bill, progressive artist, collector, educator, in Boston, oldest brother of Richard M. Hunt (1.3, 1.4)

Charles H. Russell (1796-1894), Rhode Island-born, New York City merchant, banker, railroad investor, married to Catharine Hunt's sister Caroline Howland

CLIENTS, COLLEAGUES, AND FRIENDS

Jules C.A. Allard (1832-1907), Parisian furnishings and interiors supplier, firm founded in 1859, from 1875 known as Jules Allard Fils; from 1884, owner of Maison Allard de Paris, in New York City (P.4)

Thomas G. Appleton (1812-1884), Boston merchant heir, poet, aphorist, author, arts patron

Caroline S. Astor (1830-1908), society leader, associated with Ward McAllister, originator of The Four Hundred list of socially acceptable New Yorkers

George Bancroft (1800-1891), US Secretary of the Navy, founder of the US Naval Academy, US minister to Prussia and the United Kingdom, author of best-selling *History of the United States*

Antoine-Louis Barye (1795-1875), Parisian realist sculptor, teacher of Richard M. and William M. Hunt

Henry Ward Beecher (1813-1887), brother of author Harriet Beecher Stowe, celebrity Congregational minister (4.25)

Alfred J. Bloor (1828-1917), New York City architect, critic, prominent in the American Institute of Architects (AIA)

G.-Abel Blouet (1795-1853), École des Beaux-Arts architecture professor at the time of Richard M. Hunt

Martin Brimmer (1829-1896), merchant heir, son of a Boston mayor; a founder of the city's Museum of Fine Arts (P.5)

William Cullen Bryant (1794-1878), poet and civic-minded editor of the *New-York Evening Post*

Joseph H. Choate (1832-1917), Harvard University graduate, lawyer to Richard M. Hunt, leader in the Republican Party, diplomat, and trustee of cultural institutions (P.6)

Thomas Couture (1815-1879), Parisian fine art painter, teacher of Richard M. and William M. Hunt

Thomas G. Crawford (1814-1857), American-born, Rome-based neoclassical sculptor

Charlotte S. Cushman (1816-1876), Boston-born actress, famous for both male and female roles (P.7)

Samuel Darier (1808-1884), Genevan architect, first architecture teacher of Richard M. Hunt

P.-J. Honoré Daumet (1826-1911), École des Beaux-Arts student with Richard M. Hunt, Parisian architect, teacher of Joseph H. and Richard H. Hunt (1.9)

Henri d'Orléans, Duc d'Aumale (1822-1897), son of French king Louis-Philippe, owner of the Chateau de Chantilly (P.8)

Leopold Eidlitz (1823-1908), Prague-born, New York City architect and theorist

Charles W. Eliot (1834–1926), transformative president of Harvard University, 1869–1909

Edward Everett (1794–1865), Unitarian minister, US congressman and senator, governor of Massachusetts, US secretary of state, minister to the United Kingdom, Harvard University president

Frank H. Furness (1839–1912), Richard M. Hunt student, Philadelphia architect

Rev. William H. Furness (1802–1896), Philadelphian Unitarian minister, father of architect Frank H. Furness, friend of Ralph Waldo Emerson

J.-L. Charles Garnier (1825–1898), educated at the École des Beaux-Arts, architect of the renowned Paris Opera House (P.9)

Ogden Goelet (1851–1897), with his wife Mary Wilson, builder of Ochre Court, heir to a New York City real estate fortune, related to Hunt client Elbridge T. Gerry (P.10)

William J. Hoppin (1847–1895), Harvard University graduate, lawyer and diplomat, a founder of New York's Century Association in 1847

P.-F.-Henri Labrouste (1801–1875), Paris architect of new French classicism

Hector-M. Lefuel (1810–1880), École des Beaux-Arts educated Paris architect of the new Louvre and at Fontainebleau, Richard M. Hunt's teacher and first employer (1.16)

James Lenox (1800–1880), Columbia College graduate, New York City real estate heir, philanthropist, and art and book collector (P.11)

Léon Marcotte (1824–1887), French-born, École des Beaux-Arts-trained, New York-based architect, cabinet maker, and decorator, founder of L. Marcotte & Co.

Henry G. Marquand (1819–1902), New York City railroad executive, collector, Metropolitan Museum of Art president (4.14)

George C. Mason (1820–1894), Newport, Rhode Island architect

Charles F. McKim (1847–1909), École des Beaux-Arts educated, New York City architect, a founding partner of McKim, Mead & White (P.12)

Dr. William W. Morland (1818–1876), Harvard University graduate, prominent Boston urologist

Levi P. Morton (1824–1920), Vermont-born, American minister to France, US congressman, US vice president, New York governor (P.13)

Napoléon III (1808–1873), Emperor of France, 1852–70, married to Empress Eugénie (1826–1920) (1.16)

Charles Eliot Norton (1827–1908), Harvard University's first professor of fine arts, cousin of the university's president, Charles W. Eliot

Frederick Law Olmsted (1822–1903), Boston-based landscape architect and proponent of the picturesque (5.33)

Eugène-S. Oudinot de la Faverie, known as Eugène A.S. Oudinot (1827–1889), Parisian stained-glass artist with an international clientele

Dr. Eleazer Parmly (1797-1874), a gifted poet and pioneer of dentistry as a modern medical practice (P.14)

George B. Post (1837-1913), Richard M. Hunt student, New York City architect

Henry H. Richardson (1838-1886), École des Beaux-Arts-trained Boston architect, creator of the "Richardson Romanesque"

Montgomery Schuyler (1843-1914), influential architectural critic in New York City

Alexander T. Stewart (1803-1876), Irish-born, New York City wholesaler and department store founder, art collector, early mansion builder

Russell Sturgis Jr. (1836-1909), architect, critic, prolific author, College of the City of New York professor, founding trustee of the Metropolitan Museum of Art, New York City

George Ticknor (1791-1871), Harvard University professor in modern languages, book collector (P.15)

Henry T. Tuckerman (1813-1871), New York City cultural critic, essayist, a founder of the Century Association

Richard Upjohn (1802-1878), British-born, New York City architect, a founder of the AIA

Henry Van Brunt (1832-1903), Richard M. Hunt student, critic, architect, partner with William Ware

The Vanderbilts

Alva S. Vanderbilt (1853-1933), society leader, suffragette, builder of Marble House, wife of William K. Vanderbilt, mother of Consuelo, Duchess of Marlborough (4.6a)

Cornelius Vanderbilt (1794-1877), founder of the family's railroad fortune

Cornelius Vanderbilt II (1843-1899)—oldest son of William H. Vanderbilt, brother of William K. and George W. Vanderbilt—head of the family's New York Central Railroad empire, married to Alice C. Gwynne (1845-1934), builders of the Breakers (5.22)

George W. Vanderbilt (1862-1914), youngest son of William H. Vanderbilt, book collector, conservationist, creator of Biltmore estate (5.31)

William H. Vanderbilt (1821-1885), railroad executive, principal heir of Cornelius Vanderbilt, reportedly doubled the family fortune, builder of the Vanderbilt mausoleum on Staten Island

William K. Vanderbilt (1849-1920), railroad executive, horseman, son of William H. Vanderbilt, husband of Alva Vanderbilt (4.6b)

Calvert Vaux (1824-1895), British-born, New York City architect, worked with Frederick Law Olmsted

Eugène E. Viollet-le-Duc (1814-1879), Paris architect, theorist, author, advocate for Gothic architecture (P.16)

Thomas U. Walter (1804-1887), Philadelphia-based architect, a founder of the AIA

John Q.A. Ward (1830-1910), Ohio-born, New York-based realist sculptor (3.17)

William R. Ware (1832-1915), Richard M. Hunt student, architect, founder of architecture schools at MIT and Columbia College, partner with Henry Van Brunt

Daniel Webster (1782-1852), Boston attorney, US Supreme Court orator, US congressman, US secretary of state (P.17)

Peter B. Wight (1838-1925), New York City and Chicago architect, partner of Russell Sturgis Jr.

Theodore W. Winthrop (1828-1861), New York City novelist, childhood friend of Richard M. Hunt

Richard Hunt's Légion d'Honneur medal, awarded 1884 for his Yorktown column

Richard Hunt,

Architecte, Inspecteur aux Travaux du Louvre

16, rue Taranne

Richard Hunt's business cards, a story of cosmopolitan success, as inspector of new construction at the Louvre, Paris, ca. 1854, and as America's highly decorated architect and proselytizer of establishment taste, ca. 1888

RICHARD MORRIS HUNT

CHEVALIER DE LA LÉGION D'HONNEUR

PRÉSIDENT DE L'INSTITUT DES ARCHITECTES AMÉRICAINS

MEMBRE CORRESPONDANT DE L'INSTITUT DE FRANCE

ET DE LA SOCIÉTÉ DES ARCHITECTES FRANÇAIS

ETC. ETC. ETC.

Introduction

1867 President, New York Chapter, American Institute of Architects, New York
      American commissioner, Exposition Universelle, Paris

1876 Commissioner and juror, Centennial International Exhibition, Philadelphia

1882 Honorary and corresponding member, Académie des Beaux-Arts, Institut de
      France, Paris

1884 Chevalier, Légion d'Honneur, Paris

1886 Member, Société centrale des architectes français, Paris
      Honorary and corresponding member, Royal Institute of British Architects, London

1887 Honorary and corresponding member, Österreichischer Ingenieur- und
      Architekten-Verein, Vienna

1888 President, American Institute of Architects

1892 Academician, Accademia di San Luca, Rome
      Honorary LL.D., Harvard University, Cambridge, Massachusetts

1893 President, Board of Architects, World's Columbian Exposition, Chicago
      Foreign Associate Member, Académie des Beaux-Arts, Institut de France, Paris
      Honorary member, Sociëtait Arti et Amicitiae, Amsterdam
      Royal Gold Medal, Royal Institute of British Architects, London[1]

Stand in the domed Great Hall of New York's Metropolitan Museum of Art or at the storied entrance to the Breakers mansion in Newport and ask a visitor, "So what's your opinion of Richard Morris Hunt, the building's architect?" The response is almost invariably, "Richard who?" And yet, in the Gilded Age, Hunt was a celebrity at home and abroad, more chronicled and decorated than his peers for bringing Old World civilization to New World America through architecture and art.

Recounting the life of Richard Morris Hunt risks being another homage to a dead, white architect whose design legacy is largely academic. But when viewed as a cultural leader, Hunt emerges as astonishingly relevant to the critical assessment of America's "master narrative." Tourists may not know his name, but they experience the buildings and art that he and his colleagues and patrons conceived and collected to build an American civilization. Their museums, libraries, and mansions extended what President Lincoln, on the verge of the Civil War, called "our national fabric, with all its benefits, its memories, and its hopes."[2]

The story that follows is the life and times of Richard Morris Hunt (1827–1895), the how and why of his forty-year career. Born an upper-class New Englander, empowered by wealth and kinship, and imbued

with Whig values (the centrality of history and federal support in a new republic), he came of age in a pre-professional world demanding polymathy of its selected leaders. The child of an industrious generation, he adopted its interdisciplinarity to become, literally and metaphorically, a builder of modern life.

In the 1840s, Hunt was the first American to attend the architecture section of Paris's École des Beaux-Arts, Europe's foremost school for the fine arts. He returned to New York in 1855 and built an award-winning career interweaving building and landscape architecture, interior decorating, and art collecting for commercial, civic, and residential commissions. He was an innovator of the nineteenth-century art studio and exhibition complex, apartment house, hospital, skyscraper, and residential castle, his office designing, with mixed reviews, more than three hundred projects, including the pedestal of the Statue of Liberty. He is best known for his famous, and at times, infamous, Vanderbilt family palaces, even though they represent only fifteen years of practice.

Hunt's reputation as an architect declined with modernism at the turn of the twentieth century and rose again in the 1980s when post-modernists revisited the classical canon. What endured was his genius for conceiving, founding, and managing institutions to instill the Eurocentric culture he and his generation sought for global acceptance and dominance. He had, reminisced architect Peter B. Wight, "all the elements of greatness. His was the mastermind when brought into contact with others." He had been born into power and used his gift for leadership to stay there all his life, cultivating luminaries in America and abroad who kept themselves and their friends in positions of influence. While most are forgotten today, they were men and women in journalism, the arts, politics, industry, law, and religion. They built a fortified social and financial network through family, marriage, friendship, and profession, settling in the same neighborhoods, attending the same schools and churches, and investing together in foundations of American wealth—banking, insurance, real estate, and above all, the railroad.[3]

An outcome of this clubby sharing of values and fortune was that Hunt and his clients, being intractably racist and antisemitic, accomplished big things, but without openness and inclusion. Living at a time of class revolution across the Western world and fearing their property at risk from the laboring poor, some working as servants in mansion kitchens and backstair halls, Hunt's society concurred on what was needed to define, protect, and perpetuate their ideas of a civil society. To this end they founded cultural institutions that established art history as foundational to the modern humanities. Hunt organized the first American studio based on

Dinner in the dining hall at Alva and William K. Vanderbilt's New York City chateau, ca. 1881 (detail of SC.4)

Parisian methods, which then inspired university architectural education for close to a century. He contributed to the launching of societies that promoted architecture as a profession and the artisan trades necessary for it to succeed; and he conceived of a museum of architecture before he became a founder, trustee, and donor to the Metropolitan Museum of Art that enshrined the arts as foundational to a transatlantic civilization.

For most of Hunt's forty-year career, Catharine Clinton Howland Hunt (1841-1909) was his devoted wife and collaborator. Importantly for history, she was also his biographer. Her chatty, unpublished manuscript, written after his death to memorialize his place in American history, conforms to standards of Victorian biography, a determined and "earnest exercise of information retrieval," writes one critic, encompassing "public career plus private sentimentality." The essence of this tradition was social propriety and censorship, a genteel culling of indecorous fact from family memories and letters. Representative of this editorializing is Catharine's note that Hunt's mother "burned...a great number of Mr. [Daniel] Webster's letters as they contained so much that was interesting and personal." Similarly, Catharine quoted from her husband's letters, long since missing or destroyed, an absence compounded by the dearth of Hunt's diaries, office correspondence, and records, discarded or lost when the Hunt collections made their way to a public archive. Consequently, we do not know what he thought about his work and life at pivotal moments—the deaths of his mother and brothers, his failure to win landmark commissions, and his "service" during the Civil War by proxy. Against this background, Catharine's anecdotal memoir of the people and places in her husband's life remains a cornerstone of Hunt studies.[4]

The nineteenth century was a technological era when steam, oil, and electricity, the telegraph (1844) and the telephone (1876) transformed Western life into a world of unprecedented connectivity and comparative ease of travel. For Hunt and his wife, visits to Europe were pilgrimages to better health and high art. Informed by experiences across the continent, he launched cultural initiatives that led to a generation of architects trained at home and in France who forged an American architecture, funded by wealthy clients who visited world fairs and befriended fellow millionaires abroad building country chateaus and city buildings. Together, this international plutocracy, with interconnected financial interests and aesthetic sensibilities, created a monarchy of taste.

What Hunt and his traveling clients saw was reported in illustrated print media that proliferated with photography, photogravure (1820s), and the rotary press (1843). Illustrated pages in magazines and volumes of art and architecture tracts extended American knowledge of art precedents, essential to the eclecticism Hunt and his generation practiced. He himself was a photographer, albeit briefly, and a lifetime collector of prints and engravings, of newspaper and magazine clippings of his own publicity and art issues that he and Catharine assembled in scrapbook volumes. Images he collected and drawings he preserved are largely the illustrations in this book and online images referenced in accompanying notes.

Though a grand figure in the Gilded Age, a period of big personalities and one-percenter money, Hunt was always a self-professed Yankee from Vermont, a "man of wealth," a "thorough-going American…in the usual hurry, and with a quick, nervous manner…kindly and courteous," recalled a British architect. His Plymouth Rock heritage, regional accent, and forthrightness made him, and by association his architecture, authentically American to clients and colleagues at home and abroad. This tension between the continental celebrity architect, gilding America with French-styled palaces, and common-sense New Englander, is evident in his professional names—RM Hunt, Richard Hunt, and Richard Morris Hunt— and by what he was "always known from childhood to grave, not only by his familiars but his professional brethren … 'Dick.'"[5]

The portrait on this book's cover evokes the essence of Richard Hunt, who was twenty-four when he sat for the French academician Thomas Couture. Living on the Left Bank in Paris and fluent in French, the young architect sees his manifest destiny. Three years later, he set out for home, sailing across the "Great Lake" dreaming of temples and palaces for his native land. He had become a character at once Mark Twain and Henry James, straight-talking, entrepreneurial, educated, and enterprising. Guided by duty and heritage, he would live and work to build a nation of culture and refinement.[6]

Chapter 1

No Small Potatoes

Reverend Jasper Adams, a presidential descendant and graduate of Brown University, stood before the congregation of Charleston's St. Michael's Episcopal Church in 1833. Preaching from its canopied pulpit, he expounded on God and country. "We are accustomed to rejoice in the ancestry from which we proclaimed, and well we may, for our ancestors are illustrious men. One of the colonial governors said in 1692, 'God sifted a whole nation, that he might send choice grain over into this wilderness.'"[1]

Lineage from the "sifted" few determined class and power in nineteenth-century America, a distinction conveyed by one's name. Richard Morris Hunt, born in Vermont on October 31, 1827, only sixteen months after the deaths of Thomas Jefferson and John Adams, was six at the time of the reverend's sermon and, by birthright, an entitled New England patrician. His forefathers died liberating their country from kingly rule only to evolve an aristocracy of their own. Richard's mother, Jane Maria Leavitt from Suffield, Connecticut, descended from Oliver Ellsworth, chief justice of the United States and a framer of the Constitution. His father, Jonathan Jr., was the son of Jonathan Hunt, a founder of Vermont and a lieutenant governor. His aunt, Ellen Hunt, married General Lewis Richard Morris, a US congressman from Vermont and nephew of Gouverneur Morris of New York, a graduate of King's College (Columbia College from 1784), signer of the Declaration of Independence, and minister to France. Gouverneur made the Morris family synonymous with wealth, education, and civic duty. Richard was named after Ellen's son, US Navy lieutenant Richard Hunt Morris.[2]

Vermont, home of revolutionary Ethan Allen and the Green Mountain Boys militia, embellished Richard Hunt's pedigree. Part of New France before Louis XV ceded the region to George III at the end of the Seven Years War, it abolished slavery in 1777 and became the first territory

Fig 1.11a detail, Algerian hostel

admitted to the United States after the original thirteen states. Its citizens' independence of mind and political will made for what a profile of Richard's maternal uncle praised as "integrity without compromise."[3]

The Hunts were early settlers in Brattleboro which, by the 1820s, was a milling town of two thousand citizens, living on former Abenaki lands, midway between Boston and Albany. A Dartmouth College graduate, lawyer, president of the town bank, and politician, Jonathan Hunt Jr. held office in the Vermont legislature and US Congress. He married Jane Leavitt in 1820 and they had five children: Jane, William, Jonathan, Richard, and Leavitt.

Land and banking secured the wealth of Richard's family. The Leavitts were early investors in the Northwest territory, before it became Ohio in 1803, and Richard's great-grandfather Samuel Hunt assembled acreage across New England and into Canada. As generations prospered, they lived in what they and their neighbors considered proper mansions. Jonathan Hunt Jr. built Brattleboro's first brick house at the top of Main Street, distinguished by the Greek Revival Phoenix House hotel, converted from a warehouse by a Hunt family member (1.1a-b). A staff of four looked after Jonathan's home, its size, prominent location, and illustrious history making it a place of local pride.[4]

As the United States emerged in the eighteenth century, the Hunts competed for Whig ascendancy, the "active, enterprising, intelligent, well-meaning & wealthy party of the people," wrote Ralph Waldo Emerson in 1844. While Democrat Andrew Jackson promoted laissez-faire politics benefiting white, property-owning men, Whigs sought prosperity through federal support and institutions. History was their guide, for "Forefather, Parent, Child, Posterity, Native Land...all teach us not blindly to worship, but duly to honor the past," Harvard University president Edward Everett declaimed in Boston on July 4, 1853. Respectful of wealth and custom, they contributed to a society of unequal classes, acting independently but obligated to the greatest good.[5]

Attorney and politician Daniel Webster (see P.17) was friend and colleague to his fellow Dartmouth graduate Jonathan Hunt Jr. The era's great orator and ally of the rich, including Cornelius Vanderbilt (whose fortune later transformed Richard's career), Webster spoke to the Boston Mechanics Institution in 1828, observing that America was in "a period of great activity...of growing wealth," of railroad and canal construction uniting "science and art" as the ancient Greeks had done millennia before. In this, he discerned "unambiguous indications of the growing prevalence of a just taste" and acceptance of the "principles of architecture" by which he meant the classical canon and mechanics.[6]

Fig. 1.1a Main Street, Brattleboro, Vermont, Hunt family house behind trees at top; George Houghton, ca. 1860

Fig. 1.1b Hunt's white brick childhood home, built by his father ca. 1820; unknown, ca. 1850

For Webster, the architect was obligated to privileges hard won by revolution. "Our system begins with the individual man," and must protect and further "what belongs to a moral and rational being. For the same reason, the arts are to be promoted for their general utility, as they affect the personal happiness and wellbeing of the individuals who compose the community." The practical manifestation of this politic was that civic buildings "reared by the surplus of wealth and the savings of labor" should be built "after the necessities and comforts of individuals are provided for; and not, like the Pyramids, by the unremitted toil of thousands of half-starved slaves." Observing the rudimentary state of colonial dwellings, Webster concluded that it would be "adverse to the whole spirit of our system, that we should have gorgeous and expensive public buildings, if individuals were at the same time to live in houses of mud," a proposition embraced by Hunt's clients after the Civil War.[7]

The American individualism at the heart of Daniel Webster's vision of a realized democracy was inseparable from moral propriety and faith. The Second Great Awakening of religious revivals reached its apogee under Whig power that interwove religion and politics. Party members in New England were predominately Congregational, Unitarian, and New School Presbyterians. At Brattleboro, Jonathan Hunt Jr. and his family sat in their second-row pew of the town's Unitarian meeting house, which he and fellow citizens built in 1816. Unitarians urged reason and action to build a Christian society. "I cannot but think," officiant William Wells concluded in the first sermon at the new meeting house, "that ministers and people would be better and more usefully employed, were they to spend their zeal

Fig. 1.2 Portrait of Jane M.L.
Hunt, widowed mother of
Richard Hunt; probably by her
painting instructor, Spiridione
Gambardella, ca. 1837

Fig. 1.3a Portrait of Richard and Leavitt Hunt; possibly by their mother Jane M.L. Hunt, ca. 1837

Fig. 1.3b Their sister Jane M. Hunt; Spiridione Gambardella, 1837

Fig. 1.3c Their brother, William M. Hunt; Emanuel G. Leutze, ca. 1845

in doing justice, loving mercy, and walking humbly with God, rather than in preaching and talking, and taking so much pains to know what others think...of which we can know but little, and what we do know is of small importance."[8]

Webster and Wells, one social and political, the other social and religious, expressed the practical, professional, and moral obligations that defined the life course of Richard Hunt. Independent action guided by faith, a reverence for history, and rational thought would lead him to knowledge, freedom, and happiness. The realization of these blessings, however, emanated from a liberal education.

The need for learning among a self-governing citizenry dominated thought in the new republic. "The National Welfare," Jonathan Hunt Jr. pronounced on the momentous Fourth of July in 1812, just two weeks after the young country had declared war on Britain, depended on "virtue and knowledge to be universally disseminated among the people." Debate on how to foster a virtuous society settled on volunteer associations, political parties, and government agencies for open dialogue; a free press; and institutions for literacy and knowledge. In the years ahead, as an educated New Englander and cultural leader, Richard Hunt would engage on all these fronts to further the arts in America.[9]

Richard and his family lived in Brattleboro and Washington, DC, until his father died from Asiatic cholera in 1832 while serving as a US congressman. That year, at the urging of her mother, Jane Hunt moved Richard and his four siblings to New Haven, despite Daniel Webster recommending the benefits of cultivated Boston (1.2, 1.3a-c). Living near Yale College (Yale University from 1887), she enrolled her children in school and together they attended the Unitarian church on the New Haven Green.[10]

Perhaps through her faith, Jane befriended the best-selling author and Unitarian convert Catharine M. Sedgwick. In a period of artistic engagement with Rome and Florence and support for Italian liberation, Sedgwick and her influential family aided exiled revolutionaries whose cause was the unification of Italy, the Risorgimento. They were men "marred by deep lines cut by grief, anxiety, and privation," but of "superior intelligence and education," Sedgwick wrote. In 1837 she introduced Jane to the attorney Gaetano de Castillia, the linguist and future Columbia College professor Eleuterio Felice Foresti, and the portrait painter Spiridione Gambardella. The three, representing modern professions, offered Jane's children their first sustained introduction to European culture. In family lore, their studying French, Italian, and painting, and Richard's building a brick and timber house in the family yard, were precursors to his and William's lives in architecture and art.[11]

In 1838 Jane moved to Boston so William could enter Harvard in 1840, an ineluctable choice for upper-class New Englanders. Jonathan followed his oldest brother in 1841, after he graduated from the establishment public Boston Latin School, which Richard, along with Leavitt, entered in 1839. His mother and sister recalled that Richard's "distinguishing quality from a very early age was his persistent industry." Though not studious, he was imbued with the rectitude of an educated Victorian child preparing for a post-agrarian world. In 1843 he listed daily times to rise and called for frugality and moderation. He pledged never to cheat, to strive for "the approbation of every person," and to "attend divine service regularly." Resolutely, he signed his convictions with a Cartesian flourish, "Je suis, R.M. Hunt."[12]

As the propertied widow of a congressman, Jane Hunt befriended Boston's educators and merchant elite. They represented the closed financial and societal interests transforming the colonial city into the "Athens of America," the antipode to money-centric, empire-building New York. Three intellectuals in her circle, who became advisors with Daniel Webster after her husband's death, introduced Jane to the benefits of a European education. The Unitarian orator Edward Everett, the historian George Bancroft, and the author, linguist, and bibliophile George Ticknor (see P.15) were emblematic of the self-improving, post-revolutionary New Englander. In the 1830s they studied at the University of Göttingen, where Wilhelm von Humboldt's progressive reforms were manifest in an education of choice and inquiry. Before returning to Boston, Ticknor met heroes of the international intelligentsia: Goethe in Germany, Wordsworth and Byron in England, Juliette Récamier and François-René de Chateaubriand in France. Americans impressed Europeans with their studied erudition, though their cities and artistic culture received mixed reviews.[13]

Fig. 1.4 Jane M.L. Hunt and her children (left to right), Leavitt, Richard, Jonathan, Jane, and William before sailing to France; E.L. Fisher, ca. 1843

Once back in Boston, Ticknor and Everett promoted European educational reform at Harvard, hidebound by memorization of classical texts. Their premise was that the finest minds became society leaders if they pursued fields of personal interest and affinity. A follower of Everett and critic of traditional education, Emerson wrote that men should not be drawn into conformity with the "masses, rude, lame, unmade, pernicious," but educated "to draw individuals out of them." Informed by these progressive ideals and aspirational for her children, Jane Hunt took the momentous step that determined the future of her sons as professionals in architecture, art, law, and medicine.[14]

～～～～～

When William Hunt came down with a chronic cough in 1842, doctors and Unitarian ministers advised a warmer clime, possibly in the American south, but certainly not in sensuous Italy. Pragmatically, Jane settled on Nice for the winter. Daniel Webster, recently resigned as US Secretary of State, provided letters of introduction to ministers and consuls. Foreseeing challenges ahead, he regretted her departure while hopeful for the "restauration of [William's] health." The Hunts left New York by sail packet in October 1843 (1.4). Later in life, Jane reminisced that during the eighteen-day crossing she shuddered at her undertaking, calling it "venturesome in the extreme."[15]

When he stepped onto the pier at Le Havre, Richard Hunt could not have imagined how changed his life would be, nor could the French have believed that a sixteen-year-old from Vermont would mature as America's spokesperson for French architecture and urbanism. Since the ministries of Thomas Jefferson and Gouverneur Morris and Louis XVI's support of the War of Independence, Americans had revered France for its manners, theater, and art, as the country of the Marquis de Lafayette, who fought in America's revolution, and Napoleonic civic reforms. France was then in a period of instability between the reigns of Napoléon I and Napoléon III, with novelist Honoré de Balzac's "People's Prince," King Louis-Philippe, on the throne. He had come to power after a three-day revolution in July 1830, a time of economic and agricultural crisis. Supported by the rising industrial bourgeoisie, the king ruled until 1848 in the "July Monarchy," mandated to reform religion, elections, the peerage, and royal privilege.

Jane Hunt's move to France was not exceptional. Since the 1820s American writers, educators, and collectors had settled in Paris for its arts and society. George Ticknor found it the capital of "gross and vulgar excesses," but George Bancroft thought that "England will show a stranger more [vice] in a night than France in a month...never do I expect to see a people so courteous and obliging as the French. Their pictures, their statutes, their libraries and their cabinets are open to every stranger who presents himself for admittance." Despite the risks of un-American depravity, Paris was a monument to learning, art, and architecture.[16]

Led by Italy, France, and England, Europe was so central to the lives of the American rich and educated that Horace Greeley, founding editor of the *New-York Tribune*, made Emerson's intellectual ally Margaret Fuller the paper's foreign correspondent, her columns becoming a portrait of Americans abroad. "Although we have an independent political existence," Fuller observed, "our position toward Europe, as to literature and the arts, is still that of a colony, and one feels the same joy here as the colonist returning to the parent home." This commonality of purpose did not yield shared responses. Travelers were of three species. The "servile" were in search of fine clothes, good food, and gossip. This was Fuller's least favorite, having "all the thoughtlessness and partiality of the exclusive classes in Europe, without any of their refinement, or the chivalric feeling...." The second cohort included the "conceited American, instinctively bristling and proud of—he knows not what," finding the "etiquettes of courts and camps" and church "silly." Expectedly, Fuller lauded artists and the "thinking American." He was, she wrote,

> a man who, recognizing the immense advantage of being born to a new world and on a virgin soil, yet does not wish one seed from the past to be lost. He is anxious to gather and carry back with

him every plant that will bear a new climate and new culture....
And that he may know the conditions under which he may best
place them in that new world, he does not neglect to study their
history in this.[17]

Fuller's studious, old-to-new-world artist could well constitute
a portrait of Richard Hunt. Though only in his teens when he arrived
in France, he had a natural exuberance for gathering seeds of culture,
beginning the day he arrived and traveled to Rouen. Taking the same route
in 1834, New York editor and author William Cullen Bryant wrote that
"every step of our journey reminded us that we were in an old country.
Everything we saw spoke of the past, of an antiquity without limit...
the dwellings [were] so gray, and of such antique architecture, and in
the large towns, like Rouen, rose so high, and overhung with such quaint
projections the narrow and cavernous streets." Hunt and his family spent
the night in the picturesque capital of Normandy and arrived the next
evening in Paris (1.5). Within days, the siblings, raised in collegiate New
Haven and Boston, were touring the royal Gobelins tapestry workshop and
an exhibition at the École des Beaux-Arts that introduced Richard to his
future school. Though soon to be known as the "handsomest American
in Paris," Hunt, like his peers, was besieged throughout by poor health.
Stoically he suffered through his first case of boils, impressing a local

Fig. 1.5 Paris along
the River Seine
in Hunt's time, an
empire far from
Brattleboro, Vermont.
Its "marvelous beauty,"
he told his wife,
brought tears to his
eyes; Édouard Baldus,
ca. 1860[1]

Fig. 1.6 Chateau de Petit-Val outside Paris, where the young Hunt met the era's cultural elites; ca. 1890

doctor who commented that the infection would have "killed anyone else." Under the care of the American "Mme Moulton...kindness itself," Richard recuperated at her "charming country house in the environs of Paris," the neoclassical Chateau de Petit-Val in Sucy-en-Brie (1.6). An enduring friendship developed, as it would often for Hunt, and over the years he and his wife Catharine met "celebrities of the day in arts, letters and music" at the limestone mansion.[18]

Introduced to Jane Hunt by her Boston circle, Caesarina Moulton was Fuller's American artist seeking continental culture. The beautiful daughter of a German émigré piano teacher, she became a concert soprano and married Charles Moulton, a New York and Paris real estate investor during the Second Empire. Designed for the minister of buildings under Louis XV and brother of Madame de Pompadour, the Marquis de Marigny, their chateau was in a neighborhood of aristocratic houses restored after the French Revolution by magnates building new France. As an American financier living abroad in a house of the ancien régime and frequenting a society of aristocrats and collectors, Charles Moulton, like Mr. Touchett in Henry James' *The Portrait of a Lady*, preceded the American investors and industrialists later in the century, who made Newport, Rhode Island their own enclave of stone mansions, designed by their country's leading Francophile architect, Richard Hunt.[19]

Richard's health delayed his mother's winter plans until February 1844, when she and her children headed south. She had considered Provence, but determinately independent and ignoring the prelate warning, settled on sunny Italy. Hunt's diary recounts the family's southward journey, traveling by stagecoach and steamer via Lyons, Marseilles, and Genoa where he saw "for the first time a church full of Catholics." In March the family arrived in Rome and settled into a light-filled apartment near the Spanish Steps. Rome was a city of antiquity's republics and the autocracies of Renaissance popes. Americans, as citizens of a new republic, reconciled these histories to learn from the city's centuries of art.[20]

With the Académie de France on the Pincian Hill, founded by Louis XIV in 1666, and the Italian Accademia di San Luca, founded in 1577, both closed to Americans, artists from New York and Boston living in Rome came together in the mid-1840s to draw, meeting casually in private houses and coalescing around fifteen artists. William joined the group, along with the painter Thomas P. Rossiter and future Newport architect George C. Mason, who both figured later in Richard's life.[21]

Hunt was enthralled by Italian culture and, like American Protestants before him, his response to Catholic practice was at once fascination and disdain. His lists of paintings, sculpture, and architecture, from antiquity to the Baroque, foreshadow his predisposition to the monumental and antiquarian. He was dazzled by the Vatican's porphyry and the "great mosaic work of marbles & different colors" at the Duomo in Florence. In the north were feats of industrial engineering and management—the three-mile railroad bridge at Venice and the vast efficiency of Milan's central hospital, Ospedale Maggiore Ca' Granda, established in 1456. Sculpture was integral to grand-scale architecture, and Richard and his family devoted a day to visiting Roman studios. Though not yet a high school graduate, he singled out from "fine statuary for some of our friends at home" by New York-born Thomas G. Crawford his "magnificent" *Adam and Eve*, destined for Boston's Athenaeum.[22]

In May, Jane and Jonathan returned with their mother to Paris while William traveled back to Rome to study sculpture with American Henry Kirke Brown. By carriage through a mountain blizzard, Richard and Leavitt crossed the Alps to Geneva and enrolled at the boys' school run by Protestant theologian Rev. Matthias-Alphonse Briquet (1.7). At the time, Switzerland was evolving toward a federal constitution after Napoleonic meddling in local governance. It was a sanctuary for wealthy, religious minorities, the birthplace of Jean-Jacques Rousseau, and home to Martin Luther's spiritual heir, the French-born reformer John Calvin, whose faith inspired the American pilgrims. This theological heritage, the overthrow of Jesuit control of elite education, and anti-Catholicism among New Englanders attracted Protestants to Swiss schools.[23]

Fig. 1.7 School of Rev. Alphonse Briquet in Geneva, Switzerland, attended by Leavitt and Richard Hunt; probably by Richard Hunt, ca. 1844

About twenty students, half of whom were American or English, the others French and Italian, enrolled at Briquet's school in the rural Plein Palais district of Geneva. Jane Hunt knew of Briquet through a Rhode Island merchant whose sons had attended his school. Descendants of Huguenots expelled from France by Louis XIV, Briquet's family published guidebooks and scenic photographs that tourists, like Hunt, assembled in scrapbooks of Grand Tour sights. The school master's book collecting and bibliophile engagements inspired Richard to begin his own art and architecture library.[24]

The Hunt brothers lived in Switzerland for a year perfecting their French and German. By early 1845, Richard at seventeen was plotting his future. Letters to his mother then are remarkable for their foresightedness and his settled convictions: the necessity of education, the importance of profession, and the obligation to succeed. Jane had expected her son to follow his brothers to Harvard, but shortly after New Year's Richard wrote, "I am destined to lead a military career" for which he had been "well prepared" before leaving America. A possible obstacle was his age, but "I will enumerate my several accomplishments...a schoolboy's knowledge of history...a decent knowledge of Geography.... Nearly ignorant of Greek and Latin. Know something about German, can translate easy

Italian, and understand perfectly the French." His strength was math, with "a schoolboy's knowledge of Mechanics, Hydrostatics, Pneumatics, Astronomy, & Bookkeeping--the sum total of all my *Gumption*." His focus on science, modern languages, and the absence of Greek and Latin suggests that Jane had encouraged Richard to pursue a nontraditional, self-determining path, just as she was supporting William in becoming a fine artist.

By May, Richard was refining his intentions and, importantly, his responsibilities as an American born two generations after his ancestors' revolution. "Dear Mother," he wrote "The idea that the Hunt Family which has always distinguished itself; should dry up in four 'corncobs,' 'haystacks,' or 'small potatoes,' when represented by four young men, who have had all the advantages in the world is outrageous." He was ready to apply to West Point or the Naval Academy where he could "study architecture," or "endeavor to take a degree at the École Centrale at Paris or some other first rate academy in Europe," before returning home "where an architect of the first quality would be much sought for."[25]

During this era there were no American schools of architecture; aspiring students learned at institutions teaching engineering and through apprenticeship with practicing architects and builders. Considering his familial connections and math inclinations, Hunt's melding of the military and architecture was understandable. When Hunt wrote his mother, family friend George Bancroft, then Secretary of the Navy, was endeavoring to found the United States Naval Academy at Annapolis and finally succeeded in October 1845, without federal funding. Its competition was the United States Military Academy at West Point, founded in 1802 and overseen by a student of Dartmouth and Paris' École Polytechnique. By 1826, more than a thousand men were applying to West Point annually, which included "not a small number of the sons of both the richest and the most considerable men of the country," George Ticknor wrote his wife, while monitoring the academy's spring examinations. Cadets who became teachers made engineering a path to careers in building design before Hunt and his students launched college architecture programs after the Civil War.[26]

Hunt's chosen profession became apparent when he enrolled in the atelier of Swiss architect Samuel Darier the year he settled at Briquet's. École des Beaux-Arts educated and prominent in Geneva's urbanization, Darier prepared students for application to the French school and the École Centrale des Arts et Manufactures for engineering. The drawings Hunt preserved from this time show his mastering the exacting drawing style of the French École (1.8). But Darier brought more than professional

Fig. 1.8 Seventeen-year-old Richard Hunt's drawing of an entablature with smiling dog cheneaus for his first architecture teacher, the Genevan Samuel Darier; signed "R.M. Hunt fecit. Elève [*sic*] de M. Darier," ca. 1845

training to his students. His combining of a practice and teaching, his living in an apartment house of artists and intellectuals, his founding of Geneva's architectural society, and his early support of photography, formed a model for Hunt as he became a young architect practicing in New York.[27]

By July 1845 the Hunt brothers were ending their year with Briquet. Leavitt was preparing to study law in Europe or at Harvard, and their sister Jane was learning drawing and piano nearby. Richard had determined to apply to the École des Beaux-Arts and pursue a career in architecture, a viable profession in an urbanizing world, at home and abroad. Now certain of his direction, and joined by his sister, he left Geneva for Paris on August 1.[28]

~~~~~~~~~~

Industrialization brought sustained change to European cities, made inefficient over centuries of accretion and accommodation. In Paris the king and his prefect of the Seine introduced public urinals, planted trees, installed gas lighting, paved river quays, and built early railway stations. They finished the Arc de Triomphe at the end of the Champs-Élysées, and Jacques I. Hittorff redesigned the Place de la Concorde, site of the execution of Marie Antoinette and Louis XVI. Restoring to public memory his country's long history, Louis-Philippe launched restoration projects at Versailles, where he created the Galerie des Batailles, hung with monumental paintings of French battles, including the Franco-American victory at Yorktown, Virginia. To appease the left and identify his monarchy with glories of Napoléon, he moved the ashes of the exiled emperor from St. Helena to Paris for their eventual resting place in a massive red quartzite tomb by Louis T.J. Visconti (see 1.16). To normalize relations with the Catholic Church, suppressed in the Reign of Terror, he promoted the restoration of parish churches, with supervision by architect Eugène E. Viollet-le-Duc (see P.16) and decorations by artisans later important to Hunt's American commissions.

Private wealth and modernization through the century provided years of civic and private commissions to French architects trained at the École des Beaux-Arts. The school had originated in the academies of French royal patronage, modeled after *accademias* in Rome and Florence. The 1789 revolution brought suppression of the royal institutions until 1819, when the schools of architecture, painting, and sculpture were amalgamated into the École. Catering to the upper classes, from France and other countries, the French system lacked the independence of Germany's reformed universities, with discipline, uniform curricula, and the awarding of prizes

channeling the most gifted students to administrative positions and prestige public commissions.[29]

At the École, any man, fifteen to thirty years old, French or foreign, could take the entrance exams, even several times before passing. The school required that a qualified architect (*patron*) sponsor each applicant and, after his acceptance, oversee the student's development in his atelier (1.9). Students sought out sponsors who were winners of the Grand Prix leading to study at the Villa Medici in Rome, the highest academic achievement for a French architect. Richard Hunt settled on thirty-five-year-old Hector-Martin Lefuel. He had been a student at the École with Samuel Darier and won the prize in 1839, the only fact about Lefuel that Hunt noted in his journal. Though the École was free, students paid a fee to their sponsoring architect. After passing his qualifying exams, Hunt was admitted in late 1846 to the École's architecture section, a beginner at a middling rank, 37 among 56 accepted, including several foreign-born. Hunt was the first student from the United States to enter the École, a pioneering step that initiated a rite of passage for American architects after the Civil War, when study in Paris became foundational to professional training.[30]

The École taught a method of design, not a style. French academic thought was grounded in classicism, but by the 1840s the school's methodology incorporated rational planning. Interiors were divided between principal spaces that defined a building's purpose (offices, libraries, salons, and dining rooms) and secondary ones that made it functional (halls, stairs, and facilities), organized according to use and a hierarchy of axes (see SC.6). The resulting balanced exterior and interior elevations characteristic of the Beaux-Arts building expressed its function and meaning. "A theater must have the character of a theater," wrote Charles Garnier, architect of Paris Opera House (see P.9, 5.21), "a church must have the character of a church...the details like the whole must correspond to the purpose of the monument."[31]

The École student advanced from the second to first class based on performance in competitions across essential disciplines. Professors at the school and distinguished architects judged finished sketches and rendered projects. They awarded first and second *mentions*, and medals (*medailles*) for exceptional work. Despite improving as he progressed, Hunt won only six First Mentions, including ones for a provincial theater, and a bias bridge (1.10a-b), submitted for a competition in iron construction.[32]

By the time Hunt entered the École, romantic artists and architects had embraced individualism, cultural relativity, and historical change in response to centuries of autocratic rule and dehumanization brought on by industrialization. Rejecting the timeless, transcendent purity attributed to classical buildings, favored by the aristocracy and conservative academicians, architects—inside and outside the École—forged an eclectic architecture incorporating forms from different eras and regions that conveyed a building's relation to past and present. During Hunt's École years, the *Néo-Grec* (New Greek) classicists, Henri Labrouste and his circle, promoted architectural change. Known as the Romantics (*Romantiques*), they focused on the logic of the trabeated, bearing-wall construction of the Greek temple, hence their name and predisposition to architecture from antiquity and the Renaissance. In Paris, Labrouste's groundbreaking 1850 Bibliothèque Sainte-Geneviève exemplified a synthesis of classical elements and structural transparency to reveal the library's use and place in history.

Significant to Hunt's future practice was the Romantics' exploration of architectural transitions, from Romanesque to Gothic, and, most relevantly, from Gothic to Renaissance as seen at the chateaus of Francis I (1.12, see 2.16). The transformation of an architecture from one country into a new architecture for another, as the king had adapted the Italian Renaissance to the French Gothic, and as Hunt would do in America, made buildings a reflection of national invention and progress. The opposition to Neo-Grec eclecticism was polymath architect Viollet-le-Duc, who theorized that Gothic architecture offered dynamic possibilities, applicable in iron and steel. Both camps stressed choice of materials and elements based on

Hunt's watercolor and ink drawings for
École des Beaux-Arts assignments, both
awarded First Mentions

Fig. 1.10a An iron bridge, 1847
Fig. 1.10b A theater for a small city, 1851

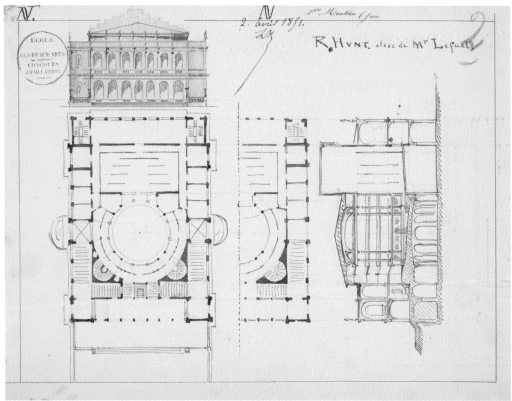

Hunt's École drawings

Fig. 1.11a A hostel in Algeria, 1851
Fig. 1.11b Archives of the National Audit
Office, 1852, its façade inscribed with lyrics
from *Yankee Doodle Dandy* (published 1842),
a traditional student jest

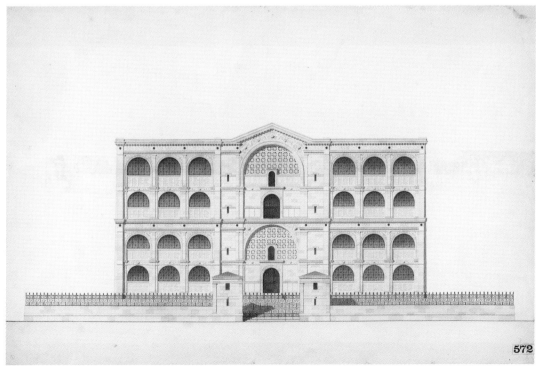

572

use and need, and the primacy of structure in the development of forms appropriate to new times.[33]

From a New England society that valued history and progress, Hunt embraced the architectural past and the rational determination of plan under a Grand Prix winner, the architect Guillaume-Abel Blouet, director of theory at the École. As an ally of the *Romantiques*, an authority on the Baths of Caracalla in Rome, and lead architect for the Renaissance-era Chateau de Fontainebleau (see 2.16, SK.2), Blouet was influential in Hunt's future career. His school assignments, preserved by Hunt in his self-historicizing archive, outlined projects by intended use, materials, and site, and the drawings required, including sections, floor plans, and elevations, in varying scale and detail. His assigned "village church" was to be "*simple*," but "a monument" for "the cult of divinity." A national assembly hall needed to follow "the [architectural] principles of simplicity and truth," which were also the "principles" of government. From this approach to architecture, Hunt learned to design buildings (a railroad station, summer house, sculptor's studio), monuments (family tomb and triumphal arch), public spaces (cemetery and city square), and furnishings (candelabra and birdcage) that were at once functional and representational.[34]

Living in a colonialist era and working from precedent, the École architect appropriated regional traditions. Since Napoléon's 1798 looting of Egypt and photographic expeditions in the 1840s, Middle Eastern architecture and interiors had entered the Romantic repertoire. In February 1851, the year Hunt attained the first class, Blouet outlined requirements for a traditional hostel run by a religious order, though one located in the Algerian desert (*Une maison hospitalière pour l'Algérie*) (1.11a). In his submission, Hunt flanked an arched entrance with stables, an axial symmetry characteristic of the Beaux-Arts building. Palms, azure tiles, and star-patterned ceilings around a fountain court evoked a tranquil civility in a country where the French had slaughtered thousands of Algerians after invading in 1830. Knowing the exotic appeal of his watercolors, at once architectural and fine art, Hunt exhibited them decades later in New York.[35]

In March 1852 Blouet assigned the design of an archives of the national audit office (*Des archives pour la cour des comptes*), on four equal floors divided into three equal parts (1.11b). For his neoclassical exterior, Hunt adapted the Bibliothèque Sainte-Geneviève. In contrast with that building's structure and meaning made transparent in iron and stone, Hunt's interpretation was heavy and unnuanced, planned with interior masonry walls. Twenty years later, he would revisit the Bibliothèque to achieve an American synthesis for the library of New York collector James Lenox.[36]

Hunt was at the École from December 1846 until September 1854, in part because of touring in Europe and America. Architecture and interiors were his focus as he traveled to England, Scotland, and Ireland in 1846, though side trips to bestselling author Sir Walter Scott's tomb and a performance of Gaetano Donizetti's *Lucrezia Borgia* (1833) were alluring diversions for the romantic mind. His first extended trip was from summer to early fall 1848, when he toured America's mid-Atlantic region and the recently populated trans-Appalachian West. Thomas U. Walter's neoclassic temple as classroom building at Girard College for poor white orphan boys in Philadelphia, Benjamin Latrobe's Catholic basilica in Baltimore, and William Strickland's limestone and iron capitol at Nashville confirmed the prospects for an American architect steeped in the methodology and classicism of the French École.[37]

The 1851 Great Exhibition of the Works of Industry of All Nations in London was a watershed moment for the arts, inspired by expositions held in France since its revolution. A committee of educators and inventors, joined by Queen Victoria's consort Prince Albert, conceived the sprawling exposition in architect Joseph Paxton's Crystal Palace, a spectacle of plate glass and iron, to improve the design of manufactured goods and, by extension, civilize the working classes. Hunt toured the fair, awestruck by displays from "oriental countries," a premonition of his forthcoming trip to the Middle East. In 1857 the exhibition's organizing committee used surplus funds to establish the South Kensington Museum for Industrial Arts (the Victoria and Albert Museum from 1899), the Science Museum, and the Natural History Museum, all in the spirit of refining the public through training and education. Twenty years later Hunt and his American colleagues would launch institutions inspired by the Victorian model.[38]

Hunt clarified his views of English and French architecture as he traveled in 1852. He found London a "murky town.... Not a church, house, shop, fountain, or monument of any kind that displays the slightest knowledge or even desire of such a thing in the way of fine arts; every detail...shows the greatest ignorance and the most profound bad taste conceivable." In contrast, the Gothic-to-Renaissance architecture of Loire chateaus was rich with potential. Lefuel, once the architect for the Chateau de Meudon and soon the chateaus of Sèvres and Fontainebleau, was making castle architecture core to Hunt's studies as industrial wealth paid for new mansions and restorations. Hunt considered still-private Chenonceau (1522) inspirational for new residential design, observing that it was "beautifully kept up, everything exists as formerly, the most interesting and comfortable chateau I ever saw."[39]

By the time of his castle tour, Hunt had learned photography, his brother Leavitt having already pioneered the new art on his tour of the Holy Land the year before. After Lefuel's American student Francis Peabody III joined Hunt in the Loire, the two "occupied [themselves] by taking views & copying designs in the interiors" at Blois (1.12). Francis I's chateau was being "beautifully restored by [Félix] Duban," an architect in the circle of Henri Labrouste, a juror of Hunt's work at the École, and restorer of Louvre interiors. He was unifying the chateau's disparate architecture and polychromed interiors, creating a narrative of the building's history dating from the fourteenth century. "It would be," commented a historian, "difficult to conceive of a monument that responded more brilliantly to the romantic imagination than the Château de Blois," running, like Hunt's own work, "the architectural gamut from massive feudal fortifications to spidery crocketed ogees and on to perfectly proportioned pairs of Doric columns." For the contemporary architect, the study of Blois showed "how architecture may be used as an evidence of civilization," wrote Hunt's student, Henry Van Brunt.[40]

Fig. 1.12 Staircase at Gothic-to-Renaissance Chateau de Blois, France, visited by Hunt in 1852, and later influential in his work at Biltmore; Hunt research photograph, ca. 1860

Fig. 1.13 Hunt's watercolor of a "Postman, woman of Upper Egypt, [Tunisian] Dey" dignitary, reflecting the allure of the "exotic" to the nineteenth-century tourist; 1853 sketchbook[2]

An École architectural education was only complete with knowledge and first-hand experience of ancient monuments central to the classical canon. At the beginning of August, Richard and William headed north, sketching in Brussels, Antwerp (see SK.5), and Düsseldorf where they dined with painter Emanuel G. Leutze. Parting in Venice (see SK.3), Hunt headed south to Rome, arriving in Alexandria by January 1853 (see SK.6). For five months, accompanied at times by the son of a US senator and the brother-in-law of his future client, Martin Brimmer, Hunt toured the Middle East, encountering beggars and bandits, swarms of "fleas" and "vermin," and bargaining with "Jews" and "Arabs." As he crossed mountains by donkey and deserts on camel, and sailed the Nile in a *dahabeah*, dressed in native clothes and plagued with boils and infection, Hunt painted, in the orientalist tradition, watercolors of local people (1.13) and escaped into Alexandre Dumas' *La Reine Margot* (1845) and sociologist Harriet Martineau's *Eastern Life, Present and Past* (1847), concluding that the Levant was no place "for ladies to visit." The trials of travel, however, did not impede Hunt's collecting "antiquities," carpets, and jewelry, nor diminish the miracle at the site of the Flagellation in Jerusalem, where "the only spring of running water" ran. By June the intrepid Americans had arrived in Athens, ground zero for architects educated in the canon, the apex of ancient architectural traditions. "I have succeeded in disentangling myself from the great oriental snare," Hunt reflected, "and though but halfway toward civilization, I feel much better" (1.14). He

found the city "fearfully hot," but cool evenings brought moon-lit hikes to the majestic Temple of Olympian Zeus and Hadrian's Gate. After traveling north through Venice, Austria, and Germany, Hunt was home in Paris by July. Wiser and informed, a pilgrim back from sacred lands, he returned to the École, writing "a happier man you do not see often. The spirit moved me and I moved with it."[41]

Hunt and his family were together in Paris, on and off, into the 1850s. The brothers rented apartments near their studies, while Jane and their mother lived together (see P.2 and P.3). By 1849, Richard Hunt was "working hard at architecture, with a manly and patriotic feeling to make himself of use at home," wrote his childhood friend from New Haven, Theodore W. Winthrop. For several years Richard and William lived along the rue Jacob on the Left Bank, where they entertained French and American friends and mixed in the life of a city that was, wrote Russian novelist Nikolai Gogol, a "vast showcase of everything produced by arts and crafts right to the last talent hidden away in some lost corner, the familiar dream of twenty-year-old men, the bazaar, the great fair of Europe." Hunt participated in this cultural souk as spectator and collector, enthralled by the tragedienne Rachel Félix, as famous for her Phaedra in Jean Racine's eponymous play as for being the mistress of three Bonapartes. An amateur in the tradition of eighteenth-century *dilettanti*, Hunt purchased new and antiquarian books, bibelots, engravings, porcelain, and antiques he discovered in bookstores, galleries, and markets, enriched by collections looted during the French Revolution and sold during subsequent regimes (1.15, see also 2.4). He was "accumulating valuable architectural works," recalled his sister, and "would deny himself almost anything to add to his collection. — He also had a taste for curios, & interesting relics — & during the Revolution of 1848 bought a number." Broke from time to time, he joined his fellow American artists in their self-anointed OMC, "Out of Money Club."[42]

After 1815, when Napoléon lost at Waterloo, until 1850, approximately one thousand Americans studied medicine in Paris. Jonathan Hunt trained at the School of Medicine (École de Médecine) and became a doctor in

Fig. 1.15 In Paris, Hunt and his brothers became collectors; sketchbook watercolor by Richard, possibly of his brother Jonathan, ca. 1850

the capital city. Leavitt, already a linguist in ancient languages, earned a law degree at the University of Heidelberg, and William continued to study art, attending Düsseldorf's Royal Academy of Art [Kunstakademie today] in 1845, renowned in America for its genre and landscape painters. Finding the curriculum constraining, as he had earlier at Harvard, William returned to Paris after a year. He entered the atelier of École-trained Thomas Couture, later joined by Richard, before finding his mentor, the realist painter of Barbizon peasants, Jean-François Millet. This experience, like Richard's at the École under Lefuel, determined William's professional practice combining painting and education.[43]

While she directed her sons into professions, Jane Hunt encouraged her only daughter in genteel arts. She herself had been raised to be a supportive wife, but to her father's disapproval, had studied drawing and painting, interests she now encouraged in her namesake. Music, needlework, and art making through copying were acceptable occupations for upper-class women. Traditionally understood as merely "ornamental" and confirmatory of a woman's femininity and elite status, these practices were in fact by mid-century a route to appointments at new schools for women and jobs in the burgeoning commercial arts. Mrs. Hunt, attentive to trends in culture, may have encouraged her daughter's training to this end, but the younger Jane did not have a career and remained unmarried, becoming her mother's companion and the family memoirist.[44]

To live in Paris at mid-century was to witness ongoing debates between church and state, argued by establishment intellectuals and reformers. With an inquiring mind, Hunt read critical texts by École classicists while collecting pamphlets and journals expressing progressive views on art. He went to church "as usual," attending sermons by reform-minded Catholic priests and Protestant preachers. In the greater field, social and political differences played out in worker rebellions. There were riots throughout the 1830s and 1840s, culminating in 1848 when Louis-Philippe fell from power and republican revolutions across Europe enflamed military suppression and autocratic rule. Near the church of the Madeleine that year, Hunt witnessed the insurrection that left fifteen hundred dead at the hands of the state. "We cannot believe," he wrote incredulously as a citizen of democracy, "they have drawn on the people." The conditions were set for the 1851 coup by Napoléon I's nephew, Louis-Napoléon Bonaparte. His declaration as Emperor Napoléon III the following year opened the Second Empire.[45]

Political upheaval and Napoleonic wars had slowed the development of Paris. After ascending to the imperial throne, and inspired by London's

Fig. 1.16 Architects Louis Visconti and Hector Lefuel (right), teacher of Richard Hunt, present plans for the new Louvre to Napoléon III and Empress Eugénie; Ange Tissier, ca. 1865

parks and Regent Street crescent, Louis-Napoléon drove a grand-scale urban renewal. Though separated by class and politics, aristocrats with inherited fortunes and the haute bourgeoisie shared the emperor's distrust of the proletariat who had rioted at the Madeleine. Now, Georges-Eugène Haussmann, the politically scheming prefect of the Seine, oversaw the city's transformation into an *"Urbs Renovata,"* an industrial-era, Augustan Rome. The objective was "an advanced civilization" of new government buildings and apartment blocks along wide boulevards that were access for government control of periodic violence by the laboring poor displaced from the city's center in the emperor's beautification campaign.[46]

On the death of his architect Louis Visconti in late 1853, Napoléon III appointed Hector Lefuel to complete the unification of the Tuileries and the Louvre, the state museum since 1793 (1.16). Lefuel, now responsible for projects employing three thousand workers, assembled an office of French and foreign-born architects, including his first American student. As he concluded his studies in 1854 Hunt was made a state building inspector, an appointment that brought him practical experience in construction and engineering. A Francophile and architect, in the tradition of Thomas Jefferson, Hunt from Brattleboro, Vermont, was now at the center of French

Fig. 1.17 Entrance to the imperial library, the Pavillon de la Bibliothèque, Louvre, Paris, by Hector Lefuel, with assistance from Richard Hunt; Édouard Baldus, ca. 1856-57

art and design. No Henri Labrouste or Charles Garnier, Hunt was a man in the right place at the right time whose abundant self-confidence, ambition, and financial independence more than made up for what he lacked in artistic vision.[47]

Lefuel's office coordinated with painters, sculptors, and craftsmen to project *la gloire* of France as embodied in Empress Eugénie and the emperor. To plan the entrance to the imperial library at the Louvre, the Pavillon de la Bibliothèque, opposite the Palais Royale on the rue de Rivoli, Lefuel engaged "dear Dick" as an assistant (1.17). One of the seven massive blocks of what is now the Cour Napoléon, the library entrance related the architecture of the new Louvre to the Renaissance entrance of the Tuileries. The pavilion was an orchestration of surface and ornament across two stories of banded columns culminating in caryatids supporting a sculpted pediment representing Art and Science. A stone monument of Beaux-Arts hierarchy, in service of order and pomp, the façade was neo-Renaissance.[48]

As the Louvre pavilion neared completion at Christmas 1854, Hunt reflected on family and country. There was no place, he wrote his mother, where the fine arts were "more needed.... Why, there are more luxurious houses put up in New York than in Paris" and if poorly designed, the "fault" lay with their architects. "Why should not our public hotels...rival or even surpass the palaces of Europe?" he asked. "It is the same thing in painting or in any branch of the Arts...." Once again, at a turning point, Hunt anticipated his future purpose with Whigish superiority. A trained architect and patriot, he was obliged to "surpass" Old World buildings with New World architecture and to "encourage" the arts at home as the Empire was doing in France. He accepted this heroic challenge, understanding that success in a nation founded on private enterprise lay with the individual.[49]

Hunt was not alone in his assessment of American culture. Theodore Winthrop had spent hours at the Louvre and was "full of plans for improving the conditions of the fine arts" at home. Their mutual friend, the New Haven-born painter Thomas Rossiter living on the Place Vendôme with his wife, Anna Parmly, shared this aspiration. Writing late in 1855 to the founders of the new American arts journal, *The Crayon*, Rossiter sent "felicitations in the success of [their] endeavor" and offered any help he could. Like Hunt, he was seeing the benefits of free education and urged support of the National Academy of Design in New York. They should advocate for its role as a "free liberal, gratuitous privilege—to a class of youth who can be aided in no other way...." He included observations on the "monster" Paris 1855 Exposition, but was looking toward New York, "for there is much to be done at home which can only be accomplished by artists making themselves formidable by numbers & influence."[50]

Opportunity in America was not all that Hunt and Rossiter shared. By early 1855, the painter and architect were planning what became Hunt's first independent project, a New York home and studio for Rossiter and his family. The double townhouse they finally built would epitomize a building that was more luxurious than many in Paris, its very boldness launching Hunt's celebrity as a hard-charging architect for new architecture as art.

George Ticknor and his generation worried that the American in Paris would lose his moral footing. "A man leaving N. England," warned a Unitarian minister, having "a moral sensibility, which our education generally produces, will continually be shocked upon his arrival in Paris. If he stays long, conscience will lose some of its power and his moral perception will be blunted…in no part of the world are all the contrivances of sensuality so concentrated as in Paris." At twenty-seven, Hunt was well settled in this city of luxury and distraction. His promotion from fifth- to fourth-class Louvre inspector afforded him more money and time to entertain, travel, study music, read, and cook. He confessed to his mother that "egotistical Dick" continued to spend money on books for "a good French library." Despite this indulgence, Hunt had not lost his way in the seductive metropolis. He had matured as a man and a thinker, recalled his brother-in-law Henry C. Chauncey, keeping the "same good lines of character." This moral steadfastness and Hunt's will to be more than "small potatoes" decided his return to America.[51]

On learning of his pending departure, Hector Lefuel cautioned his young colleague against uncertain prospects in a nation that regarded architecture not as an art, but as a mechanical trade. He could offer Hunt "any government position within his control if he would remain in Paris." But set on his course of action, and after visiting Rossiter's "monster" Exposition Universelle where William exhibited paintings, Hunt sailed for home in September 1855, his art and books already crated and shipped.[52]

Richard Hunt had been raised a Unitarian Whig in a privileged society of statesmen, intellectuals, and businessmen that entrusted the realization of a prosperous and cultured democracy to the educated individual, supported by clergy who advocated for deeds over moral piety. To become an informed and contributing citizen, he had followed the scholarly path forged by his parents' generation. He had befriended artists and educators and become a seasoned traveler, a connoisseur of opera, art, and cuisine, of marbled interiors, gilded furnishings, and museum collections. Critical for his intended profession, he had received an atelier education and experienced the power of an integrated practice in service to socio-political ends, of architecture, sculpture, and interior design conceived together for a signifying whole greater than its constituent parts. The road forward had been humbling at times, never winning a coveted École "*medaille*" and losing competitions to stronger talents, outcomes that steeled the young architect for contests after the Civil War.

As Daniel Webster's "rational being" and Margaret Fuller's "thinking American," Hunt was ready to plant foreign seedlings at home, to "practice his profession in the United States," wrote family friend and former president Martin Van Buren to architect Richard Upjohn, "more as a matter of taste, and to reap its Honors, than for immediate pecuniary advantage." Inculcated into two post-revolutionary societies and from a background of public service, Richard Hunt understood that action brought social change. In the years ahead he would use his training and privilege to engage in public dialogues, interweaving new institutions and building monuments to "civilize" his native land.[53]

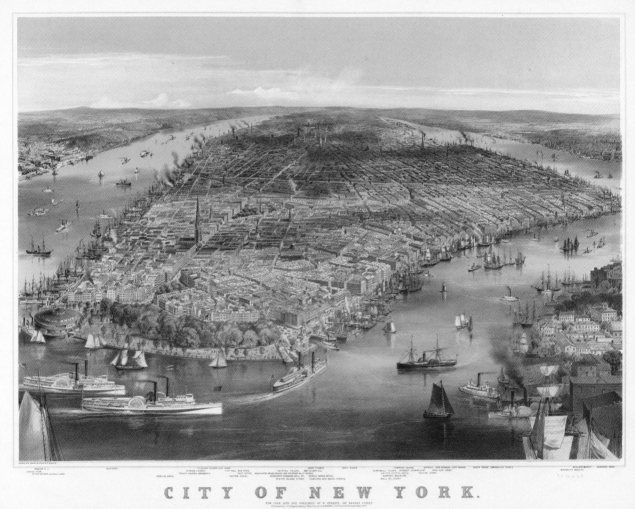

CITY OF NEW YORK.

NEW YORK, LITH. AND PUBLISHED BY N. CURRIER, 152 NASSAU STREET.

Chapter 2

Soldier of the Crayon

Richard Hunt returned to America, confident, even arrogant in his belief, that a professional architect could exceed, as he had written his mother, "the palaces of Europe." Now his Yankee common sense told him that only New York was rich enough for his fierce ambition.

The Empire City before the Civil War was America's financial and transportation hub, more daring and economically diverse than rivals Boston and Philadelphia (2.1). Cornelius Vanderbilt was consolidating the New York Central Railroad, and banking, insurance, real estate, and commerce generated staggering riches for those at the top. By mid-century just over one percent of the city's 800,000 residents owned seventy-one percent of its wealth.[1]

Financially, Gotham was in league with London and Paris, but lacked the art and architecture that leaders believed benefited and refined all classes. Thomas Jefferson's view that "great cities are great sores on the body politic" was now "a vulgar and shallow opinion," wrote *Putnam's Monthly Magazine* in 1855, the year Hunt returned to New York. The very "concentration of intelligence and power" in the modern city, where neighbors lived with "good manners, grace, good morals, honesty, and true religion," made it a place of civilization led by the rich and educated, the nation's privileged civilizers. To meet their civic obligations to engender "civility" over "barbarism," they turned to Europe for artistic and institutional inspiration.[2]

Financially independent from a paternal inheritance, Hunt rented a studio in the University Building (1837) at the University of the City of New York (New York University—NYU—from 1896) on Washington Square (2.2). The English-inspired, Gothic Revival residence and work space became home to new institutions advancing American culture, including the New York Academy of Medicine, the American Geographical Society, and

Fig. 2.1 New York City, as it looked when Hunt returned from Paris; his New-York Tribune tower and Statue of Liberty would transform the skyline with new heights; Charles Parsons, Currier & Ives, ca. 1856

eventually the American Institute of Architects (AIA). Cornelius Vanderbilt was nearby on Washington Place, while established merchants lived in Greek Revival houses along the square. Shipping magnate Samuel S. Howland, his wife Joanna E. Hone, and their seven children, had lived at No. 12.[3]

Now a committed author, Theodore Winthrop set his 1861 bestseller, *Cecil Dreeme*, at the University Building. In his Gothic mystery of sexual identity, he evoked his childhood friend Richard Hunt in the novel's architect, "a fellow of the practical and artistic natures well combined." He lived in a crenelated collegial building, his "Rubbish Palace" rooms displaying European "plunder...models of the most mythological temples, and the most Christian spires and towers. There were prints and pictures, old and young. There were curiosities in iron and steel, in enamel and ivory, in glass and gem, in armor and weapons.... Fact, beauty, and fun were all represented in his museum." Though no images of Hunt's rooms are extant, we glimpse the extent of his collecting in photographs (2.3) of the bronzes and enamels, embroideries, and architectural elements bequeathed to his sons Richard and Joseph Howland Hunt and displayed in their New York houses [4]

Dr. James Wynne, writing for the *New-York Evening Post*, was so impressed by Hunt's collections that he included him in his 1859 compendium of fifty-one New York bibliophiles. Hunt was in esteemed company, joining historian George Bancroft, architect Alexander J. Davis, public library patron William B. Astor, and the city's Catholic archbishop. He claimed to own three to four thousand volumes, largely acquired in Paris, of which close to two thousand were as "complete a set of work relating to architecture as it was in [Hunt's] power to possess." Associated with these were books on "painting, sculpture, interior decorations, and the ornamental and useful arts of different epochs."[5]

Hunt collected for subject, provenance, and bindings. From the extant "Library of Richard Morris Hunt" at the Library of Congress, we know that volumes on French architecture before 1800 were his focus. He bought from dealers and auctions, seeking editions owned and authored by architects. An exceptional prize with an autobiographical connection was Hunt's copy of the multi-volumed *Architecture française* (1752-1756) (2.4) by Jacques-François Blondel, regally bound in red leather and gold stamped with the arms of the Marquis de Marigny, builder of the Chateau de Petit-Val where Hunt was a guest of its nineteenth-century owners, the American Moulton family.[6]

In addition to his books, Hunt reportedly owned five thousand photographs of "views of celebrated monuments and edifices." As black

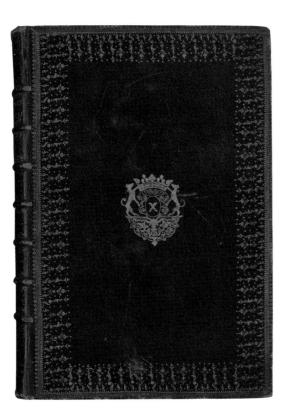

Fig. 2.4 *Architecture françoise* (1752-1756), from the library of the Marquis de Marigny, brother of Madame de Pompadour, a prized edition in Richard Hunt's library of more than three thousand volumes

and white images of historic buildings and interiors were fundamental to the design of historicist buildings and restorations, Hunt collected images by leading photographers Édouard Baldus, Charles Marville, and Bison Frères. He believed, Wynne wrote, that an architect's drawings facilitated conception, but only photographs gave a "perspective view" and revealed a building's "effect."[7]

Exceptional in his interviews, Wynne concluded by noting Hunt's art plunder:

> This collection contains many interesting relics of Egyptian, Roman, and Grecian Antiquity, and is particularly rich in specimens of more modern art illustrative of different epochs, among which are many articles of household furniture, [such] as curious clocks of different ages, and articles of domestic use, as well as many rare ornaments taken from venerable edifices as they existed in the middle ages. There are a large number of specimens of windows of stained glass arrayed in this era, and numerous church ornaments and altar-pieces, some of which are of exquisite workmanship. Among these latter are the doors and frontispiece of a tabernacle in solid silver, and an elaborately bound missal, garnished with massive silver designs, taken from an old Cathedral in Holland, which are especially worthy of notice.[8]

In disposition Hunt was a plain-speaking New Englander, but his book and art collecting were Parisian, inspired by Alexandre du Sommerard and a generation of architect/collectors and dealer/collectors, including Émile-Auguste Reiber and Émile Gavet, influential in Hunt's mansion practice. An early archeologist, and a "gentleman of fortune and a distinguished antiquarian," Sommerard lived in the Hôtel de Cluny where he "gathered about him the most complete collection of civil, military, and religious objects of art of the middle ages extant, which he arranged with great care in chronological order" (2.5). Americans in Paris, Hunt continued, were awed by "this remarkable specimen of the remains of the venerable mansions of Paris of the sixteenth century," and the "singular curiosities which each apartment opens to their view." His own collecting of books and photographs, of handmade objects "of different ages," secular and religious,

Fig. 2.5 Hôtel de Cluny, Paris (a museum after 1843); the Gothic-to-Renaissance residence housed an arts collection that inspired Richard Hunt, already a collector in the capital city at the time of this painting; Pierre A. Poirot, 1850

Fig. 2.6 Thirty-Fourth Street, Fifth Avenue, New York City, Caroline and William B. Astor Jr. house (1856); Alexander T. Stewart white marble Second Empire palace (1870); when asked by the department store founder what he thought of its "Greek" architecture, Hunt replied: 'Well...it may be Greek to you, I assure you it is Greek to me, but I don't think it would deceive the smallest little yellow dog that runs down the street"; H.N. Tiemann & Co., 1893[3]

of varied materials and utility, suggests that Hunt, like Sommerard and his followers, conceived his collection as a didactic enterprise dedicated to the history of design and architecture, an antiquarian approach that would inform his leadership in the arts after the Civil War and choice of French Renaissance design for the American palace.[9]

Allied with Hunt's collecting for civilization was his architectural practice, dedicated to building monuments to edify and ennoble a young nation. The Emersonian cult of the individual that shaped Hunt's essential character made America fertile ground for romantic, eclectic architecture based in Western history. Since 1810, the Classical movement, seen by Hunt on his 1848 tour of the South, and the Gothic Revival, exemplified by NYU's University Building, were bookends of international architectural practice. Steamship travel to Europe and buildings by immigrant architects from Germany, England, and France had broadened acceptance of the Romanesque and polychromed English Gothic, associated with John Ruskin, the Victorian artist and theorist on architecture. Over the coming decades Hunt would explore these traditions while becoming a standard bearer for French planning and design, furthering its mandate that architecture should reflect its use and meaning.

By the 1850s, New York had evolved from the Greek Revival to a new eclecticism. Along Broadway was Richard Upjohn's Gothic Trinity Church (1846) and Trench & Snook's Renaissance Revival marble and iron

Fig. 2.7 House and studio of fine artist Thomas Rossiter, as first envisioned by Hunt—a Venetian Gothic palazzo; Richard Hunt, ca. 1854–55

department store (1846) for Irish immigrant Alexander T. Stewart. The German Round-Arch-style Astor Library (1853) by Berlin-born Alexander Saeltzer was at Astor Place. In this international "melting pot" of European style, Richard Hunt opened his career with a Parisian house for the artist Thomas Rossiter on Thirty-Eighth, west of Fifth Avenue.

Treeless streets of high-stooped brownstones gave New York what Protestant residents considered an "unostentatious magnificence," exemplified by the house Griffith Thomas completed for Caroline and William B. Astor Jr. at Fifth Avenue and Thirty-Fourth in 1856 (2.6), the year Hunt launched his Rossiter project. He had initiated plans while still in Paris by "amplifying and adding to" a sketch by the artist, conceiving a Ruskinian Venetian Gothic palazzo, possibly inspired by Rossiter's painting, *Venice*, awarded a Gold Medal at Paris's 1855 exposition (2.7). Dr. Eleazer Parmly (see P.14), Rossiter's father-in-law, a Vermont-born dentist and real estate developer, would pay the costs.[10]

Throughout his career Hunt expanded on what others had originated, bringing his sense of the theatrical and grand to projects uniquely affordable by wealthy clients. German-born Detlef Lienau and likely Parisian Léon A. Marcotte, students of Henri Labrouste, introduced the Neo-Grec style to New York at the Fifth Avenue brick and brownstone house (1850) of banker Hart M. Shiff. Hunt followed this lead with the Rossiter double house and studio, abandoning his original Gothic

Fig. 2.8 Thomas Rossiter house and studio (1857), New York City; photograph signed "My first work/58 RMH," ca. 1875

Fig. 2.9 Thomas Rossiter house and studio, first-floor plan for Venetian version, ca. 1854–55

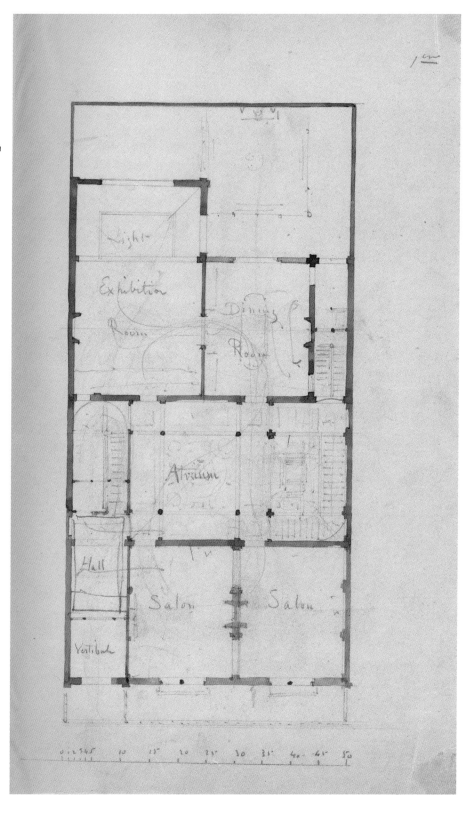

concept for a plan drawing on the French Renaissance Revival of Hector Lefuel's Louvre and the classical New Greek. He called for a Louis XIII-style red brick and limestone exterior but settled on yellow stone, with contrasting brownstone pilasters and window surrounds (2.8, 2.9). The extant interior plans for the Venetian version suggest an interweaving of private and public rooms around a skylighted, balconied stair—the "atrium"—a feature of Hunt's later houses that brought light to dark interiors.[11]

The Rossiter columned façade was fragmented, but imposing. When construction began the adjoining lots were undeveloped, but by the 1880s the house to the east had elements of Hunt's design, possibly by a builder working for Parmly, ironic considering what ensued between Hunt and the doctor. The overall effect on the street lacked the brownstone consistency that antebellum New York found appropriately reserved, but the Beaux-Arts had arrived, wrote critic Montgomery Schuyler, a "beneficial influence in the prevailing chaos" of eclectic styles.[12]

On completion of the Rossiter house, Hunt boldly lodged a contentious lawsuit against Parmly. The doctor refused to pay Hunt's five-percent fee for design and oversight, citing the architect's failure to sign a contract and his having spent twice the estimated $25,000 cost of construction, due to the house's "atrium hall," carved stone, and a neo-Baroque bookcase, an early sign of Hunt's taste for ornamented interiors. Hunt countered that changes late in construction had made expenses soar.[13]

If money was the public justification for the trial, the prejudice that architects faced in pragmatic America was its subtext—that professional design offered little worthy of compensation. To justify his fee, Hunt outlined for the jury how his office had proceeded. First, he shared schematic sketches with his client. On approval, he employed two draftsmen and hired Joseph Wells, the English-born architect of preacher Henry Ward Beecher's renowned congregational Plymouth Church of the Pilgrims in Brooklyn. Together, the men produced more than two hundred drawings, with Hunt choosing materials, selecting finishes, and guiding quarry work, a profession he knew well from supervising construction of the new Louvre.[14]

The doctor claimed to have never paid an architect in the past, relying on his carpenter/builder and tradesmen for planning, compensating for labor and materials, not design. When Parmly's contractor was asked if an architect was ever required, he responded no, that if "a ground plan and elevation" is needed, a "mechanic can go to a library and take down a book on architecture and ask the owner to select anything he likes...." However, if the owner wanted something "different," a professional was required. The Rossiter house, he sneered, "was different from any other I ever saw in my life...."[15]

With the right to compensation for creative input at stake, star witnesses at the trial included English-born architects Jacob Wrey Mould and Richard Upjohn. They supported Hunt's claim that his drawings had value, with the latter stating he charged a one-percent fee for preliminary sketches not used. "You as a lawyer," he told the plaintiff's attorney, "when you give your opinion, do not charge for pen, ink and paper, but for your opinion."[16]

In a split verdict, the court obligated Parmly to pay half of the five-percent fee as compensation for Hunt's "different" design, determining that the doctor had already compensated others for supervision. For Hunt, and his profession, the decision had long-term significance. Trained architects were now entitled to payment for conceptual work, a privilege distinguishing them from tradesmen who dominated American architecture. Emboldened, Hunt would continue to press for acceptance of architecture as a creative, thinking profession.[17]

During the Rossiter project, Wells had overseen construction while Hunt worked for Philadelphian Thomas U. Walter, then expanding the US Capitol in Washington, DC. Hunt's intention had been "to see how public buildings were constructed," knowing from Paris that government commissions became cultural monuments. He was in Walter's office from March until June 1857 as the Capitol's iron-framed dome was under construction, to be crowned by *Freedom*, sculpted by Hunt's acquaintance in Rome, Thomas G. Crawford. In his letter of engagement, Walter referred to Hunt as an "assistant," though Hunt, elaborating on his role, claimed at the Parmly trial that he had been "supervisor to the whole bureau" of Walter's staff. Walter permitted Hunt monthly trips to review the Rossiter project, and then encouraged him to permanently return to New York. There is "little to do in my office beyond copying," Walter wrote, "...too mechanical an occupation for a mind like yours...my own conviction is, that it will be better for you to remain in New York, where you have so good an opportunity—to build up a flourishing business."[18]

~~~~~~~~

Undaunted by the Parmly trial and determined to succeed as New Yorkers invested in high culture, Hunt secured his next two commissions, both arts-related: an artist's studio and exhibition space at Tenth Street between

Fig. 2.10 Richard Hunt outside his Studio Building (1858) at West Tenth Street, New York City, ca. 1875

Fig. 2.11 Hunt's atelier in his Studio Building, New York City; S. Beer, New York, ca. 1861

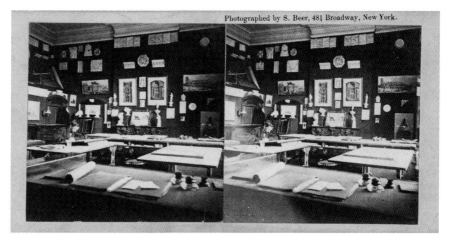

Photographed by S. Beer, 481 Broadway, New York.

Fifth and Sixth Avenues for James B. Johnston, heir to a mercantile fortune, and a private gallery in Weehawken, New Jersey.

Hunt's Tenth Street Studio building (1858) was Neo-Grec in design and indebted to contemporary French architecture (2.10). A circle-in-square motif at the first floor in contrasting stone ran rhythmically across the brick exterior, a grid of compressed Renaissance elements reflecting the interior space. Approximately ninety-eight by ninety-four feet, its core was a court lit by skylights. The arts center housed a two-story ground-floor gallery for public exhibitions and twenty-three studios above, with sleeping lofts but no kitchens. Hunt consistently advanced new building types, and his Tenth Street courtyard plan was later adapted for apartment houses and hotels.[19]

Attended by a concierge, as was customary in France, Tenth Street was an immediate success when it opened in 1858. Every room was rented and tenants over the years included Paris-trained polymathic artist John La Farge, Hudson River School painter Frederic E. Church, and the French landscapist of American scenes, Régis F. Gignoux. Hunt leased adjoining studios (2.11) that he furnished as a Beaux-Arts atelier, where apprentice students worked at drafting tables, inspired by books, architectural casts, and photographs.[20]

The studio building signaled the rise of the financially independent American artist and the civilizing intentions of New York society. Until this time, there had been studios at Union Square and along Broadway, but Johnston's development created an artist collective strategically located in a neighborhood of Fifth Avenue collectors, university faculty, and Samuel F.B. Morse's National Academy of Design (founded 1825) at Thirteenth Street and Fifth Avenue. Light-filled and architecturally advanced, Hunt's studio complex became a gathering place for men and women creating, buying, and, significantly, writing about art and architecture.

Print media was requisite to the emergence of American art before the Civil War. Illustrated books, newspapers, and magazines tracked and guided the progress of the fine arts and public taste. Professional publications made stars of early critics, the Gothic Revival architect Russell Sturgis Jr., Alfred J. Bloor, and Montgomery Schuyler, all colleagues and friends of Hunt. William J. Stillman, co-founder of *The Crayon*, which published the AIA's early meeting proceedings; Theodore Winthrop, author of *Cecil Dreeme*; and Henry T. Tuckerman were all writers in residence at Tenth Street. Heir to a Boston banking fortune and son of a Unitarian minister, Tuckerman was a regular at Hunt family dinners and a fellow bibliophile. Social and gregarious, he profiled upper-class life in New York and Newport, Rhode Island, and promoted art ideals that Hunt realized in buildings and civic engagement. He was a founder of the Century Association in 1847, the arts and literary club at Eighth Street off Fifth, where Hunt was elected a member in 1855, followed by landscape architect Frederick Law Olmsted and Calvert Vaux in 1859.[21]

Three years before Hunt and his colleagues launched the Metropolitan Museum of Art in 1870, Tuckerman published his *Book of the Artists*. He bemoaned that New Yorkers could only view paintings and sculpture at art societies and residential galleries of private collectors. Hunt himself was drawn into their circle when Newark mayor William Wright commissioned a private gallery, possibly for his recent purchase of French artist Rosa Bonheur's monumental painting, *The Horse Fair*, later given by Hunt's client Cornelius Vanderbilt II to the Metropolitan Museum. In New York, the banking Rothschilds' representative in America, August Belmont, built a gallery next to his Fifth Avenue house, and blocks away was John Johnston, railroad executive and brother of the Studio Building developer. He hosted private receptions in his residential gallery where the interdependent worlds of art and finance met. Hunt visited an exhibition there with his relative—through his wife's Howland lineage— Theodore Roosevelt Sr., father of the twenty-sixth US president; bibliophile James Lenox; and dealer Samuel P. Avery, who with his wife, Mary, founded Columbia University's Avery Architectural and Fine Arts Library, in memory of their son and Hunt student, the architect Henry O. Avery.[22]

Engagement with the arts and building a practice were two aspects of Hunt's career. The third was arts education. At the time, Americans learned architecture through apprenticeship and engineering. By the 1850s new schools and institutes teaching drawing and design took hold, inspired by programs at London's South Kensington Museum and supported by manufacturers seeking to improve product design. In New York, Richard Upjohn offered informal training three years before he and his colleagues founded the AIA in 1857 to professionalize architecture through education and standards of practice. As the industrial economy needed new building types and Americans abroad seeing Old World architecture, the times were right for change.

Before his return to America, Hunt and his brother William imagined a New York school of art and architecture taught by practicing artists. After settling at Washington Square, Hunt launched an atelier the year Upjohn founded the AIA. His teaching was École-based, but unlike in France, students completed academic assignments while also working in Hunt's practice, first in his NYU rooms and later at the Tenth Street studio. The Rossiter draftsman George Bradbury was an early pupil, joined by men who became leaders of the architectural establishment as practitioners, educators, writers, and spokesmen: Henry Van Brunt, Charles D. Gambrill, George B. Post, William R. Ware, and Frank H. Furness.[23]

Furness was a son of the Rev. William H. Furness, the Boston-born minister of Philadelphia's First Unitarian Church. A lifelong friend of Emerson, an abolitionist and advocate for the arts, the senior Furness called for the cultivation of "beauty, a natural desire" to bring harmony to American life and improve the "useful arts." Hunt stopped by the Furness home in 1857 while returning to New York from Washington during his stint with Thomas Walter. Frank Furness recalled that Hunt had "the reputation of being by far the brightest man in the École des Beaux-Arts...." A "bunch of joyous, energetic nerves," he did not have "the thoughtful look which he bore in later years." Frank was already studying architecture but after meeting Hunt and marveling at his fast-penned, "cobweb" drawing style, his professional path was set.[24]

Hunt differentiated between English and French training. In England, the apprentice learned through copying project drawings, work that any "John Chinaman" could do. The French, valuing imagination and theory, assigned a problem to "exercise" the student's "mind" and in "that way it [taught] him, or cultivate[d] his imagination, from the very start." Drawing was the basis of art and architecture, and Hunt considered himself a valiant "soldier of the *crayon*" [French for pencil]. "Draw, draw, draw," he told his students. "It will ultimately give you a certain control of your pencil, so you can more rapidly express on paper your thoughts in designing."[25]

Antiquity's canon was foundational to Hunt's approach, his students learning to draft plans "on rigidly scholastic lines, and the vertical developments in the elevations...in strict classic form according to the method of the French school" (see SC.6). Even "if you never practice classical architecture, you get a certain idea of proportion that will never leave you, and that is essential in good designing in any of the different schools." That said, Hunt had a "large catholicity," recalled Furness, and encouraged study of every period. The contemporary architect was inspired by an "idea, not slavish adherence" to precedence.[26]

Hunt's New York atelier was a step toward institutionalizing architecture as a fine art in America and a sign of emerging professionalism in middle-class life. At mid-century, "professional" meant the comprehensive knowledge of a field, achieved through training and apprenticeship. The reward was democracy's promise of self-subsistence in an economy dependent on specialization. Europe had led the way with progressive universities and institutes, and now competitive America was founding societies and four-year college programs. William Ware in 1868 organized the first American professional architectural school, founded at the Massachusetts Institute of Technology (MIT). In 1881 he moved to Columbia College in the City of New York (Columbia University from 1896) and established its architecture department at the School of Mines, which included civil engineering. The model for his programs, he wrote, was "a direct outcome of the Tenth Street Studio."[27]

Hunt and his generation understood that by working together they could advance their chosen profession, setting standards for architectural practice and, through built work, further public acceptance of architecture as an art in advanced societies. In founding the AIA with Hunt and eleven other architects, Richard Upjohn believed that this could be achieved by promoting "branches of the arts and sciences" and "the scientific and practical perfection of its members...not just individual architects."[28]

Thirty-year-old Hunt, one of the five American-born founders of the AIA and the institute's only École-trained architect, became chairman of the national institute's Library and Publications Committee, 1858-70; president of its New York chapter from its founding in 1867 until 1870; and national president, 1888-91. His final years were critical as the AIA confronted the federal government over the poor quality of its buildings and collaborated with the Western Association of Architects, established in 1884 by Daniel Burnham, Louis Sullivan, and their community of Midwestern architects.[29]

The AIA developed as a network of clients, critics, university presidents, artists, landscape architects, and clergy, including the Rev. William Furness, who established architecture as an art and promoted its allied disciplines to ennoble society through fine design. During Hunt's tenure as the New York chapter president, members expanded the AIA reach internationally, electing his teachers and colleagues, including Samuel Darier, Hector Lefuel, Charles Garnier, and Eugène Viollet-le-Duc, as honorary members of this American circle of influence.[30]

The AIA focused on professional standards and terms. Broadly, it cohered around a definition of architecture as the three-dimensional expression of an idea conveyed by the language of style, material, and plan. In revealing a building's use and organization through elevations, the American romantic architect contributed to social transparency. Alfred Bloor, quoting from the book of Luke, told his fellow AIA members in 1869 that: "We live in an age when 'there is nothing covered that cannot be revealed, and hid that shall not be known' after so much history was written…in the small interests of evanescent power and individual vanity…. [History now] is written over again in the interests of Truth and the education and welfare of the whole community."[31]

At the AIA, secular classicism and ecclesiastic Gothic were contested histories. Prague-born Leopold Eidlitz posited that the fifteenth century had seen a "blind return to the Classic styles." "Feudalism," however, had given "birth to Gothic Architecture" and "laid the foundation to free and representative forms of government." For Hunt, "each style of architecture owes its existence to the religion which is coeval with it." Gothic should "give way to another style (in Protestant countries at least)," just as it had in the humanist Renaissance that followed the medieval "Dark Ages." French architecture incorporating both Gothic and classical elements was Hunt's point of departure for buildings in a nation undergoing a secular Renaissance.[32]

To substantiate the relationship of historic buildings to new design, Hunt presented his "History of Architecture" to the AIA in 1857. The talk was neither published nor commented on in *The Crayon*, possibly because it was a draft of Hunt's entry on architecture published two years later in the popular *The New American Cyclopedia*. There he laid out a narrative indebted to the Romantics and archeological evidence, weaving a matrix of eighteenth- and nineteenth-century thought. Supported by mechanics and engineering, architecture was the "art of building," encompassing civic, military, and naval design, fields garnering privileged government commissions. Egypt, Greece, and Rome originated the Western arch and column. But from the Christian era to the humanist Renaissance, ancient traditions had been transformed. French and Italian architecture defined this evolutionary past, with German Gothic and

English Palladian playing contributing roles. As for "modern architecture," the "elements of the nineteenth-century architecture would seem to be purely eclectic," but the exception to this practice was the "French school, the Romantique wherein the Grecian rather than the Roman elements were introduced…portraying simplicity, grace, purity, harmony" through the integration of form, structure, and decoration. Iron was modernity's material, permitting light and space at an industrial scale, as demonstrated by England's Crystal Palace pavilion. Its application in prosperous America would lead to "new architectural features."[33]

Hunt's essay was a manifesto for emerging architects and the general public, biased to classical "beauty" in its ancient and Neo-Grec manifestations, yet accommodating new materials. From his Eurocentric vantage, there were no American buildings worth discussing, neoclassical or otherwise, making the country a tabula rasa whose future lay in the rational determination of plan. Knowing and honoring the past and responsive to the present, the architect could conceive an architecture appropriate to its time and place.

Excepting his history lecture, Hunt's focus at the AIA was building the institute's print collections, funded by his relatives, colleagues, and clients. Despite its common protocol of admission by ticket, the AIA library of books, photographs, and engravings came to educate a broad community, the "engineer, the journalist, the college professor, the student, the merchant and clerk, the broker, consul, clergyman, physician, lawyer, banker, artist painter, carver, silversmith, carpenter and stone cutter." This breadth of public interest was a change from the past due to European travel, a "higher tone of culture," and "partial escape" from the practicalities that had dominated life in the early republic.[34]

～～～～～～

New York was home for Hunt, and as a single man he befriended leaders in business and the arts who were later important to his practice and institutions he founded. Similarly, his ties in Boston were deep in what Oliver Wendell Holmes Sr. called the city's "Brahmin" elite, a society of financial and social leaders, descendants of Pilgrim founders and British aristocrats. They made Boston New York's competitor as their city grew from 93,000 residents in 1840 to 137,000 a decade later, with Irish immigrants and Central Europeans working the city's textile mills and railroad. This growth brought the Back Bay development, a grid of tree-lined blocks around Commonwealth Avenue "similar in its effect to that

Fig. 2.12 Hunt's 1860
Dr. William Morland
residence (right) at
Newbury and Arlington
Streets, French
Neo-Grec classicism in
Boston's new Back Bay
development, ca. 1880

of the Champs Élysées in Paris or the Unter den Linden in Berlin," wrote
its likely planner, architect Arthur D. Gilman. Hunt's singular contribution
was at the corner of Newbury and Arlington Streets opposite the Boston
Common, three adjoining houses (1860) for the prominent Harvard-
educated urologist Dr. William W. Morland, treated as a freestanding block,
forty-five by ninety foot, faced in gray-green Canadian freestone (2.12). Its
string courses, bay windows, cornices, and continuous Mansard roof were
features of Gilman's nearby Parisian William D. Bates house of the same
year, but Hunt's row was coolly Neo-Grec, stressing mass through recessed
headers, inscribed floriate motifs, and shallow reveals.[35]

With a community of prominent local architects, including Henry
H. Richardson and the Ruskinian John H. Sturgis, Boston never became
a center for Hunt's practice. But the city's summer resort at Newport
evolved into his enduring showcase. An entrée to this art and society
retreat was his brother William, as determined for the future of American

Fig. 2.13 Catharine and Richard Hunt house (acquired 1864), Hill-Top Cottage, Newport, Rhode Island; ca. mid-1870s

painting as Richard was for architecture. He had moved there in 1856 after marrying Boston merchant heir Louisa D. Perkins, a power alliance to a family of art collectors.[36]

The seaside town of Newport on Aquidneck Island faces the Atlantic Ocean and sheltering Narragansett Bay. It was a refuge for Portuguese Jews in the colonial period, when the British and Americans waged battles until the Comte de Rochambeau occupied the town from 1780 to 1781. That latter year he joined the Marquis de Lafayette and George Washington to defeat the British at Yorktown, Virginia, an event important to Hunt as a designer of the battle's 1884 monument. Early nineteenth-century trade and industrialization bypassed the once prosperous outpost, but railroads and steamships in the 1850s brought Southern plantation owners and Northern merchants escaping summer heat. By 1858 Newport had become a "delightful watering-place, though usually considered as merely a fashionable place of resort,... nevertheless quite rich in artistic associations," with its colony of American artists in residence during the summer months. At the north end of Bellevue Avenue, William purchased Hill-Top Cottage, originally a two-story, Greek Revival villa before a prior owner added a new first floor (2.13). Working on parallel tracks, Richard launched the Tenth Street Studio building as William built a carriage house (see 5.7b) at the back of Hill-Top's tree-shaded lot, where he taught drawing and painting in a first-floor classroom and second-floor studio.[37]

In 1860, Hunt was finishing the Morland houses and recovering from dysentery in Providence as the guest of New York banker David Duncan and his wife Fannie. Disbanding his New York atelier, he brought students Edward Quincy and Frank Furness to Newport where they studied art in William's studio, joined by John La Farge and brothers Henry and William James, back from Europe. Newport, wrote Henry, was "the one right residence, in all our great country, for those tainted, under whatever attenuations, with the quality and the effect of detachment from their experiences of Europe."[38]

Professional success did not guarantee acceptance in class- and money-conscious America, but the right house, clubs, and marriage improved the odds, as William Hunt knew when he married his Brahmin wife. In the summer of 1860, thirty-two-year-old Richard met the Duncans' friend, eighteen-year-old Catharine Clinton Howland, known as Kate. An heir to one of America's greatest shipping fortunes, she was a Mayflower descendant through John Howland and the youngest of six sisters and a brother who lived at NYU's University Building at the time of Hunt's studio there. Their deceased parents were Joanna Hone and Samuel Howland of Washington Square. Samuel and his brother Gardiner G. Howland had expanded the family's merchant business to South America, and in 1832 Gardiner's son William E. Howland and cousin William H. Aspinwall reorganized the firm as Howland & Aspinwall (see P.1). They introduced clipper service to China, founded the Pacific Mail Steamship Company, and financed the Panama to California railroad just before the Gold Rush in 1848. A devout Episcopalian who worshiped at New York's Trinity Church and funded Paris' American cathedral, Aspinwall was Catharine's cousin and guardian. He became a patron of new cultural institutions, some designed by Richard Hunt, and was one of New York's early collectors of old master paintings.[39]

Kate was dark-haired, social, and welcoming, an "exuberant sultana" remarked a New York society diarist. Richard's sister Jane found her "very amiable, straightforward," and unlike the wives of her other brothers, "respect[ful]" of their critical mother. Catharine and Richard shared a sharp, observant humor and were devoted to their influential families. Personally, he had "a captivating animation [and] a frank sincerity," wrote Henry Van Brunt, and "these qualities, combined with the dignity of his bearing and his manly beauty, made him a notable individuality."[40]

Over the course of the summer Hunt courted Catharine at teas and society balls before proposing in September 1860. Even though his daughter was the wife of James Renwick Jr., architect of the Norman Romanesque Smithsonian Institution (1855) in Washington, DC, William Aspinwall and family allies met Hunt's proposal "with violent disapproval and opposition." Richard was a gentleman, Catharine wrote, but his humor and "independence" in thought "meant to them only eccentricity... the fact of a man following an artistic profession was to his detriment...." Overcoming the long tradition of actors and artists as social outsiders remained a challenge for Hunt and his associates throughout the nineteenth century, but because of urban efforts to advance art and architecture, Henry James Sr. could write in 1851 that though the artist "had been from the beginning always a very suspicious individual in the moral regard... whether he be naughty or virtuous, we seek him and honor him...."[41]

Ever determined, Richard ultimately prevailed, and Catharine accepted his offer with an independence and authenticity that would be characteristic of her life. On April 2, 1861, they married at Richard Upjohn's Gothic Episcopal Church of the Ascension (1841) on Fifth Avenue, around the corner from Hunt's Tenth Street studio, and honeymooned at Niagara Falls, as his parents had done forty years before. Ten days later Confederates bombarded Fort Sumter, launching the Civil War. The upper-class Seventh Regiment of the New York Militia (see 2.2), including Hunt's childhood friend Theodore Winthrop, headed south to battle as Hunt and the Century Association organized a members' Union regiment. Advised that his recent dysentery would render him vulnerable in combat, Hunt accepted the club option to pay another to serve in his place, par for men of his class and a decision later questioned for its morality by his wife. On his release from military duty, Richard and Catharine, accompanied by his mother, sailed for Le Havre in May.[42]

Catharine's inheritance and Hunt's work and investments paid for six trips abroad during their marriage, with two lasting more than a year. To read Catharine's remembrances of these sojourns, when she and her children were sick in Paris and Richard took cures at German spas, is to experience nineteenth-century life of new convenience—trains, ships, gas light, running water, heating, ventilation—and debilitating illness before advances in sanitation and medical care. Richard suffered for decades from dysentery, boils, gout, and fever, which rarely kept him from his demanding practice.

Catharine and Richard joined his siblings Jane and Jonathan on arrival in Paris. At first the newlyweds stayed at a hotel near Hunt's Pavillon de la Bibliothèque and then shared an apartment with New Yorker John N.A. Griswold and his wife Jane Emmet. An associate of Catharine's brother-in-law Charles H. Russell and later a president of the Illinois Central Railroad, Griswold was the uncle of architecture critic Mariana A. Griswold Van Rensselaer and cousin to tobacco heir Pierre Lorillard IV, who sold his Newport house, the Breakers, to Hunt's client, Cornelius Vanderbilt II. In Paris, Griswold negotiated for Hunt to design a summer cottage in Newport (see 2.19–2.21b), the first of many commissions he received from this privileged and interrelated world.[43]

The city was as Hunt had left it six years before, his "old confreres" leaders in new architecture he was bringing to America. Accompanied by Lefuel, Catharine and Richard reviewed Félix Duban's restoration of the Louvre's Gallery of Apollo and strolled along the new Avenue de l'Impératrice (Avenue Foch from 1929) and through the Bois de Boulogne, seeing buildings in the fashionable rustic style. Alone Hunt toured the neighborhood bordering the Parc Monceau. He knew the empire's bankers, the Pereire brothers, had acquired the seventeenth-century *quartier* to develop a neighborhood of classical limestone mansions for collectors, financiers, and industrialists, much as Fifth Avenue evolved along Central Park. At the end of July, Richard and Catharine joined Leavitt in Derbyshire, England. He had graduated in law (1856) from the University of Heidelberg and was practicing in New York while continuing his scholarly study of the ancient world. He too was honeymooning, with wealthy Katherine Jarvis from Vermont. After visiting Chatsworth house in Derbyshire, Catharine and Richard headed south to the Isle of Wight, famous for the Italianate Osborne House and its pristine Swiss chalet, designed by Prince Albert for Queen Victoria (2.14 and 2.15a). The Hunts and the American painter William P.W. Dana and his family rented a thatched-roof cottage in Bonchurch, where the artist and architect sketched along the English Channel.[44]

By fall the Hunts were back in Paris, living in an apartment on the Champs-Élysées and waiting for the birth of their first child, the future architect Richard Howland Hunt. Domestic help, sometimes obliging, often intrusive, was a leitmotif of Catharine's honeymoon memoir. There was

Fig. 2.14a Catharine (seated left) and
Richard Hunt on their honeymoon
with American artist William P.W.
Dana (seated right) and his young
family, Ventnor, Isle of Wight,
England, 1861

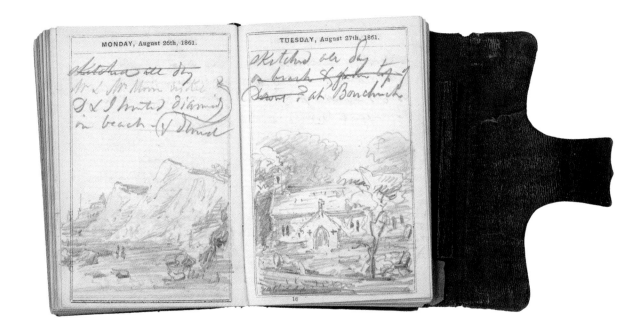

Fig. 2.14b Richard's 1861 honeymoon diary

Fig. 2.15 Richard Hunt's model of an ocelot at the Paris zoo; cast in bronze by Antoine-Louis Barye, 1861

MODELED·BY
RICHARD·MORRIS·HUNT.
1861.

"trouble with dishonest servants" until Clémence, "a great tall grenadier of a woman, reigned supreme over the pots and pans." In general, however, French staff "belonged to the old regime...who considered your pockets and your interest," refusing miserly tips.

   With his practice in mind and art allied to architecture, Hunt studied plants and modeled animals at the city's historic botanical garden under supervision of the *animaliste* Antoine-Louis Barye, a teacher of William Morris Hunt (2.15). They collected and promoted the sculptor's work, prized in America and abroad for its realism after neoclassicism. Catharine and Richard's son was born in March, and following trips to the resort at Biarritz on the Atlantic, to Fontainebleau (2.16) and a visit with Jean-François Millet and his family nearby, the Hunts sailed for home in April 1862. On their first trip abroad together, Hunt had renewed friendships in Paris' art community and shown his young wife developments in French architecture and urbanism that would influence his practice through the Civil War. From these novel and educating experiences, Catharine had come to see Paris "with new eyes."[45]

<p style="text-align:center">~~~~~~~~~</p>

From Christmas 1862 until 1886, Catharine and Richard Hunt lived in the wealthy neighborhood near Fifth Avenue and Thirty-Fourth Street

Fig. 2.16 Horseshoe Staircase (1634), Chateau de Fontainebleau, France, a touchstone for Hunt's American castles; Hunt office research photograph, ca. 1870

Photographed by S. Beer, 481 Broadway, New York.

after purchasing the somber brownstone at 49 West Thirty-Fifth owned by his mother. Howland family friends, the ultra-wealthy John J. Astor III and his wife, Charlotte Augusta Gibbes, lived nearby, only a garden apart from her sister-in-law, the society doyenne and future Hunt client Caroline S. Astor (see 2.6). The decoration of the Hunt reception rooms was fashionably cultivated—mahogany and gilded furniture upholstered in gold damask, "Turkish" carpets, dozens of paintings, sculptures, and bibelots; the bedrooms in contrast were spare and color-themed (2.17). In 1864 Richard and Catharine purchased Hill-Top Cottage from William Hunt and established their way of life for thirty years, spending fall and winter in New York and spring and summer at Newport, attended by servants they brought from Europe to serve in their life of discreet luxury.[46]

The Hunts had eventually five children: Richard ("Dickie" or "Dick"), Catharine ("Kitty"), Joseph ("Dody" or "Joe"), Esther, and Herbert. They sent their oldest sons to new, British-style, American boarding schools and the École des Beaux-Arts. To Catharine, Richard was a devoted father and her entrée to the international creative elite. "Their hospitable home," reminisced family attorney Joseph Choate (P.6), "was always an object lesson in culture and refinement...thronged with great artists, scholars, musicians, actors...no such celebrities came to America without wanting to know them," all introduced to Catharine by her famous husband. For Richard, his marriage, certainly in part strategic, placed him among the Episcopal rich. Given his oft-publicized background and society living, his social standing was inevitably a draw to status-conscious clients. But fame and wealth were not entirely advantageous, some dismissing his career as the indulgence of a privileged life. In the beginning, a journalist recalled, contractors thought Richard had "altogether too many new ideas to suit their conservatism.... The fact is, said one contractor...'Mr. Hunt could never have made a living at all if he hadn't had a rich wife.'"[47]

Heeding the reserve of her class, Catharine rarely discussed race, religion, and politics in her husband's biography, remarkable considering they lived through the Civil War that brought 620,000 military deaths, out of a population of some thirty-one million, between April 1861 and the war's end four years later. From their heritage that revered tradition, and the sacrifices of family and friends, the Hunts' sympathies lay with the Union and the Republican Party of abolitionist Whigs. Joseph Howland, Catharine's brother and Richard's neighbor at the University Building, rose to brevet brigadier general and fought at the First Battle of Bull Run; Leavitt Hunt became a colonel and served at Malvern Hill; but childhood friend Theodore Winthrop died at the Battle of Big Bethel.[48]

Catharine and Richard's mutual contribution to the war effort was on behalf of New York's Metropolitan Fair, held over three weeks in April 1864 to fund medical services. They collaborated on the event's art committees, joining collectors, architects, and artists. The National Guard armory on Fourteenth Street near Sixth Avenue was the fair's main building, but when the number of donated items for sale and auction exceeded expectations, management added an annex at north Union Square. Hunt oversaw construction of this temporary space and decorated its corridor baronially, with banners hung from poles (see page 8).[49]

The arts exhibited at the fair reflected the era's reverence for the past at the intersection of industrial globalization and nationalism. Frederic Church's *Niagara* (1857) and Emanuel Leutze's *Washington Crossing the Delaware* (1851) were blockbuster paintings in the main gallery, while a poem by Goethe was on display with letters from Beethoven, Rossini, and Verdi. There was the Arms and Trophies Room and the popular Curiosity Shop selling "staples of Art museums—ancient carvings, bronzes, stained glass, Venetian glass, Gobelin tapestry," and other material arts like those in the Hunt collection.[50]

By the time the fair closed, the organizers had raised one million dollars and advanced cultural progress. "The surprise and delight exhibited by the thousands...who visited the Picture Gallery," wrote Henry Tuckerman, "has suggested to many, for the first time, and renewed in other minds more emphatically, the need, desirableness, and practicability of a permanent and free Gallery of Art in our cities." New York, as the "third metropolis of the civilized world," would benefit from such an institution as a "promoter of high civilization."[51]

The Civil War reset the social order of New York. The merchant class Roosevelts and Johnstons forged financial and social alliances with new industrialists to pay for the war. In 1861 these wealthy citizens, calculating the loss of cotton trade, debated the benefits of abolition. But then fearing that slavery was sustaining the South's military edge and that a prolonged conflict would strain the nation's prosperity, three hundred professional and business leaders rallied for the Union in launching the Union League Club of New York. At times clubs were perceived as threats to democracy, a fear addressed by a founding member, Frederick Law Olmsted. There were those who would like to establish a legal aristocracy, he wrote, but any member should only belong to America's "hereditary natural aristocracy," men of accomplishment, "descendants of the alms bearers and of the dukes of our land...," bearing "old colonial names." They should be men in science and business, of "good stock, or of notably high character," joined by successful "clever men" in letters and the arts. There should be, however, no place for "men of leisure."[52]

Richard Hunt exemplified Olmsted's Union League member, a descendant of colonial founders and a "clever" man of rising influence. He attended the club's organizing meeting in 1863, joined its arts committee, and decorated the club rooms at Madison Square. Two years later, he oversaw the League's temporary monument to Abraham Lincoln, placed in the square during the assassinated president's funeral procession along Broadway—a bust on a white marble pedestal and black dais. In this and its broad efforts on behalf of advancing a unified nation during and after the war, the Union League, wrote Catharine, "stood for all that was best in the Republican party."[53]

New Yorkers continued their civilizing endeavors throughout the national conflict, but Hunt, already accustomed to professional success, was left behind. His proposals for cultural projects went unrealized—a museum in Central Park, a neo-Gothic mercantile library in Brooklyn, homes for the New-York Historical Society, the Academy of Music, and the American Institute. Notably he lost to Peter Wight the 1861 commission for the National Academy of Design at Madison Square, his arcaded proposal utilitarian in contrast to Wight's exuberant palazzo in the transitional Venetian Gothic style, heralded by John Ruskin in his influential *The Stones of Venice* (1851-53). But these disappointments paled in comparison to Hunt's unrelenting but failed pursuit to design entrances to Central Park, the city's most ambitious public space landscaped by Frederick Law Olmsted and Calvert Vaux.[54]

Olmsted was born in Hartford, Connecticut, five years before Hunt and was a model of George Bancroft's transformative figure at a critical juncture in history. He put landscape architecture on the map as the nation moved from country to city. America, Olmsted wrote, could not "gain in virtue, wisdom, comfort," unless through the "advance" of great cities, where public spaces and parks, like beautiful buildings, were forces for moral order and peace. He shared this Euro-inspired vision with his partner, the English-born Vaux, who came to America in 1850 as the partner of Andrew Jackson Downing, the first American-born landscape architect.[55]

In 1848, a year after Hunt entered the École des Beaux-Arts, the New York merchant Robert B. Minturn and his wife Anna M. Wendell toured Europe and the Middle East. On return, and impressed by London, Paris, and Vienna, they called a meeting of gentlemen New Yorkers to discuss a "large park for walking and driving." Such an amenity would enhance the city's reputation abroad. "We are tired of having everything boorish and coarse and unfeeling called American," wrote park supporter and editor George W. Curtis. Since Alexis de Tocqueville in the 1830s, Parisians and Londoners had looked down on the wealthy metropolis for its materialism lacking refinement, its self-interest over civic commitment. Downing and newspaper editor William Cullen Bryant backed the Minturns' appeal, and in 1853 New York set aside almost eight hundred acres north of Fifty-Ninth Street, between Fifth and Eighth Avenues. The Board of Commissioners of Central Park awarded the design to Olmsted and Vaux for their picturesque "Greensward Plan." By century's end a wasteland of swamps, scrub, and granite outcroppings had become a reimagining of America's native landscape, a retreat from the commercial hustle three miles south.[56]

Competition to design gateways to the park's southern entrances brought a clash of egos. A railroad attorney and ally of the state's governor, Andrew H. Green had been influential in creating the park's board and became its dominant member. In 1860 Green presented drawings for simple iron gates and rough stone walls at the park's perimeter, likely by Vaux and Jacob Wrey Mould. Charles Russell, Hunt's brother-in-law, introduced Richard to the project. The board accepted his proposal for gateways and set construction to start in 1864. When work did not proceed, Hunt pushed his case by exhibiting plans and renderings at the National Academy of Design in April 1865. Vaux, colluding with Olmsted behind the scenes, objected to Hunt's design as formal and grandiose. On learning of the exhibition, he lobbied the Commission directly and in the press. "The hour has come...for a clean statement and a good-humored square hit," Vaux wrote Olmsted. In response to the ensuing negative publicity enflamed by Vaux, Green stopped the advancement of Hunt's plans in May 1865.[57]

For all their outward gentility and moral posturing, mid-century competitors ruthlessly defended their art ideals. Hunt pitched battles at important junctures, always forthright in debate. For his park entrances, he appealed to the court of public opinion, as he had at the Parmly trial. From the 1840s, the intelligentsia enlisted new printing technologies to promote their cultural authority. In 1866 Hunt self-published a thirty-six-page booklet with a deceptively benign title: *Designs for the Gateways of the Southern Entrances to the Central Park*. The format followed English manuals for landscape design, but the text and illustrations were polemical, rebutting a scathing critique by *New-York Tribune* critic Clarence C. Cook, prodded by Vaux. The essays were by Hunt's friend and frequent collaborator, the attorney and art enthusiast William J. Hoppin, first published in William Cullen Bryant's newspaper, the *New-York Evening Post*. Hoppin wrote anonymously as "Civis," but the thinking was Hunt's.

The park gates were thematic, a Beaux-Arts sculptural ensemble transforming the European, aristocratic tradition of allegorical sculpture into a four-part monument to democracy, with gates to war and peace bracketing ones to the arts and commerce. Hunt intended to transform the plaza outside the park's Fifth Avenue entrance into an American Place de la Concorde, where neoclassical buildings would frame a memorial

Fig. 2.18 Proposed entrance to Central Park at Fifth Avenue, New York City, from Hunt's self-published polemic, *Designs for the Gateways of the Southern Entrances to the Central Park*; Hunt office rendering, lithograph, 1866

column to Henry Hudson (2.18). Hunt intimated in his publication that this alignment, both in Paris and in his imagined New York, was indebted to the Piazza del Popolo in Rome (1818), a reference suggesting republican origins. Between Fifty-Seventh and Fifty-Eighth Streets, along the west side of Fifth Avenue, Hunt anticipated a Louis XIII-style hotel or house anchored by a corner tower, similar to the one George Post built, at Hunt's suggestion, when he extended Cornelius Vanderbilt II's mansion along the same block thirty years later.[58]

The opposing positions of Olmsted and Hunt in *Designs for the Gateways* exemplified landscape debate throughout the period. Vaux and Olmsted stood for Ruskin and Gothic England, for naturalized landscape signifying virtue in nature. Rustic and informal, theirs was "an American park," argued Cook, with no place for the "spirit" of the "10th Street Studio building." Hunt's designs were too "elaborate and too monumental," his ornamentation too French and imperial, signifying admiration for Napoléon III and his recent anti-democratic coup d'état in Mexico. "We don't like to be reminded of such rif-raf as the French Emperor," Cook sniped.[59]

A never-failing voice for École classicism and urban planning, of built monuments in a cityscape of supporting scale, Hunt rebutted the opposing positions and projected into the future. If New York was to "be any thing but an overgrown provincial town," declared Civis, "an unmeaning, dreary waste of brick and brown-stone fronts—it must have some marked architectural centre" along the avenues and streets framing and leading to the park. Hunt's gateways were not "too elaborate and monumental," but appropriate for the "street architecture which will surround the Park, provided this architecture is to be of the character which the location demands." The entrances would not disturb Olmsted and Vaux's "poor imitation of the wildness of nature," but create a visually symbolic and practical transition from urban to rural.[60]

Hunt's published "hit" is as close as one gets to his thinking about the interrelationship of architecture to the urban environment, his published plans Parisian in their conversion of existing streets into axes to signifying monuments. In his view, the scale, classicism, and geometry of French architecture were appropriate to the inevitable monumentality of city development and the future functioning of a "metropolis." Finally, in 1868, the Park's board compensated Hunt for his gateway designs, but the lost opportunity rankled for life. When he and Olmsted came together twenty years later at Biltmore in North Carolina, Hunt doggedly returned to the subject.[61]

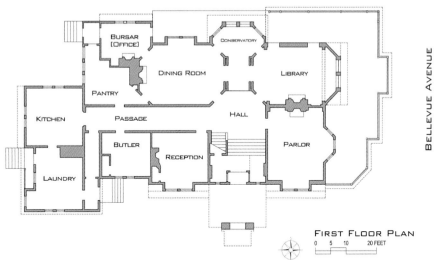

Fig. 2.19 Jane and John Griswold cottage (1864), Newport, Rhode Island, was American French Normand; Michael Froio, 2019

Fig. 2.20 Griswold cottage, axial first-floor plan; James B. Garrison, AutoCAD, 2021

Hunt's predisposition to high-art and classical monumentality deepened as the decades passed, but he was never immune to the vernacular. Though many of his New York efforts faltered during the Civil War, his Newport practice flourished. Between 1862, when he began the John Griswold house, and 1869 when his mansion practice began, Hunt either renovated existing mid-century villas or built what the rich, with self-conscious modesty, called their summer "cottages." His early Newport houses were rarely reviewed at the time, but were acknowledged as distinct and surprising as "novel and attractive, as well as very peculiar." Montgomery Schuyler thought they were of "no great architectural importance...though they were not without considerable results in their day in bringing about a more intelligent and artistic treatment of the vernacular construction...."[62]

Hunt approached the Griswold cottage and its detached carriage house in response to 1840s wood-framed American architecture by Richard Upjohn and Leopold Eidlitz and what he had seen on his travels in northern France. Elevations articulated by boards applied to clapboard, suggesting, but not mirroring, interior structure, gave the exterior an ordered, rational rusticity (2.19). The interior was similarly composed, its Beaux-Arts progression a departure from interlocking plans of related French and German villas (2.20, 2.21a-b). The porte-cochère opened to a three-story stair and vestibule that led to an elongated octagonal library and dining room (see page 10), connected by a hall parallel to the porch. Wood interiors were part of the American country house tradition, but Hunt introduced neo-Renaissance details, further enhancing the cottage's modern continentalism.[63]

Along with structural legibility, color entered architectural debate in the nineteenth century when Abel Blouet and Henri Labrouste rendered Greek and Byzantine monuments in chromatic hues. Their interpretations were radical at a time when architects and historians, following the writings of Johann J. Winckelmann, assumed that antiquity had been in unpainted stone. By the 1850s, color theories in France and England, new building materials, and chromolithographed pattern books made color a unifying element for building exteriors and interiors, harmonizing architecture and nature. At the annual meeting of the AIA in 1867, the Ruskinian Richard Upjohn told the membership that "color is the vitalizing principle of architecture.... See how the yellow tint of a sunset enlivens the most tame and contemptible building. We cannot have a permanent sunset," but through paint and stained glass, the architect could "approximate" natural effects. When building supplies became available again after the Civil War, Hunt oversaw the painting of the Griswold house in a palette native to Newport. The applied boards were earth brown, the clapboard sunset yellow, and the window sashes forest green. The diamond-patterned slate roof, derived from Norman models, was cloud gray and maroon.[64]

Hunt's successful practice and presence in art circles made him a rising star in a society bringing professional architecture to America. Remaining *au courant* required travel to old and new buildings, the foundation of a historicist practice. To this end, in 1867, as Newport projects were under way and the Central Park debacle unresolved, Hunt and William

Hoppin, with Catharine and five-year-old Dick, traveled to Europe. As became their custom, the Hunts first stopped in London where Robert Browning, the dramatic poet, and Catharine had a "long talk" at a reception for the city's "great men" after a levee at Buckingham Palace. By April 1 they were in Paris for the opening of the Exposition Universelle on the Champ de Mars, which Hunt attended as commissioner to the American Fine Arts Committee. He was a juror to the architecture section, dominated by eight French architects, including Hector Lefuel and Félix Duban.[65]

Like its predecessors, the fair attracted millions of visitors over seven months, the "elite of the civilized world." Intended to promote material and moral well-being, as well as the "dignity of all labor," the exhibition was an international competition among nations seeking global influence. Luxury goods and mechanical inventions conveyed a spirit of optimism and Western progress, while paintings lent by Hunt's clients William H. Osborn, Henry G. Marquand, and James Pinchot promoted American art. The presentation of antiques to be "imitated" and the promotion of private collecting by the Gallery of the History of Work, managed by Alexandre du Sommerard's son Edmond and others, were goals that guided Hunt's work and avocations.[66]

Hunt's commitments as juror to the architecture section did not distract from his collecting. He acquired books on architecture and design (see SK.12), photographs by Charles Marville, and plaster casts of sculpture from the twelfth through seventeenth centuries. A society high point was the imperial ball at the Tuileries in June, where he and Catharine in court dress were presented to the emperor and empress. Considering his relationship with Lefuel, and the fame of his brother William, whose painting *La Marguerite* Napoléon III had selected for purchase at the 1852 Paris Salon (see 3.14), the emperor certainly knew of Richard Hunt. The architect later recalled that Lefuel had wanted to present one of his designs to the court and recommend that he oversee its construction in France, but Hunt declined the offer and never carried out a project abroad.[67]

After the ball the Hunts left Paris for Charlemagne's palace at Aachen and then traveled through Holland, Sweden, Norway, and Russia, collecting jewelry and precious boxes, local costumes, and liturgical vessels. Hunt sketched wooden medieval and modern churches outside Oslo (SK.10) and noted the dimensions of German Leo von Klenze's New Hermitage (1838) in St. Petersburg, impressed by the city's "grand public buildings and palaces on grand scale." From the north they went to Berlin, a center of architecture by Karl Friedrich Schinkel whose 1830 neoclassical Königliches Museum (Altes Museum from 1845) was founded in 1823 to cultivate public

Fig. 2.21a–b
Griswold cottage
stair, opposite, and
Renaissance Revival
library, above; Hunt
articulated structure
with applied strips
and altered classical
proportions for light
and air; Michael
Froio, 2019[5]

knowledge of the arts. After visiting George Bancroft, recently appointed American minister to Prussia, and traveling by train with the young Lewis Carroll (Charles Lutwidge Dodgson), author of the recently published *Alice's Adventures in Wonderland*, who conjured up magical tales for Dickie, they returned to Paris and luxury at the Bristol Hotel on the Place Vendôme. Their Louis Vuitton trunks packed with new plunder, they sailed for home in the fall. Hunt had again pursued aspects that defined him and his career—the acquisition of books and photographs, of art and objects for an architect's library and museum, and the review of new and old buildings, both the vernacular and academic.[68]

"I think that to be an American is an excellent preparation for culture," wrote Henry James in 1867. "[W]e can deal freely with forms of civilization not our own, can pick and choose and assimilate and in short (aesthetically etc.) claim our property wherever we find it." Assimilation defined the course of Hunt's career as he entered his early forties, an established figure in the movement to bring refinement and professional design to brick and clapboard America, influencing the work of his students and the institutions he and his clients founded. In the coming decade his office would succeed by designing buildings of a new scale and structural complexity as new wealth and peace afforded the French Renaissance-style architecture he made his own, negotiating the Gothic-Classical divide by synthesizing elements of both.[69]

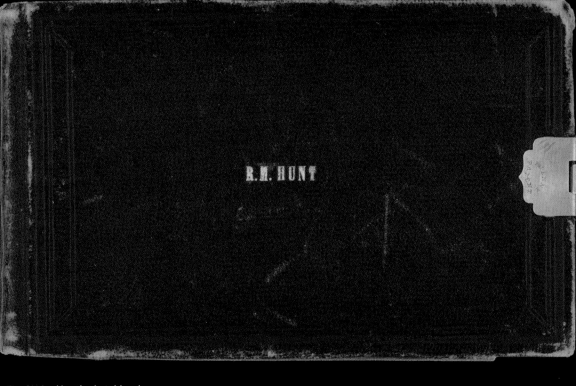

Fig. SK.1a Hunt's sketchbook,
dated by Catharine Hunt, 1852

Sketchbook Portfolio

Echoing a centuries' old dictum of Western artists and architects, Richard Hunt told his students, "Draw, draw, draw, sketch, sketch, sketch!... It will ultimately give you a certain control of your pencil, so that you can more rapidly express on paper your thoughts in designing."

Hunt himself drew his way through the École des Beaux-Arts and forty years of professional life, recording in sketchbooks places and people he encountered, noting purchases of books, plaster casts, bottles of cordials for his cellar, and expenses at luxury European spas and hotels. Ancient and modern architecture, flora and fauna, mountain passes and sea vistas, civic and residential interiors, engineered structures, and polychromed details were all in his purview as his generation's renowned antiquarian, the cultivated gentleman architect with the demeanor of a four-star general.[1]

Fig. SK.1b Polychrome details in Rome, 1852

SK.2

SK.3

SK.4

SK.5

Fig. SK.2 Hunt wrote "first class in drawing at Fontainebleau," ca. 1848

Fig. SK.3 Palazzo Cavalli-Franchetti, Venice, 1852

Fig. SK.4 Family dogs in Paris, ca. 1851

Fig. SK.5 William Hunt "admiring Rubens picture Antwerp" at Cathedral of Our Lady, 1852

SK.6

SK.7

SK.9

SK.10

SK.8

SK. 11

Fig. SK.7 Beau Séjour hotel, Lausanne, Switzerland, April 24, 1885

Fig. SK.8 Romanesque apse, Basilika St. Aposteln, Cologne, Germany, 1874

Fig. SK.9 "Dody [the future architect Joseph Hunt] in Paper cap-Nice, Chmas 1874"

Fig. SK.10 Tyristrand Kirke (1857), Christian H. Grosch, Norway, July 24, 1867

Fig. SK.11 Measured drawing, Protestant Great Church (Grote Kerk), The Hague, 1867

Fig. SK.12 Books purchased from Lenoir-Rapilly, Paris, 1867

SK. 12

Chapter 3

A Robust and Vivacious Temperament

As the peripatetic Hunts traveled to Oslo in 1867, Ralph Waldo Emerson delivered his address, "Progress of Culture," at Harvard's Unitarian church. Democracy was at a critical moment in post-slavery America, its cities "rude," their architecture "tent-like when compared with the monumental solidity of medieval and primeval remains in Europe and Asia." History had proven that solutions depended on the educated citizen, self-helping and searching, undeterred by obstacles, "strong enough to hold up the Republic."[1]

A year after his speech heralding the national work to be done, Emerson met forty-one-year-old Richard Hunt in New York. He was struck by their "spirited" conversation "loaded with matter, & expressed with the vigor & fury of a member of the Harvard boat or ball club," expounding "fine theories of the possibilities of art." Reminding the philosopher of his local policeman, Hunt's regional accent was in "ludicrous contrast with the Egyptian & Greek grandeurs he was hinting or portraying." The architect was a "thinking soul...horsed on a robust & vivacious temperament. The combination is so rare of an Irish laborer's nerve & elasticity with [art historian Johann J.] Winckelmann's experience & cultivation, as to fill one with immense hope of great results." To the Sage of Concord, Hunt was an American genius, able to transform "tent-like" America into a society of white marble temples, already envisioned by artists and architects in the Greek Revival. A few years later, Hunt made Emerson's "My Men" list of eighteen contributing Americans. He was the only architect among business and cultural superstars, including sculptor Horatio Greenough and Henry David Thoreau of Walden Pond.[2]

Fig. 3.32 detail, Paris Commune

The North's prophesy that the Civil War would purge America of its coarse materialism and launch a Golden Age of Greece proved illusory. Instead, post-war carpetbagging and laissez-faire politics ushered in what Mark Twain cynically tagged the "Gilded Age" of uber wealth and devastating urban poverty. In the eight years after 1865, capital to manufacturing quadrupled, railroad miles doubled, and three million immigrants arrived on American shores, driving the national population to more than forty million. New York thrived, its financial markets and trading soaring, hobbled only by periodic recessions and panics.[3]

Despite this astounding prosperity, a journalist cautioned in 1871 that "commerce" was not the primary goal of "civilized communities," but the "magnetism of intercourse" foundational to urban life. Libraries, museums, and office towers, creating a public forum, needed to be civic monuments, not for the "value they possess," wrote Theodore Winthrop, but as reflections of "power & progress."[4]

As a purveyor of Franco-American culture, Hunt ascended to the top of his profession when economic *and* civilizing forces took hold after the Civil War. Whereas he had built only fifteen projects before 1867, by 1880 his office had completed seventy-five buildings and monuments. Excepting for years of financial bust, his draftsmen and assistants, from two to an estimated thirty at its peak, handled a steady flow of commissions. By the 1870s, these professional men were managing project development. To mixed success, Hunt remained their leader/collaborator, communicating through letters, sketches, and telegrams when traveling abroad. During his European tour in 1888, he navigated rocky relations with mining industrialist William Borden, building a city chateau in Chicago, and lost an important New York commission to George Post, Hunt's student and then competitor, when office assistant and architect Maurice Fornachon "bungled in his interviews with C[ollis] P. Huntington," éminence grise of the Central Pacific Railroad building a Fifth Avenue mansion.[5]

Hunt initiated projects intuitively, in notebooks and on tracing paper, yellow pads, and letterhead. From time to time, he painted pictorial watercolors (see 5.14). Office architects prepared renderings, detailed elevations, and plans that grew in number and precision over the decades. They collaborated with a circle of mechanical trades and Parisian decorating firms that realized the era's gilded interiors. Learning from his Rossiter debacle, Hunt oversaw construction contracts that had evolved by the 1870s into printed forms. He learned to insist on supervision, requiring travel by rail and carriage. This burden lessened after his oldest son joined the firm in 1887, but surviving letters from the late 1880s and

Fig. 3.1 Stained-glass cartoons, gouache; Eugène Oudinot, ca. 1844, from Hunt's scrapbook collection[6]

early 1890s while working for the young George Vanderbilt attest to Hunt's beck-and-call life catering to entitled clients, even when an on-site architect reported to New York.[6]

The nineteenth century was an era of systemic change, documented in unprecedented ways as primeval fields and forests gave way to iron and steel. Hunt joined this archiving movement, collecting hundreds of photographs and illustrations that he cataloged for reference in project development. His files included furniture and costume illustrations, portraits of architects, engravings of ruins and gardens, stained-glass studies, and clippings about buildings he designed and art and architecture of his time. He, and later Catharine, assembled this documentation in scrapbook albums and created folios of his sketches, plans, and renderings that became a visual autobiography of his practice (3.1, see also Scrapbook Portfolio). This forty-year pursuit of knowledge and history made Hunt's print collections an encyclopedic *aide-mémoire* and reference library, intended for the museum of architecture he first envisioned in the 1850s, but never realized.[7]

By middle age Richard Hunt was a celebrity, an art critic finding him:

> a picturesque figure, stalwart for his inches [he was not tall], and with something in his carriage as well in his manner of speech that made you suspect the military officer rather than the artist. His head was handsome; it conveyed even an impression of stateliness,

at times, under the gray hair. But the air of stateliness was fleeting. In the main, Hunt was prodigiously vivacious, almost a Frenchman in some of his quick passage of talk, and the talk itself was explosive. He liked pungency and never failed to introduce it into his discourse, no matter what the occasion.

Office staff remembered their boss as affable, direct, and generous, swearing his way through meetings. He had an "utter hatred of anything in the nature of unfairness in practice, unfairness in conduct or sham in general," recalled George Post, and he was "sympathetic" with anyone and anything connected to the arts. Determinately hardworking and energetic, he returned to his studio "puffing like an express train" after "two chicken sandwiches and one cup of tea" at lunch. He encouraged men to join his profession and offered experienced counsel, sometimes resented and rebuffed. Chicago architect Louis Sullivan, cold to Hunt's charisma, was sixteen when he called on the "architectural lion...in his den," who went on about his "mighty man's tale of his life in Paris with Lefuel."[8]

Hunt spoke infrequently in public and published little. He did not discuss his client work, and what thinking guided his practice we know from a handful of surviving letters and speeches. Nevertheless, his revised "Architecture" entry in Thomas G. Appleton's 1873 edition of the *American Cyclopedia* offers insight into his practice after the Civil War. Building design now encompassed all structures except "defense and ships," a change distancing architects from engineers and opening their field to residential and commercial design. Overall, as a profession, architecture was in two classes, "the barbarous art of those nations which lie outside the circle of civilization, and the second comprising historical styles." This line in the sand was consistent with Paris' 1867 world's fair, when Western societies presented history as one of increasing refinement and the arts as a sign of evolution from the primitive to civilized.[9]

Hunt stood for classicism, promoting the French "*néo-grecque*" or "*romantique*" that had "showed enough vigor to throw aside the methods of the ancients and to create new forms." Exemplary were Félix Duban's Palais des Études (1839) at the École des Beaux-Arts, the Column of July by Joseph-Louis Duc (1840), later influential in the design of Hunt's Yorktown column (see 4.23), and Henri Labrouste's Bibliothèque Sainte-Geneviève (1851), revisited by Hunt for his Lenox Library (see 3.8). These works had guided French architecture and "sensibly modified" German neoclassicism. Even though that architecture's "general effect [was] bareness and hardness," it was "impossible to deny to the best

Fig. 3.2 Philanthropist James Lenox's Gothic Revival red brick and limestone Presbyterian Hospital (1872) at Fourth (Park) Avenue, New York City; beyond, Hunt's classical Lenox Library rises between Madison and Fifth Avenues; ca. 1873

Fig. 3.3 Presbyterian Hospital ground-floor plan; James B. Garrison, AutoCAD, 2019

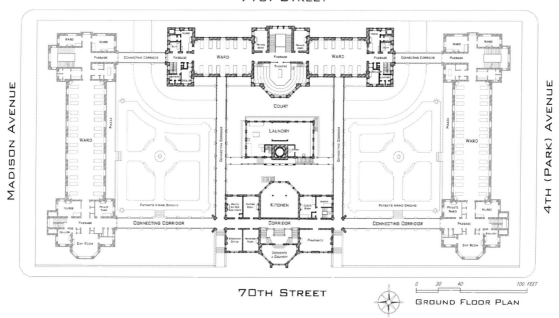

works of [Karl Friedrich] Schinkel and [Leo von] Klenze a good measure of admiration," a tempered view reflecting Hunt's recent trip to northern Europe and an early sign of his work for Harvard at century's end. He praised architects Eugène Viollet-le-Duc and Jean-Baptiste-Antoine Lassus for their Gothic restorations but judged them as "timid and ineffective," except when the rounded Romanesque arch was used, a view confirmed by his 1867 tour of new buildings in Paris and significant to his own work at Princeton and West Point (see 4.2a-b, 5.43). American architecture itself had no place in history, except for the Greek Revival, but students educated in new programs, including his own, were introducing École discipline to architecture at home.[10]

Hunt practiced what he preached, first for city buildings and colleges educating sons of the bourgeoisie. In an astonishingly short period, his office advanced the urban townhouse and apartment building, art studio complex, hospital, and business tower. Though he competed for major civic and business projects, he lost repeatedly to George Post and competitors in the commercial field, pressed by engineering and scale, but succeeded as a residential romanticist.

Hunt's first realized civic project was New York's Presbyterian Hospital (3.2). Commissioned by James Lenox (see P.11), its campus was between Seventy and Seventy-First Streets and Madison and Fourth (Park) Avenues on farmland Lenox inherited from his father, soon to rise in value as business development pushed city residents northward to Central Park. Having evolved from the incoherence of his Rossiter house, Hunt designed the hospital with bravura, informed by sanitary and ventilation standards that developed after the 1832 international cholera pandemic that killed his father. Paris' Hôpital Lariboisière (1856) and Philadelphia's Hospital of the Protestant Episcopal Church (1851) influenced Hunt's plan for buildings enclosing an open court (3.3). The reception wing and its second-floor, steepled chapel faced south to Seventieth and north to an operating theater and ward along Seventy-First. On the exterior, clipped, recessed limestone headers and banding across pressed red brick were Hunt's reconciliation of new French Gothic and the polychromatic effects of English Gothic, already familiar to New Yorkers from 1860s work by Jacob Wrey Mould.[11]

The hospital opened in 1872, but Hunt did not live to see its campus completed, as was the case with his courtyard plans for Yale's Theological Hall and the Metropolitan Museum of Art (see 3.22, 5.49a-b). In comparison with New York's civic architecture, the Presbyterian buildings were literary and picturesque, a "French treatment as practiced by Viollet-le-Duc," wrote a Chicago critic. But Montgomery Schuyler echoed the sentiments of many, writing that the "vigorously-grouped, picturesquely-outlined and aspiring mass" was diminished by its "confused and 'spotty'" color.[12]

Neo-Grec/neo-Gothic projects contemporaneous with the Presbyterian Hospital were Hunt's four-story office building in Providence, Rhode Island (ca. 1869), and his brick Stuyvesant Apartments (3.4), commissioned by Rutherfurd Stuyvesant, a twenty-six-year-old real estate heir, member of the Century Association, and trustee of the Metropolitan Museum of Art. His and other patroon families were developing apartment buildings on their New York properties, leased under restrictive covenants. Americans accustomed to the single-family home resisted living next door to tradesmen, but apartments, known as "French flats" after developments in Second Empire Paris, ultimately defined New York. They provided affordable space at a time of urban expansion, and their advanced design contributed to public taste, as defined by the rentier class.

The Stuyvesant (1870) at Eighteenth Street between Irving Place and Third Avenue was the first American apartment building identified as such, preceded by the apartment hotel in New York and Boston. Hunt had designed a small, multi-unit building on Wooster Street (ca. 1855), but now set out to make a livable block like those in Paris. In Boston Hunt treated the Morland houses as an *hôtel particulier* under one roof. At the Stuyvesant he divided its Mansard story with four dormers and introduced French doors at the second floor to suggest a row of adjoining but independent houses. There were sixteen apartments, four to a floor, and four studios under the roof for the artists needed to design and build New York (3.5). The eight-room Stuyvesant apartment offered a private bath and dumbwaiter kitchen, luxury amenities that won Hunt critical praise for civilizing apartment life, which was often associated with the dilapidated immigrant tenement downtown.[13]

An immediate financial success, the Stuyvesant attracted prominent tenants, including Calvert Vaux and landscape painter Worthington Whittredge, and it inspired the entrepreneur Paran Stevens, manager of high society's white marble Fifth Avenue Hotel at Twenty-Third Street and Madison Square. In 1870 he commissioned Hunt to design Stevens House, New York's first luxury apartment building, a Neo-Grec/ Gothic chateau serviced by a passenger elevator. Hunt followed the plan of a residential hotel—eighteen apartments above sidewalk stores—but introduced the novel addition of servants' quarters in the attic.

Though influential in the planning of residential and hotel buildings through the 1870s, Stevens House was a financial failure and eventually

Fig. 3.4 Stuyvesant Apartments (1870), New York City; the red brick and stone street façade suggested a townhouse row, signifying home to renters; ca. 1875

Fig. 3.5 Stuyvesant Apartments plan; new convenience, comfort, and hygiene refined apartment living; James B. Garrison, AutoCAD, 2021

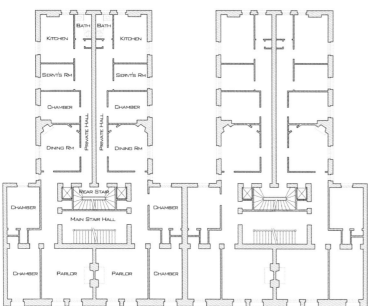

TYPICAL APARTMENT FLOOR

EIGHTEENTH STREET

0   5   10   20 FEET

converted to a hotel by Stevens' widow, Marietta R. Stevens, whom Hunt sued in 1878 for final payment. Her attorney countered that poor engineering and oversight had driven up costs, though Paran Stevens had only contracted for design. Hunt's lawyer was Joseph Choate, his childhood friend from Beacon Hill and their generation's omniscient attorney, counsel to Alva Vanderbilt and the Astors. He played on Marietta's pretentions and the era's social distinctions. A grocer's daughter, she was rumored to have ended the engagement of her son to the future author Edith Wharton to prevent him from inheriting his father's fortune, due to him on marriage. To courtroom applause, Choate traced Marietta's social climb and triumph after "the arm of royalty [New York and Newport society] bent to receive her." And how had she "reached this imposing eminence?" he asked rhetorically. "Upon a mountain of unpaid debt." Class warfare won out when Hunt was awarded his payment. Once again, he had contributed to a public understanding of professional architecture and affirmed, by inference, that architects, though slow to be considered artists, had rights, regardless of their clients' superior wealth and position.[14]

Just as urban expansion drove apartment development, so did it create demand for commercial space. From the late 1860s, Hunt designed low-rise offices and warehouses before chateaus and monuments consumed his studio practice. Though he continued to build in brick and stone, he experimented with iron screens of windows and shallow pilasters for commercial offices and store fronts at New York's Union Square and along Broadway (3.6), his storefront for financier Royal Phelps five-story building (1872) presaging innovations by Chicago's Adler and Sullivan in the 1880s.[15]

Hunt's advocacy of iron illuminates his evolving relationship to the place of history in design, unexpected considering his devotion to established precedent. Egyptian, Greek, Roman, and Gothic architecture had "weighed *long and heavily* on the mind of the public," he explained. Now, it "would be in vain to attempt to bind the public down to the architecture of past ages" given the era's new materials and needs. Iron, originating in antiquity, was an "appropriate" material for maximizing light and space on narrow lots and could be preserved through painted polychromatic effects as the "ancients" had done.[16]

Except for his Central Park gateways, we know little of Hunt's disappointments, but as an innovator of new forms his unsuccessful bid for the Equitable Life Assurance tower at Cedar and Broadway in 1867 must have rankled. Orchestrating new heights was unchartered territory for the nineteenth-century architect and Hunt, along with Henry Richardson, proposed multiple-story window arcades, an influential approach that

Fig. 3.6 Van Rensselaer Building along Broadway (1872), New York City; its painted neo-Moorish iron façade attracted customers to a fashionable drygoods store; hand-colored photograph, ca. 1872

Hunt used for his 1870s office buildings. But both architects lost to Arthur Gilman and Edward H. Kendall, assisted by George Post. Financed by life insurance sold during the Civil War, Equitable's fireproof brick, granite, and iron tower, an integrated rhythm of pilasters and arched windows over nine stories, was New York's first elevator skyscraper.[17]

Hunt succeeded in securing two office commissions, designed and built from 1873 to 1876. His red pressed brick and green sandstone Delaware and Hudson Canal Co. building at Courtland Street was an expressive breakaway from the contemporary office block, its rows of windows in shallow arches and floors separated by ledges becoming standard elements in later commercial design. His ambitious *New-York Tribune* office tower for a client asserting his vision after the historic legacy of a predecessor would become a city landmark.

~~~~~~~

Fig. 3.7 Printing House Square, New York City; the First Amendment thrived opposite City Hall; from left: Brooklyn Bridge terminal (1883), George Post's domed *The New York World* tower (1890), the *New-York Sun* building (1872), Hunt's 1875 *New-York Tribune* headquarters, and the *New-York Times* tower (1889), also by Post; Detroit Publishing Co., photochrom, ca. 1900

Newspapers were among the century's contributions to the "magnetism of intercourse" and a shared culture, introducing architectural commentary to 1850s news coverage. In the 1870s they conveyed their rising influence by building architecturally advanced headquarters at New York's Printing House Square near the Brooklyn Bridge (1869–83), office blocks that literally towered over existing six-story buildings. After *New-York Tribune* founder and outspoken abolitionist Horace Greeley died in 1872, the paper's new owner and editor, Whitelaw Reid, hired Hunt to design the *Tribune*'s new offices on the site of its 1843 building at Spruce and Nassau Streets (3.7). Reid's fifteen-point competition memorandum specified the requirements of a newspaper publishing house: editorial and office space on the upper floors and printing presses in the basement. New features included rental space above street-level stores and a tower for Reid's balconied office, symbolically overlooking Federal-style City Hall.[18]

Though hard to discern from the scant extant drawings, Hunt's contribution to office design was known in the period to have been not only architectural, but also technically innovative. Until the 1880s, architects were project engineers, and Hunt worked with Robert G. Hatfield and competed against Leopold Eidlitz and George Post. After the devastating citywide fires in Chicago (1871) and Boston (1872), fireproofing was on every developer's mind. At the Tribune building and the Coal and Iron Exchange, Hunt pioneered the use of light-weight terracotta hollow-block floor construction, enclosed iron vertical supports, and brick or concrete wall partitions. On the exterior he used, as others did for commercial work, fire-resistant hard red brick, articulated by contrasting granite lintels, sills, clock-tower base, and cornice.[19]

An intimation of post-Civil War luxury and possibly Hunt's first employment of the noted firm, Herter Brothers provided the Tribune's street-level baronial banking and counting room interiors. The two-story entrance, faced in mixed woods and imported red, gray, and black marble, and lit by bronze chandeliers, led to the main stairs and two passenger elevators for tenants. The Spruce Street entrance elevator was an express to the paper's basement, first, eighth, and ninth floors, an arrangement that expedited production while separating labor from professional tenants, including Hunt's studio, which moved to the tower in 1881. More than one hundred and fifty offices received steam heat, gas lighting, and water. Pneumatic tubes and electric annunciators made the tower state of the art.[20]

At 260 feet from sidewalk to top of spire, the ten-story Tribune became the city's tallest building and one of the largest blocks of rentable space. Its corbelled tower after the Medici Palazzo Vecchio in Florence, dramatic coloring, French roof, and recessed details gave the headquarters an overscaled picturesqueness and rationality, as suggested by Reid at the tower's opening on the *Tribune*'s thirty-fourth anniversary in 1875. No doubt parroting Hunt, the publisher explained that "every ornament has its uses; the position of every stone is dictated by the necessities of construction; and the whole work exhibits the overruling influence of a consistent idea." Introducing crisp Neo-Grec details and segmental arches, Hunt had brought American scale to lessons learned from French commercial buildings and yet met the dual demand of romantic thought, that architecture reflect its history and respond to modern necessities. But ultimately, as at his second apartment buildings (1871, 1873) for Rutherfurd Stuyvesant, he had struggled to reach the required height, his blocks of multiple stories earning scathing reviews. "The Tribune Mausoleum," reported the penny-daily *Sun*, was a monument to Hunt's "fitfulness and eccentricity," awkwardly scaled on its angled site along Printing House Square. Hunt had also failed with his proposal for the nearby Western Union Telegraph Building, a commission won by George Post and finished the same year as the Tribune. Though both men had called for stress-relieving arches, and, as at the Tribune, projecting wall-bearing piers, Post had achieved an ornamented, muscled grandeur expressive of a global brand.[21]

Notwithstanding its inherent stumpiness, the Tribune contributed to the verticalization of New York's skyline and the potential for French rationalism at multiple stories, its gridded exterior, stone detailing, arcaded bays, and shallow reveals entering the lexicon of office design. Along with Presbyterian Hospital and Central Park, the tower manifested the faith in fine architecture and urban planning to transform the American city into a dynamo for social uplift. This objective was at play again when leaders founded new museums and libraries.

In 1871 New York landowners gathered on a winter evening to explore uptown development. Real estate attorney Simeon Church held forth, responding to studies showing that the railroad, while good for business, was luring middle-class New Yorkers to clean and verdant suburban towns.[22]

> We are true citizens of New York…. With pride we see her reach her iron arms across the Continent, to invite the treasures of the East; and send her commercial flag unto every Sea and Ocean. Still greater is the pride with which we contemplate in the future her rocky heights and waste places filled with palaces, and monuments dedicated to Art and Science, which her Princes know how to build—her streets throbbing with the pulsations of her great industrial life, her commerce enriching and her civilization blessing every nation. Great abroad, she struggles now for breath at home…. Give New York a chance to grow, and she will achieve her own destiny, and become, not merely the Queen City of the Continent, but the IMPERIAL METROPOLIS OF THE WORLD.

Business leaders, educators, and clergy concurred with Church. To the frustration of architects and artists, however, work on behalf of culture was contingent on private money. There was "uniform opposition to and distaste for governmental interference," wrote a cleric for a monthly arts journal in 1877. And furthermore, "the lack of hereditary titles, or laws of primogeniture, [made] the founding of a 'family' practically impossible." For these reasons, the rich turned to "expenditure for public purposes as the best way of leaving behind them an honorable name" inextricably linking private patronage to public institutions, founded by Richard Hunt and his circle. In Second Empire France civic architecture and art glorified the state, but in America, through Hunt's transposition of French aristocratic aesthetics, new buildings would embody the civilizing contributions of private wealth.[23]

A New York landowner with the education and deep pockets to realize public projects was James Lenox, a Columbia College graduate. His Scottish immigrant father, like John J. Astor, made a fortune in trading and real estate after the American Revolution. Lenox worked in the family firm before dedicating himself to collecting Shakespeare folios, early Bibles, and European and American art, which he assembled over forty years in his double townhouse on lower Fifth Avenue.

Rare book dealer and native Vermonter Henry N. Stevens found Lenox "a man of few words and few intimate friends." Richard Hunt was one of the chosen and their relationship suggests how he cultivated his society clients. Though the staunchly Presbyterian bachelor disapproved of Hunt smoking cigars, Lenox's sister recalled that the architect's brownstone was the only one "her brother ever visited outside his own family home." Over long walks in Newport and through the exchange of rare gifts their friendship deepened after the Civil War.[24]

Twenty years before Andrew Carnegie made it his mission, Lenox devoted a share of his fortune to building libraries. At the end of 1869, his Presbyterian Hospital well under way, Lenox commissioned Hunt to design a public library for the Fifth Avenue portion of his farm. He donated the land, $300,000, and his art and book collections. As the state was approving the library's incorporation, led by a six-member board of Lenox family members and Hunt relatives and colleagues, Hunt presented preliminary plans and broke ground in 1870. Maurice Fornachon oversaw construction as Lenox meticulously tracked expenses, his library costing $540,000 by 1875.[25]

To plan for Lenox's diverse collections under one roof, Hunt turned to contemporary French libraries known to his patron. The bibliophile had lived in France during the Second Empire, when peace and prosperity brought new funding to public libraries in cities seeking cultural status. Like chateaus, these new institutions often combined books and fine art in single buildings. Hunt initiated design empirically, beginning with sketches and elevations. Preparatory renderings for the Lenox show his predisposition

Fig. 3.8 Lenox Library, New York City, looking northeast from Fifth Avenue, with Hunt's Presbyterian Hospital beyond; probably photographed January 15, 1877, the day after the library opened; Charles S. Farrar[7]

to Hector Lefuel's sculptural romanticism as he moved through iterations of a neo-Renaissance palace to achieve what he described in 1859 as Neo-Grec "simplicity, grace, purity, harmony." His awareness of the library-gallery at Grenoble (1870) by École-trained Charles-Auguste Questel and the Bibliothèque de Sainte-Geneviève was evident, his Lenox library being a fractured balance between classical unity and structural articulation that he continued to explore.[26]

The completed library (1877) was 192 feet wide and 114 feet deep, in gray ashlar limestone (3.8). Pink stone columns flanked the twenty-four-foot oak and iron entrance doors. The rear elevation in exposed structural brick faced east over a grazing field to Lenox's Presbyterian Hospital at Madison Avenue. The library was Athens to the hospital's Mont-Saint-Michel, one a secular temple to learning, the other a sanctuary for Christian care (3.9a-b, 3.10a-b). Hunt was praised for his Beaux-Arts ordering of space: bookrooms in the south wings and the janitor quarters between staircases to the second-floor statuary hall, reading rooms, and art gallery.[27]

A January blizzard on opening day in 1877 piled snow and ice onto roof-top skylights, eliciting public criticism of the darkened gallery below. As for

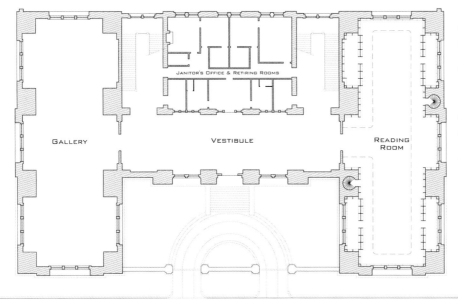

Fig. 3.9a–b First-floor, top, and second-floor, bottom, plans, Lenox Library; James B. Garrison, AutoCAD, 2021

Fig. 3.10a–b First-floor reading room, opposite top; second-floor sculpture hall, opposite bottom, Lenox Library; ca. 1900

GALLERY

VESTIBULE

JANITOR'S OFFICE & RETIRING ROOMS

READING
ROOM

FIFTH AVENUE

FIRST FLOOR PLAN

0 5 10   20   50 FEET

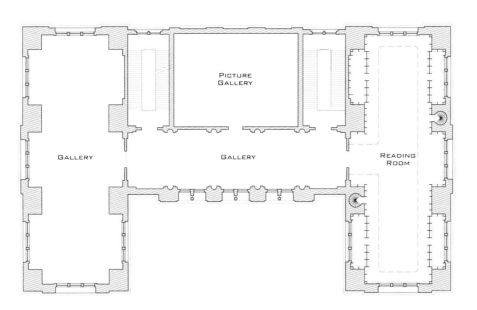

PICTURE
GALLERY

GALLERY

GALLERY

READING
ROOM

SECOND FLOOR PLAN

0 5 10   20   50 FEET

the architecture, it was disturbingly new. In a paean to the Gothic as "true originality," *The New York Times* wrote during the library's construction that Hunt's "pseudo-original" style revealed all the "striking defects of modern classic architecture." His failure to respect canonical proportions was a disappointment considering his successful integration of Neo-Grec and Gothic elements at Stevens House five years before. Montgomery Schuyler, however, was farsighted, finding the Lenox "academic and individual" in its École plan and precedents, its "massiveness...artistically accentuated." Unique for its time, the library's "largeness and liberality" made it "perhaps the most monumental public building in New York...."[28]

Lenox's choice of an uptown location and classical architecture, anticipating the City Beautiful movement at century's end, set him apart from the Astor family and its eponymous Romanesque library at Lafayette Place. His choice of architect, a collaborator with shared ambitions, had been astute. After receiving a rare volume from Lenox as the library was under construction, Hunt thanked his fellow bibliophile. "I shall always value it...as a souvenir of the many pleasant interviews occasioned by our united efforts in creating a monument which I hope will be worthy of the name it bears."[29]

If family monument was Lenox and Hunt's personal objective, surpassing the Bibliothèque Nationale in Paris and London's British Library was their public stance. But nineteenth-century patronage for social progress through education and fine architecture had limits. When lobbying corrupt state senator William M. "Boss" Tweed, Lenox wrote, "I desire as possible to keep together the different objects included in the act [of donation], and to make them a humanist adjunction & ornament to the City of N.Y." However, "to throw open such collections of statuary, pictures etc. and of books likewise to the examination of the public at all times, indiscriminately...would lead to injury and in time irreparable loss...." To this end, the Lenox, like the Astor, became a semi-public research institution, accessible on application. For years the press sniped at the library's privileging private need over public good, reporting that galleries had no chairs and readers were being regularly evicted according to "control and regulations." Similar to guidelines that governed the Metropolitan Museum of Art and Central Park, these restrictive conditions were alleviated only at the end of the 1880s when progressivism tempered the class prejudices of governing trustees imposing their civilizing standards.[30]

As the Lenox Library was in development, the Union League Club of New York held a special meeting of its Art Committee in late 1869. Colonial-era descendant and Hunt family friend, attorney John Jay, had returned from Paris impressed by its support of the arts and was now urging fellow members to found a city art museum. As in the development of Central Park, New York's cultural inferiority was at issue, its fine art holdings paltry by comparison with collections abroad. Poet and editor William Cullen Bryant opined that funding such a museum would be difficult, but a Congregational minister observed that the "improvement of each individual man and woman, in all that is noble and beautiful and good," would be a compensating reward. As representative of New York's architectural community, Hunt commented wryly that it would be easier to erect a museum than "to fill the building when we have it." He had already led an unsuccessful campaign at the AIA to create a privately funded museum, a State Academy of Architectural Art, modeled on the South Kensington Museum.[31]

Inspired by London, Union League members were receptive to its Art Committee and at the close of its meeting committed to soliciting funds for a Metropolitan Museum of Art. John Johnston's $10,000 was the largest donation, followed by William B. Astor at $2,500 and Richard Hunt, meeting his peers, pledged $1,000.[32]

Within a year, New York's society of trustees and donors founded both the American Museum of Natural History (1869) and the Metropolitan Museum of Art (1870), allying science and art as colleges were doing in their curricula. The state voted for incorporation of both institutions and the city leased the art museum land in Central Park. Olmsted and Vaux feared urban development would despoil their bucolic retreat, but overlord Andrew Green believed his park and the Metropolitan shared a commitment to public enrichment. Businessman William Aspinwall, and attorneys Joseph Choate and William Hoppin, joined social reformers and artists, including sculptor John Q.A. Ward and Richard Hunt, as the Metropolitan's founders and first board of trustees. For twenty-five years, Hunt was an informed advisor and patron on the board, but practicing new French classicism in an era of Gothic civic design circumscribed his role as architect until he triumphed in 1893 as lead architect for the museum's signature Fifth Avenue wing.

By the time Metropolitan trustees were considering architects for their museum, Hunt had submitted plans for the New-York Historical Society's Museum of History, Antiquities, and Art to be built on grounds adjacent to Central Park's historic Arsenal at Sixty-Fourth and Fifth Streets (see SC.7). The project ended because of insufficient funds, and Hunt's Second Empire submission failed to promote his candidacy as the Metropolitan's architect. In 1871 the museum's board, including trustees Olmsted and Green, awarded their project to Gothic revivalists Calvert Vaux and Jacob Wrey

Fig. 3.11 *Mother and Child*; Catharine Hunt was in Boston posing for her portrait with son Richard when she learned of President Lincoln's assassination, April 15, 1865; by her brother-in-law William Morris Hunt, 1864-65[8]

Mould. They also won the commission for the Museum of Natural History, besting Hunt's new Louvre-inspired design.[33]

Costing less than a half a million dollars, the Metropolitan Museum, in Central Park at Eightieth Street, opened in 1880. President Rutherford B. Hayes attended the ceremony and trustee Joseph Choate delivered the principal address. American collecting of masterpieces was not yet in reach, he explained, but over time "higher forms of beauty would tend directly to humanize, to educate, and refine a practical and laborious people...." Critics lambasted Vaux and Mould's brick and granite building, though they approved of its skylit interior court, recommended by Hunt and fellow members of the museum's architectural committee (see 5.48). Compared with Sturgis and Brigham's Ruskinian Boston Museum of Fine Arts (1876), New York's public gallery was a hulking Gothic warehouse.[34]

Inaugural exhibitions at the Metropolitan were selections from private collections and paintings by William Morris Hunt, already exhibited at the Boston museum (founded 1870). Witty and authoritative, William advocated for American painting and art education as his brother was advancing architecture. He taught women in his Boston studio and published the pragmatic *Talks on Art* (1878), informed by his Barbizon years studying under Millet. To New Yorkers he was an art star, known from submissions to the National Academy of Design. When he exhibited *Mother and Child*, his portrait of Catharine and her first child, New York's *Evening Post* wrote that, while there was a concern for provincialism in American painting, William's depiction of maternal love "addressed itself to the art-public of the world, but would be best appreciated in Paris" (3.11). It was among the finest works at the 1866 exhibition, high praise when Winslow Homer's Civil War memory of the same year, *Prisoners from the Front*, hung in a nearby gallery.[35]

At the 1869 Union League meeting, Hunt recalled that he and William had urged New York to purchase the celebrated Giampietro Campana Collection of antiquities. He explained that its ancient metal artifacts, ultimately purchased by the Louvre, had "changed the modern workmanship of gold" at a time when cultivating artisanal work was imperative for revivalist architecture and interiors. To this end, the Metropolitan Museum itself mounted didactic displays and in 1880 launched an industrial arts education program. Hunt participated as a judge of student assignments and was a member of the museum's exhibition committee. His personal loans to the Metropolitan, some of which were no doubt displayed at its opening, included French, Russian, and Italian silver that could advance American craftsmanship.[36]

Hunt was not alone in his promotion of skilled trades. Collecting and the domestic arts were occupations open to women, and Catharine, who acquired antique jewelry, lace, fans, and textiles, contributed to her husband's museum loans and to exhibitions for charities they supported. Among them was the Society of Decorative Art of New York, founded in 1876 by interior designer Candace T. Wheeler. By training women artisans, she made decoration a career opportunity. Her inspiration was the South Kensington Museum and London's Royal School of Art Needlework, which exhibited at the Philadelphia Centennial. Catharine became vice president of Wheeler's society and Richard a member of its advisory committee, leasing the Society space in a building he owned on East Twenty-First Street. When Wheeler organized her annual fundraising exhibitions, Hunt's clients and friends participated. Further support came from selling embroideries by Society artists to decorating firms and private collectors, including Alva S. Vanderbilt.[37]

Hunt's engagements, as club organizer, museum donor and board

Fig. 3.12 Virginia and William Osborn house (1870), Fourth (Park) Avenue, New York City; a critic found this double-townhouse of a railroad millionaire and art collector "showy, with much ingenious detail," exceptional at a time when "no man's house in New York was built for him"; ca. 1875[9]

member, collector, and architect, made him omnipresent in New York art circles, a role he cultivated through the 1870s and 1880s. A beneficial outcome of his contributions were commissions from business leaders and the artists they supported. Three clients from these interconnected worlds were William H. Osborn, Martin Brimmer, and John Ward. They all commissioned double townhouses whose contemporary architecture was in striking contrast to existing brick and brownstone rows.

Osborn exemplified the executive client in Hunt's practice after the economy recovered in the 1860s. Son of a Massachusetts farmer, he began his career in the China trade before becoming an owner and manager of the Illinois Central Railroad. One of his partners was colonial descendant Jonathan Sturges, who made his first fortune in the grocery business. Osborn and Sturges were collectors of American art and became benefactors of the Metropolitan Museum. In 1853 Osborn entered New York's bourgeois society by marrying Sturges' daughter Virginia, whose sister Amelia married financier J. Pierpont Morgan. The Osborns built in upper-class Murray Hill, at Park Avenue between Thirty-Third and Thirty-Fourth Streets, next door to the adjoining houses of Sturges and his son Frederick, designed at the same time by Henry Richardson and Hunt's student Charles Gambrill (1870) (3.12). Their four-story brick block was plain and reserved compared with Hunt's Neo-Grec double house, a grid of arched windows, pilasters, and stone panels shallowly carved to accentuate the continuous mass of the brick facing.[38]

As the Osborn residence proceeded, Hunt designed two houses (1870) on Beacon Hill for his childhood friend, Martin Brimmer, a Harvard graduate, son of a Boston mayor, and heir to a merchant and real estate fortune (see P.5, 3.13). Courteous and dryly humorous, a friend to George Ticknor and William Hunt, Brimmer wrote a book with his wife on religion and art in ancient Egypt. "There was in Mr. Brimmer nothing of that austere look which comes from holding on to property and standing pat," recalled John Jay Chapman, poet and critic of the Gilded Age. "And besides this, he was warm; not, perhaps, quite as warm as the Tropics, but very much warmer than the average Beacon Street mantel-pieces were."[39]

A Massachusetts state politician in the 1850s, Brimmer turned to philanthropy after the Civil War and became to Boston what James Lenox and Henry Marquand were to New York, a builder and patron of art, religion, education, and health institutions. For Brimmer, industrialization and the "immense progress in mechanical reproduction" were introducing art and refinement to the working classes who would soon have, through industrialization, the leisure to visit new museums and theaters. The outcome would be public recognition that art was "an essential element of human life: the parallel of ugliness with vice and of beauty with holiness...." Enlightened and moral, the American city would be "fully up to the standard of Florence" in the Italian Renaissance.[40]

Together the Osborn and Brimmer houses exemplified Hunt's continued exploration of the Neo-Grec and sculptural Second Empire and their owners' gutsy willingness to advance American culture through the new. Montgomery Schuyler found the Brimmer houses "restless" and "animated," a local critic discerning an "adaption of Neo Grace [sic] details, moulding, &c. in the form of a chateau of Francis I of France." This choice of royal lineage, adopted by Hunt's later clients, may have been due to the heiress and Boston Brahmin Marianne T. Brimmer, whose brother joined Hunt

Fig. 3.13 Marianne and Martin Brimmer houses (1870), Boston, in brick and buff stone suggesting a French Renaissance chateau; ca. 1875

on his tour of the Middle East. "[L]arge, imposing, handsome, blonde and infantile," John Chapman wrote. "She was a queen-bee, twice as large and twice as handsome as other women; and she wore Damascened brocades and ostrich feathers, and had eyes as blue as the sky." Her bravura style and love of "*luxe*" explains the extroverted exuberance of her house's exterior in contrast with Virginia Osborn's reserved presence along Park Avenue.[41]

The Brimmer houses, in face brick and buff stone, were two separate residences that Hunt, as he had for Dr. Morland across the Boston Common, unified with a Mansard roof. The Brimmers lived in the larger house east of the corner, its entrance opening to a foyer warmed by a "monumental

J. A. WHIPPLE. 297 WASHINGTON STREET, BOSTON.

Fig. 3.14 Brimmer Second Empire salon with contemporary French and American paintings, including William Hunt's 1854 *La Marguerite* (above desk); J.A. Whipple, ca. 1890[10]

chimney" in the "style of an old French chateau." The dining room beyond overlooked a garden at the back, and stone stairs led to the second-floor library and salon (3.14). Damask upholstery, machine-woven carpeting, and contemporary French and American paintings made these rooms fashionably Second Empire. They were well known to Hunt and his society of intellectuals and culture makers. In 1888 Martin Brimmer invited him to dinner with *The Atlantic Monthly* editor, James Russell Lowell, and Harvard biologist Louis Agassiz. "I predict if you come, your architecture will feel the good effects of it forever after," quipped the host. Brimmer assured Hunt that his older brother would concur. "Wm Hunt & I are always of the same opinion."[42]

The continentalism of Hunt's first city residences reached the heartland a year after the Brimmer and Osborn houses. Following the Great Chicago Fire in 1871, department store founder Marshall Field commissioned a house on Prairie Avenue, the city's premier residential street. Born in Massachusetts and descended from Pilgrim settlers, Field devoted his life to business. He married Nannie D. Scott, daughter of an Ohio ironmaster, and became a benefactor of the Field Museum of Natural History and John D. Rockefeller's University of Chicago.

The Field house was Hunt's first city mansion (1873), a French eighteenth-century *hôtel particulier* made modern, a robust American interpretation of Second Empire models that had already inspired Henry

Richardson's Dorsheimer house (Buffalo, New York, 1871) and Arthur Gilman's Samuel Hooper house (Boston, 1861) (3.15). Structure and decoration were integrated, sandstone headers continuous at the string course and cornice defining red brick panels. For the interiors, Hunt returned to the French fashion that inspired his Griswold house in Newport, angling the octagonal dining and living rooms for garden views. The lavish patterned and paneled first-floor interiors (3.16a-b) by L. Marcotte & Co. were in the ornately patterned Aesthetic style that valued the handcrafted and exotic over the machine made.[43]

Field had been bold in his choice of an East Coast architect, reaping the rewards of fine design. The merchant, a critic wrote, was commendable for "turn[ing] his back upon the Chicago architects, who had done so little to beautify their city," building a house "large, costly, and elegant both in its exterior and interior...a good example of Mr. Hunt in his best moods...

Fig. 3.15 Nannie and Marshall Field house (1873), Chicago, Hunt's first city mansion, a brick-and-stone *hôtel particulier* for a department store founder; ca. 1880

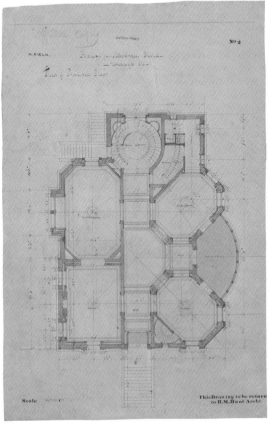

Fig. 3.16a Field house, entrance hall, in the Aesthetic style, by L. Marcotte & Co.; ca. 1884

Fig. 3.16b Field house, first-floor plan, geometrically conceived; Hunt office; ca. 1873

not built to frighten the inhabitants, as was one of his efforts [the Brimmer house] at about the same time in Boston." Furthermore, it would "always be a fine example of house architecture for our citizens to contemplate." Hunt had achieved what he and his clients sought, professional architecture in service of social status and the societal good.[44]

~~~~~~~~

John Ward was an influential artist-client in Hunt's early practice. Like Hunt, he was an advocate for art institutions and education, earning the sobriquet "Dean of American Sculpture" to Hunt's "Dean of American Architecture." He was president of the National Academy of Design and a founder of the National Sculpture Society in 1893, serving as its long-term president, joined by Hunt in executive positions.

Ward commissioned Hunt to design two New York house-studios (1869, 1882) (3.17a-b). The first was between Fifth and Sixth Avenues at Forty-Ninth Street. Hunt settled on a Neo-Grec, gray plaster cement façade, ornamented with low reliefs and incised arabesques, in startling contrast to the adjoining brownstone houses. Decorated by Pottier & Stymus, the first-floor interiors included a small studio at the entrance and a two-story modeling room in the rear. The residence was on the upper floors.[45]

Public sculpture in America had already taken hold when Hunt and Ward brought the expressive naturalism of French sculptor Pierre-Jean

Fig. 3.17a-b Anna and John Ward house and studio (1869), New York City, preliminary (left) and final elevations, Hunt office, ca. 1869

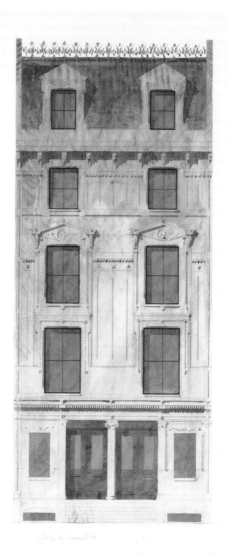

Fig. 3.18 Studio at Ward's 1882 New York City house with the sculptor, foreground right, statue of industrialist William E. Dodge, left, actor Steele MacKaye in topcoat, the model for the Seventh Regiment memorial soldier (3.20), on platform, and Pilgrim memorial, far right; ca. 1883[11]

David d'Angers to park and city square monuments (from *monere*, to remind) that venerated establishment values (3.18). Catharine Hunt wrote that "Ward did the sculpture" and Richard "furnished the drawings for the pedestal and studied up the inscriptions." His École training, archeological interests, and surviving plans support this characterization of Hunt as the partners' conceptual center, skilled at expressing in three dimensions client intentions.[46]

Hunt and Ward's first collaboration was a memorial in Newport to Commodore Matthew C. Perry, a Rhode Island native and naval officer legendary for opening Japan to Western trade (3.19). Perry's daughter Jane was married to the monument's patron, German-born Jewish financier August Belmont who had converted to his wife's Episcopalian faith. The sculpture, advancing Belmont's place in the Christian elite, was sited in historic Touro Park opposite the Griswold house. Hunt's granite pedestal was broad and squared to support the statue of related proportion. Perry stood as a Roman emperor, lifting his cape to reveal his naval uniform. Ward's ability to imbue military and business heroes with immediacy, while conveying a classical dignity, brought him years of prestige commissions.

The abolitionist *New-York Tribune* reported on the statue's dedication in 1868. Due to the efforts of a local judge, as well as Colonel Thomas

W. Higginson, a Unitarian minister and Civil War leader of Boston's African-American brigade, seven to eight thousand spectators attended, including children, "not all of one color." For the dedicating minister, the memorial was a sign of America's emerging appreciation of art and design, for "culture and refinement of a people is surely indicated by their taste in sculpture."[47]

The appeal and meaning of the Perry statue were direct by comparison with Hunt and Ward's Civil War memorials. Honoring the service and sacrifice of citizens warring against one another was inevitably problematic. Poet Walt Whitman, who tended the wounded in Union hospitals, struggled with bearing memory to the nation's loss. Realist author William Dean Howells, who lived out the war in Venice as an American consul, considered the tragedy a national disgrace. Memorials should contribute to the future peace, he wrote, but officials needed to deliberate when "choosing their sculptors and architects.... Home talent is a good thing when educated and developed, but it must be taught in the schools of art."[48]

Hunt's first Civil War memorial was in 1867, a modest fourteen-foot, bluestone and red granite wall tomb for Colonel Percival Drayton in New York's Trinity Church, a collaboration with French émigré carver Léon Larmande, and possibly Frank Furness. That same year the Seventh Regiment Memorial Association commissioned Hunt and Ward's only built New York monument to army sacrifice (3.20, see 2.2). The commission represented Hunt's second opportunity, after his Central Park gates, to

Fig. 3.19 Commodore Matthew Perry memorial dedicated in 1868, Newport, Rhode Island; in the 1870s, sculptor John Ward added the bas-relief to Hunt's pedestal; Michael Froio, 2020

Fig. 3.20 Seventh Regiment monument dedicated in 1874, Central Park, New York City; Hunt and John Ward honored both the regiment's sacrifice in the Civil War and its cultural leadership; Michael Froio, 2020[12]

introduce a Beaux-Arts sculpture ensemble to American city planning. His initial proposal was a gathering of mourning figures at the base of a pedestaled soldier, to be installed at his Warrior entrance gate. However, the regiment, derided as a citadel of dandified privilege, was not seeking sentimentality, but ennoblement as civic leaders of the bourgeoisie. After Olmsted and Vaux endorsed a solitary figure, Hunt and Ward settled on a modest twenty-one-foot-high granite and bronze monument, installed at the Sixty-Ninth Street West Walk. Instead of conveying the pathos of war, their anonymous infantryman was an "ideal citizen soldier—the man of culture, refinement, and social position."[49]

For creative professionals and their financial backers, culture in the nineteenth century meant religion, education, and the arts, interrelated as fields of interest and improvement. There was no sophistication without knowledge of art and religion, and no art and religion without education. Hunt and his clients understood this matrix and turned to funding culture for societal advancement.[50]

Hunt's contribution to education was as a teacher and practitioner of Beaux-Arts planning. His role in religion was as an architect of churches and seminaries, a core component of successful architecture firms even during the gradual secularization of society. In 1867 the intellectual theologian and pastor, Yale College graduate Horace Bushnell, spoke at the dedication of his Congregational Park Church in Hartford. "The greatest buildings of the world are not palaces, or forums, or amphitheatres, but temples." The Colosseum may have seated more than any church, but it was no more than a "prodigious freak of royal barbarity." Any religion with staying power "comes to the flower, sooner or later, by asserting visibility and permanence in stone." Hunt, a doer of great things, failed to win a major church commission, but he succeeded in the movement to expand divinity schools, furthering his dual practice dedicated to architecture and education. Two years after Bushnell held forth in Hartford, his alma mater commissioned Hunt to design its Theological Hall (later East Divinity Hall).[51]

At the time of the commission, Hunt was working on Scroll and Key Hall. Some fraternities were secret societies that built windowless club houses in classical and Middle Eastern styles expressing their agnostic mysticism. Yale's Skull and Bones society, founded in 1832, was already ensconced in its Egyptian-style "tomb" when Hunt began his work for Scroll and Key. Only one pavilion of his ambitious plan for two wings was built at the corner of Wall and College Streets (1869) (3.21). Hunt would have considered his Moorish-Byzantine fantasy of horseshoe arches and

Fig. 3.21 Scroll and Key Hall (1870), Yale College, New Haven, Connecticut, opposite, for a secret society that admitted only members to its windowless Moorish Revival clubhouse; Michael Froio, 2020

Fig. 3.22 Yale Theological Hall (1870), New Haven, Connecticut, and Hunt's adjoining neo-Gothic Marquand Chapel (1871); ca. 1872[13]

colored-stone bands wrapping four sides as the intersection of Greco-Roman and Eastern architecture, a transitional style.[52]

Associated with medieval scholasticism and Christian morality, Gothic traditions were dominant in academic architecture. At the time of the Theological Hall commission, Russell Sturgis Jr. was transforming Yale's campus along College Street into an Anglo-American Gothic row, supported by the theological school's Ruskinian building committee. Hunt laid out a plan for four buildings around a court at the corner of Elm and College Streets. Its first building, in red and black brick, trimmed in stone, was about 45 feet wide and 164 feet long. For the committee his initial design had been Gothic, but evolved, as contemporaries noted, into a Neo-Grec and French Renaissance synthesis (1870) (3.22). The classroom core on the first floor was between two blocks, one chamfered at the corner so that the school's library looked out, on axis, to the New Haven Green. Suites and bathrooms for about sixty students were on the floors above.

Hunt met the school's programmatic requirements, combining convenience and historic reference, using brick buttresses to express the building's plan transparently, extending them through the exterior walls and across the brick-faced interior corridor to separate first-floor classrooms, to rationally mark "interior sub-divisions" along "architectural

lines" he explained to college patrons. As for light and air, steam heat was "more economical and cleaner...the plan is so laid out that every room gets direct sunlight—a feature of great importance, not only for cheerfulness, but for hygiene."[53]

As Theological Hall neared completion, Hunt designed a chapel (1871) to the east, the only other building he oversaw in his courtyard plan. The exterior was finished in brick and stone matching the adjoining Hall, its cruciform interior vaulted in southern pine, the transverse ribs braced by hammer-head brackets. The French Gothic exterior, singular among Hunt's built churches, was likely at the request of Huguenot descendant Frederick Marquand who funded the chapel in memory of his wife, Hetty Perry. The older brother of Henry Marquand, soon to be Hunt's client,

Fig. 3.23 Second Academic Hall (1881), Hampton Normal and Agricultural Institute, Hampton, Virginia, near the mouth of the Chesapeake Bay, a harbinger of America's architecture of structure without decoration; Michael Froio, 2019[14]

Frederick had been president of his family's New York silver and jewelry business. A patron of civic and religious organizations, he served as trustee and donor to Virginia's Hampton Normal and Agricultural Institute (Hampton University from 1984).[54]

The American Missionary Association, a Protestant abolitionist society, led by the thirty-seven-year-old Civil War brigadier general Samuel C. Armstrong, opened the institute in 1868 and dedicated it to training African-American teachers and community leaders. To fund his enterprise, he cultivated the white society of Northern philanthropists, many in the circle of Richard Hunt, for whom race was complex. Catharine Hunt recalled that at the time of New York's Metropolitan Fair for Civil War medical supplies, Leavitt Hunt, serving in the Union Army, shipped a "contraband darkey" north "C.O.D." to work at the event and the Hunts' Hill-Top Cottage in Newport. This singular reference in Catharine's biography of Richard reflects her society's ambivalence toward abolition, on the one hand supporting opportunity for all while on the other remaining entrenched in the era's racism.[55]

Armstrong associated architecture with moral inspiration, and he commissioned buildings signifying his commitment to post-war civilization. In 1869 he hired Richard Hunt to design Hampton's first permanent building, Academic Hall. Its plan was a Greek cross, 110 feet by 85 feet, its timber-frame finished in red and black brick made by students living in tents along the Hampton River. Funded largely by the Reconstruction-era Freedmen's Bureau, the three-story building was light-filled from shallow-profile windows capped by brick arches and separated into pairs by buttresses running from the first to second floor.[56]

For Booker T. Washington, the college's renowned graduate, it fulfilled Armstrong's expectation of enlightenment through architecture. The *Up from Slavery* (1901) memoirist vividly recalled his arrival in 1872:[57]

> To me it had been a long, eventful journey, but the first sight of the large, three-story, brick school building seemed to have rewarded me for all that I had undergone in order to reach the place. If the people who gave the money to provide that building could appreciate the influence the sight of it had upon me, as well as upon thousands of other youths, they would feel all the more encouraged to make such gifts. It seemed to me to be the largest and most beautiful building I had ever seen. The sight of it seemed to give me new life. I felt that a new kind of existence had now begun—that life would now have a new meaning.

After Academic Hall burned down in 1879, Armstrong commissioned
a fireproof replacement (1881) (3.23). Hunt followed the general's request
for no decoration, retaining the original cruciform plan, now 110 feet by 75
feet, and marking corner piers and floor and ceiling divides in a grid of red
brick against stucco, empaneling the sides as he did in brick and wood
throughout the 1870s. Accommodating a recitation hall, offices, assembly
room, and an attic dormitory for thirty-five students, the new building
reflected the American trend toward structure over ornament and narrative
meaning. The building remains striking for its austere, rational legibility,
a moment when Hunt forewent the picturesque for what Montgomery
Schuyler called a building that was simply a "thing itself."[58]

Fig. 3.24a Virginia Hall (1879), Hampton, left, ca. 1885, a secular cathedral fulfilling the Unitarian Rev. Samuel Osgood's 1874 call for American architects to transform "broad acres into fair landscape, with soaring spires and smiling homes"[15]

Fig. 3.24b Virginia Hall entrance; Michael Froio, 2019

Virginia Hall (1879) was Hunt's second commission at Hampton, paid for by private donations and built with student labor during the depressed 1870s. In the long shadow of slavery, Armstrong sought to "dignify labor," his new building rising like a chateau-cathedral from the war-torn countryside, its design indebted to English and continental civic buildings (3.24a-b). The five-story, T-shaped brick residence, a central block terminated by corner pavilions, and piers defining arched window bays, accommodated one hundred twenty women and twelve teachers, student and faculty dining rooms, kitchens, a library, a space for manufacturing clothes, and a two-story chapel.[59]

The civilization movement that Armstrong brought to the ravaged South evolved across America as industrial prosperity came to small cities and towns along the railroad. Hunt joined building and landscape architects in this national gentrification, notably designing a church and library at Matteawan (Beacon today), New York, funded by Catharine Hunt's brother, Joseph Howland. Made a brevet brigadier general for bravery in the Civil War and at New York's Draft Riots, he was a local banker, philanthropist, and state treasurer. His wife Eliza Woolsey from Rhode Island served as a wartime nurse and published her collected letters.[60]

Fig. 3.25a Eliza, wife of Joseph Howland, seated in Hunt's music pavilion (1873) at their estate, Tioronda, Matteawan, New York; ca. 1874[16]

Fig. 3.25b William A. Johnson & Son organ, Opus 411 (1873), opposite; Michael Froio, 2019

The Howlands lived near Matteawan at Tioronda (a Haudenosaunee term for "the place where two waters meet"), their Hudson River estate landscaped by neighbor Henry Winthrop Sargent. The influential horticulturalist, and friend of Andrew Jackson Downing and Frederick Law Olmsted, had recently published a European house and garden guide for wealthy tourists when the Howlands commissioned Hunt to design a music room for their moody 1861 brick, wood, and stone villa. The house, by English-born Frederick C. Withers, derived from continental sources that similarly influenced Hunt's cottage architecture and nearby Howland Circulating Library (later Howland Cultural Center).

When completed in 1873, the part-octagonal, French Gothic Revival Howland pavilion was a sacristy to Withers' cottage. Inside, Hunt's predisposition to color and drama was present again, an imposing Renaissance Revival fireplace in glazed red-orange brick and a polychromed organ dominating the wood-vaulted room, its ceiling inspired by churches Hunt would have seen traveling through Normandy villages (3.25a-b).[61]

Hunt's Franco-Norwegian Presbyterian Church at Matteawan was dedicated in July 1872, only a month before the opening of the nearby Howland library (3.26a-b). Sixty-five feet deep and roughly forty-five feet

wide, it exemplified Hunt's animated vernacular—slate hung walls, colored brick window surrounds, steeped pitched roof, and bracketed eaves. Its squared plan was a respite from the exterior's bright cacophony. The library visitor entered through a low-ceilinged hall, past a stair to a second-floor apartment, to be awed by the square, light-filled reading room that soared more than thirty feet. It was an illuminated, engineered sanctuary for contemplative study, its bracing and slatted ceiling inspired by Viollet-le-Duc's treatise on iron structure (*Deuxième Entretien*, 1863) and the fifteenth-century Protestant Great Church (*Grote Kerk*) in The Hague (see SK.11), which Hunt sketched and measured in 1867.[62]

Fig. 3.26a Howland Circulating Library, Matteawan (Beacon), New York, dedicated 1872; Michael Froio, 2019

Fig. 3.26b Library's reading room, opposite, a chapel for learning (gallery added 1894); Michael Froio, 2019

Tioronda's vaulted music room reflected the demand in post-war America for specialized interiors and lavish homes, alluring to the romantic mind imagining tales by Scott and Hawthorne and operas by Verdi and Donizetti. Adept at finessing such intersections, Hunt continued to bring trends in French home architecture to Newport, albeit at a new and grander scale. Emboldened by privileged clients who toured the Old World, he elaborated his 1860s vernacular style while sustaining his École approach to plan. In 1870 he built The Corners for the Shakespearean actress Charlotte S. Cushman (see P.7), an international star who lived in Rome during the 1850s and was partner then with American sculptor Emma Stebbins.

Planned in a cross-axis on an elevated site to meet Cushman's demand for a "sea" and "sunsets" view, The Corners was a French Normand villa, its wood exterior empaneled, its interiors octagonal, as at the nearby Griswold cottage (3.27). Commentators remarked on Hunt's eccentricity, the Civil War abolitionist hero Colonel Higginson paradoxically writing in racist terms that The Corners was the "wildest turn of an insane kaleidoscope, the petrified antics of a crazy coon—with a dance of intoxicated lightning rods breaking out over the roof." Journalist Martha Lamb sensed

Fig. 3.27 The Corners (1870), Newport, Rhode Island, a monumental villa in wood for Charlotte Cushman, America's celebrity tragedienne; ca. 1870[17]

the "painted towers" of the much-admired, poetical Chillon castle at Lake Geneva. "Red, yellow, brown, and green," wrote a local columnist, probably about The Corners, "are being put on the same building in a very fanciful manner, after the Swiss style which is just now all the rage." Hunt himself had looked at chalet architecture to design his 1867 Newport villa for the widowed New York heiress, Rebecca J. "Mrs. Isaac Colford" Jones.[63]

Hunt's lifelong attraction to the decorated played out in his rustic houses contemporaneous with The Corners and Howland library. Wealthy Boston litterateur Thomas G. Appleton's 1871 cottage and Henry Marquand's 1873 Linden Gate were Grimms' fairy-tale imaginings of steeply pitched, slate-patterned roofs, trussed gables, jerkin heads, and surfaces encrusted in stone and colored brick conjuring up the medievalism of northern European suburban villas.[64]

Reimaging existing houses contributed to Hunt's rise as society's architect. The year he began the Appleton cottage he transformed art collector Mary A.D. Bruen's matter-of-fact rubble stone house (1851) by local architect Seth C. Bradford into a Euro-American villa (3.28a-b). Its neighbor to the south off Bellevue Avenue was Bradford's fireproofed brick and Massachusetts granite Chateau-sur-Mer (1852), built for the New York merchant William S. Wetmore. On his death in 1862, his son George inherited the chateau. Yale- and Columbia-educated, a member of Skull and Bones, George became a Rhode Island governor and US senator. After

Fig. 3.28a–b Mary Bruen rubble stone house (1851), left, Newport, Rhode Island; ca. 1855; the house after Hunt's 1872 continental upgrade, right; Michael Froio, 2020

their honeymoon in Europe, he and his wife, Edith M. Keteltas, employed Hunt in building campaigns, from 1873 to 1880, to modernize their house through design.

Raising the existing Mansard roof to a Parisian pitch and framing entrances in granite Neo-Grec surrounds, Hunt brought Second Empire scale to Wetmore's chateau (3.29). A new stair from the porte-cochère was lined with moralizing *Fables* of Jean de la Fontaine, introducing pictorial light to the dark interior, as murals of sky and trees transformed Parisian libraries by Henri Labrouste. Beyond this entrance the dining room and library opened to a three-story hall, their neo-Renaissance interiors supplied by Florentine craftsman Luigi Frullini, likely discovered by Hunt at the 1867 Paris Exposition (3.30a-b). In their ambition, the interiors belonged to the 1870s trend, in America and abroad, of professionally decorated rooms aspiring to period authenticity. The chateau's architecture and interiors were in contrast to the neighboring home of the same years by Henry Richardson for George Wetmore's sister Annie and her husband William Watts Sherman. Its Anglo-American details and horizontality now superseded Hunt's vertical Norman style for cottage architecture as he moved to limestone palaces for the vacationing rich, competing with peers in the European plutocracy building their own country palaces.[65]

By the 1870s Hunt was prospering from multiple projects for individual clients. In Newport, William R. Travers, a Columbia-educated New York

lawyer whose daughter married society artist Walter Gay and lived in Paris, hired Hunt to remodel his house at Ochre Point (1872) and to build a commercial block (1871) along Bellevue Avenue (3.31). For this development, Hunt drew again on the European vernacular, wrapping the second floor in a grid of ornamental bracing on brick siding, the third story animated by bracketed eaves, gables, and dormers. This was architecture as literature, evoking medieval streets then being restored in Europe and longed for by Hunt and his well-traveled clients.[66]

Hunt's rusticated cottages influenced the work of Philadelphia's Frank Furness, Boston's Peabody & Stearns, and Newporter George Mason. Similarly, his Travers block guided future development. As Newport became a resort renowned for Hunt's mansions, the Bellevue shopping district

Fig. 3.29 Edith and George Wetmore house, Chateau-sur-Mer, after 1870s renovations, Bellevue Avenue, Newport, Rhode Island; Hunt transformed it into a Second Empire country mansion, his first at the ocean resort; Michael Froio, 2020

Fig. 3.30a Renaissance Revival library, Chateau-sur-Mer (ca. 1876), Florentine decorator Luigi Frullini; cornice plaques to Raphael, Dante, and Michelangelo, alongside Washington and Lincoln, reflected the Old-to-New-World spirit of the times; ca. 1884

Fig. 3.30b Library bookcase; Michael Froio, 2020

extended south to include McKim, Mead & White's tennis and theater club, The Casino (1881). The New York-based architects were deferential to their older colleague, and though advancing a new American vernacular, in contrast to Hunt's unwavering Eurocentricity, their gabled and shingled building continued the scale and horizontal divisions of his adjoining development.

The Travers block was nearing completion and Chateau-sur-Mer progressing when international events revealed the underlying instability of Hunt's seemingly omniscient world. France suffered the humiliating end of the Franco-Prussian War, followed by the Commune riots when workers set Paris ablaze, torching aristocratic monuments (3.32). It was a "miracle," Jonathan Hunt wrote his mother in June 1871, "that I should have escaped when so many others have been frightfully massacred." The socialists had fomented the "refuse of the workers" against the "Bourgeoisie," causing the Empire to fall. Two years later, America's Great Panic of 1873, from monetary policy, speculation, and losses in the devastating Chicago and Boston fires, triggered an international depression that stalled Hunt's architectural practice. In December that year he caught pneumonia after a snowy afternoon reviewing a homesite in Poughkeepsie, New York, for celebrity preacher Henry Ward Beecher. Catharine assumed management

Fig. 3.31 Travers block (1871), Newport, Rhode Island; Hunt's retail and lodging development conjured up Europe's romantic medieval streets, alluring to the town's wealthy summer residents; ca. 1890

Fig. 3.32 The burning of Paris in the Commune riots confirmed the importance of "civilizing" society; Michel-Charles Fichot, *Paris Incendie*, colored engraving, 1871

of Richard's studio while he recuperated at home. Though not fully recovered, on doctor's orders he sailed for Europe in May 1874, joined by Catharine and three of their five children.[67]

The Hunts' year abroad, intended for rest and recuperation, was a trauma of poor health and family loss. Between their own illnesses and their children's bouts of scarlet fever, Catharine and Richard stayed at healing spas and toured Germany, Switzerland, and Italy, where Richard painted and sketched churches in the Romanesque style made fashionable in America by Henry Richardson (see SK.8). In Paris, Jonathan committed suicide, the forty-eight-year-old doctor to the poor slitting his throat. Catharine snobbishly remarked that he had lived unwed with a "little *lingère*," a French laundress "not of [Jonathan's] class." They had a daughter, Jeanne, later confined to the asylum at Charenton, driven mad by violence during the Commune. Richard arranged for his brother's burial in Paris' Père Lachaise cemetery and shipped his library and art back to America.[68]

War-time defeat and violence traumatized Paris, but the city rose again in the Belle Époque of the Third Republic, a period of colonialization and scientific invention, of Worth gowns, Impressionist paintings, and Jules E.F. Massenet's comic opera *Manon*. Monuments to establishment culture, the burned-out Hôtel de Ville and Hôtel de Salm, home of the Légion d'Honneur, were restored and honored. By fall 1874 when Hunt was

in the capital city, Charles Garnier's Paris Opera house was nearing completion, a late but influential summa of Second Empire art and architecture. Hunt and his family headed south to Nice for Christmas in the pine-scented hills above the Bay of Angels (3.33), where they celebrated the end of a very grim year.

Over several exceptional days, Hunt joined sixty-year-old Viollet-le-Duc at the Chateau de Pierrefonds north of Paris, a trip they had anticipated in 1867 (3.34). The French architect's reforming spirit, polymathy, and advocacy of new materials and integration of decorative and fine art into projects were shared by Hunt. His writings on buildings, interiors, and furnishings from the Middle Ages to the Renaissance made him an international voice for architecture as structure and function, popularized by Hunt's student Henry Van Brunt, who translated *Entretiens sur l'architecture* (1863-72) into English. Viollet-le-Duc had been restoring the fourteenth-century Pierrefonds for Napoléon III since 1857, reimagining crumbling piles of stone as a towered Gothic fortress, its deep mullioned windows in blocks of dressed stone, massing, and polychromed interiors (see 5.38a-b) influencing Hunt's work after his return to America in May 1875.[69]

Over the twenty years since he first returned to America, Hunt had used his education and social position with an unrelenting determination to be both cultural leader and architect. A preacher for public education in

Fig. 3.33 After a year of poor health and loss, the Hunt family spent Christmas above the Mediterranean in Nice, France, where Hunt painted flora and fauna and this view to the city's Bay of Angels; watercolor, sketchbook, 1874

Fig. 3.34 Chateau de Pierrefonds, France, visited by Hunt in 1874 with its restoration architect, the spokesperson for Gothic architecture in France and America, Viollet-le-Duc; Emmanuel Lansyer, the architect's student, ca. 1868

taste and beauty, Henry Ward Beecher first met Hunt around 1859 when he was planning a new Pilgrim Church in Brooklyn. Arriving at Hunt's Tenth Street studio unannounced, he inquired if the architect knew anything about acoustics. Then-student George Post recalled that Hunt characteristically quipped in response, "Not the first _____ thing!" Despite this initial uninspiring retort, Beecher was later convinced by planning for a home, not built, that Hunt had become over the years "one of the few men in his profession who are artists rather than artisans," a hard-won distinction and a resounding endorsement for Hunt and architecture as a fine art.

Now, an adventurous purveyor of French-inspired architecture, designing buildings that adapted precedents to the needs of contemporary life and attuned to trends at home and abroad, Hunt would turn to lessons learned from his Lenox Library and Pierrefonds to move from structural articulation in brick and wood to stone and sculpture to realize the Medician longings of the Gilded Age.[70]

Chapter 4

Desirable Elements for Wealth

After their return from Europe in 1875, the Hunts rallied friends and colleagues to promote Philadelphia's 1876 Centennial International Exhibition, where examples of the nation's industrial progress awed more than ten million visitors from across the globe (4.1). Catharine, a commentator wrote, "with a mind full of learning, particularly in archeology, and with her husband behind her, inspired by his researches," produced *tableaux vivants* at the Union League Club of New York, portraying moments from the nation's past. Richard, as a juror for the fair's exhibits in "Architecture and Engineering," solicited leading architects to participate. Gambrill & Richardson, George Post, and Richard Upjohn contributed plans and renderings while Hunt, for his part, exhibited drawings demonstrating the breadth of his practice and willful determination. His selections—the neo-Moorish Van Rensselaer "iron building," Lenox Library, Tribune tower, and his rejected Western Union Telegraph headquarters and Central Park gateways—were his bona fides for urban development.[1]

Toward the end of the exhibition, Hunt presented his impressions to the AIA. At home, "art-education of the masses" at new schools and museums was expanding public knowledge of fine design, while across the Western world, a "great architectural revival" had ensued following London's technologically advanced Crystal Palace (1851). In Paris and Vienna, urban renewal had swept away "dismal streets of the middle ages" for "broad and noble thoroughfares in harmony with the requirements of the day." That said, Hunt supported France's restoration of historic

Fig 4.21 detail, Statue of Liberty, New York Harbor

On the image: *Centennial 1876* / *Phila^d. P^a*

churches and chateaus, but accepted the sacrifice of America's eighteenth-century buildings to advance its emergent civilization.[2]

As for the Centennial's buildings, their eclecticism and proportions were "squatty," "clumsy," and lacking in "monumental grandeur," though architects had met practical requirements using glass, iron, and steel. American building plans on display illustrated overwrought and ornamented structures, the exception being drawings from Massachusetts for an asylum, hospital, grammar school, and college. A solution to this poor Yankee showing was the adaptation of Beaux-Arts methods that could lift the native architect to the "elevated position" of his peers in France.[3]

The work Hunt exhibited in Philadelphia and his praise for Massachusetts were signs of prosperity and the prestige of public work. Though he frequently failed in commercial competitions, as the call for an American style and technology came to determine form, he succeeded in designing churches and seminary buildings, his picturesque approach suited to the sensibilities of institutions seeking images of moral order and tradition.

Hunt built only six of the thirteen churches he designed, informed by his decided views of ecclesiastical architecture, presented at the 1877 Fourth Annual Congress of the Episcopal Church. A consensus held that new churches, too eclectic and ornamented, did not represent Protestant reserve and humility. One presenter cited Eugène Viollet-le-Duc and called for structures of "our time and country...." Emlen T. Littell of the New York AIA believed that America's founding in "the English Church" and "the English nation" made Gothic design appropriate. To seek new solutions would be "perilous."[4]

The outspoken voice of continental history, supporting global reach and countering Anglo-Saxon nationalism, Hunt responded in two parts, first by archeologically tracing Western architecture, followed by an assessment of Christian interiors and their functionality. The Byzantine basilica— the "'ecclesia,' or place of assembly"—represented a transitional architecture between the classical Greco-Roman and the Gothic, its cruciform plan "symbolical [and] appropriate" for the recent "change of ritual" requiring the assembly of celebrants in democratic "harmony and equality." Advances in engineering, eliminating columns at the crossing, made this community possible.[5]

At the time of the Episcopal Congress, Hunt was already planning a chapel for Princeton (chartered in 1746 as the College of New Jersey, Princeton University from 1896). After the Civil War its president James McCosh liberalized the curriculum along lines pursued by Harvard's Charles W. Eliot, Hunt's childhood friend. McCosh shared his generation's faith in fine architecture to advance spiritual growth, and in a period of rising post-war enrollment, he commissioned buildings by professional architects. As early as 1873, he turned to Henry Marquand to fund a new chapel. The financier had not been college-educated, but his son Allan, a graduate of Princeton and its first professor of art and archeology in 1883 (his uncle Frederick Marquand endowed the chair), advised his father in cultural projects that would bring "credit upon the name of Marquand," long associated with money-making and commerce.[6]

Hunt was already the architect of Marquand's Newport cottage, Linden Gate, when the millionaire selected him as the chapel architect. McCosh was specific about a site near Italianate Nassau Hall and wanted a visible landmark of collegial faith, with a belfry "as high as the tower of Babel." When construction began in 1881, Hunt had in 1879 already designed for the Princeton Theological Seminary (founded 1812) two faculty houses and the school's Lenox Library, all funded by James Lenox. Seventy by sixty feet, the red brick and brownstone building was strikingly classical, its interior a court framed by books and lit by clerestory windows.[7]

The Marquand Chapel, completed in 1882, was Hunt's adaptation of the Romanesque, 130 feet long and 88 feet wide in rough-cut Trenton brownstone harmonizing with buildings nearby (4.2a-b). The plan was cruciform, its porch, apse, stair, and 140-foot venting tower expressing

Fig. 4.2a Hunt's Romanesque Marquand Chapel (1882), Princeton, New Jersey; after 1885

Fig. 4.2b Chapel's wood vaulted interior; after 1897[18]

the building's function. Steam-heated and illuminated by electric light and Tiffany stained glass, the sanctuary was open and welcoming, its wood vaulting and supports inspired by Viollet-le-Duc's *Entretien* which Hunt had referenced for his Howland library. The altar was under a half-dome, faced with Ravenna-style mosaics. Hunt specified motifs for the entrance and chancel curtains, woven by artists at the Society of Decorative Art under Catharine's supervision.[8]

A student review of the chapel was astute, noting that Hunt, who believed that "all church decoration should be symbolical," had turned to the Roman basilica for the apse, Gothic vaulting for the transept, and the Turkish mosque for the minaret-style tower. Though there were "no unique specimens of architectural style," they were "more or less symbolic of [the church's] use." Hunt had given form to church history, denominationally and architecturally, as President McCosh was seeking an incorporative American Protestantism.[9]

Hunt sustained a long practice in part because of his at times pragmatic adapting to trends in architecture, rather than pursuing an individualistic path. The Marquand Chapel's Romanesque aspect may not have been entirely of Hunt's choosing. By the late 1870s Princeton administrators were under the sway of their critical success, Witherspoon Hall by William A. Potter. "They were then crazy on the Potter style," wrote Allan Marquand to his father, "and wanted uniformity." The hulking dormitory, completed in 1877, was indebted to the transformative work of Henry Richardson, Hunt's rival for America's most influential architect, at home and abroad.[10]

Like Hunt, Richardson was raised Unitarian and aspired to West Point before studying at Harvard and the Paris École. He spent the Civil War in France and returned to America in 1865, partnering with Hunt's student Charles D. Gambrill in New York before moving to Boston where his Episcopal Trinity Church (1877) secured his reputation, its Byzantine plan undoubtedly influencing Hunt's presentation at the Episcopal conference. Hunt had competed for the commission, and like his losing proposal for New York's National Academy of Design (1861), his plan—a stone block, Latin-cross nave and transept pierced by Romanesque lancet windows—was merely serviceable when compared with his sculptural work indebted to Francis I and the Second Empire.[11]

The Marquand Chapel was Hunt's first built response to what became known as the Richardsonian Romanesque. Though he and the Boston architect shared École planning, Hunt's exterior elements were always discrete and legible, in contrast to Richardson's work seen by Hunt as "bold and fertile in conception, and broadly treated," bearing "the stamp of genius," an approach that came to be considered, at home and abroad, distinctly American.[12]

As he expanded his practice, Hunt continued to advocate for professional architecture. He promoted the necessity of independent architects in government work and entered public debate. In 1875 New York legislators assembled a committee of Olmsted, Richardson, and Eidlitz to review the neo-Renaissance state capitol at Albany, then under construction to plans by English-born Thomas Fuller. In person and in print, Hunt and members of New York's AIA argued against the committee's proposed Romanesque changes, "an agglomeration of incongruous forms," that would "vitiate instead of educat[e] the taste of the people." Consequently, the capitol would become a moral and aesthetic failure, condemning the "architectural skill" of a generation. Though the revisions were ultimately incorporated, Hunt had advanced a premise of new design, that only "utility" and "unity of style," by which he meant a coherent eclecticism, could advance an uplifting, professional architecture, an objective he finally realized at Chicago's 1893 exposition (see 5.45) of classical buildings.[13]

~~~~~~~~

Professionally, Richard Hunt flourished in the Gilded Age, but illness and loss shadowed life at home. Catharine was stricken by typhoid fever, and whooping cough and measles plagued their children. Jane Leavitt Hunt died in 1877 at seventy-six, a determined figure estranged at times from her children. She had been, Catharine reminisced, a woman of "tremendous pride of family and race...her children [owed] her much, particularly William and Richard, whose artistic abilities she encouraged," when men of their class did not pursue art professions. At her own choosing, she was buried next to her parents in Connecticut, not with her husband in Vermont.[14]

Despite his maternal support and renown, William Morris Hunt died suddenly in 1879. The decade had been one of crisis for the booster of art and education. The Great Boston Fire of 1872 reduced his studio and painting collection to ashes, and the following year his wife Louisa ended their rocky marriage, only to enter an asylum later. The popularity of his work in decline and exhausted from painting murals at the new Albany Capitol, William retreated to the Isles of Shoales where he stayed at a local hotel with poet and artist Celia Thaxter. In early September, she found the fifty-five-year-old painter dead in a nearby pond. Some believed his death was accidental, but others assumed suicide. "William put an end to his wild, restless, unhappy life," wrote Bostonian Marian Hooper Adams, who killed herself six years later. "Perhaps it has saved him from years of insanity, which his temperament pointed to." His "resentful" wife, who had separated William from his children and family, did not attend the funeral in Brattleboro, where he was buried next to his father, his grave marked by a black granite slab designed by Richard, starkly engraved with his brother's name and dates.[15]

In less than four years, Hunt had buried his mother and two brothers, leaving him the surviving nova of his competitive family. Leavitt, a once promising attorney and intellectual, was sunk by speculative investments and became a gentleman farmer in Vermont, while Jane, alone after the death of her mother, moved to California where she lived out most of her life as a watercolorist. Richard remained in New York, bolstered by career and money, and supported by his empathetic wife, known for her maternal warmth and dedication to his career.[16]

Circumspect as her class required, Catharine did not dwell on her family's hardships, but persevered as Richard's collaborator. "The decade between 1870 and 1880 found New York at its best," reminisced a columnist at century's end, though the 1873 financial panic had "left a necessity of caution in expenditure," before the "worship of the Golden Calf" in the 1880s and 1890s. On specified days William Aspinwall and John Johnston opened their private collections to a select public. There were club readings of Shakespeare's sonnets and tales of Renaissance Italy, society benefits and balls in August Belmont's gallery, "a room to command the respect of Europe." The Academy of Music presented *Lucia di Lammermoor* and *Lohengrin,* and Catharine's friend and confidante, Swedish soprano Christina Nilsson, sang Marguerite in Gounod's *Faust,* a celebrated event that opens Edith Wharton's *The Age of Innocence* (1920), her portrait of this genteel society and its entanglements with parvenu Julius Beaufort, a riff on the Belmont name. Pictorials followed the lives of litterateurs and opera stars, the infamous adultery trial of Henry Ward Beecher making headline news. Stuyvesant, Astor, Hoppin, and Roosevelt were prominent names among the "well born, well-educated and fashionable." They were an "aristocracy...a smaller and less glittering one than [later], but it was far more elegant, well bred, exclusive and distinguished," always welcomed at the "delightful house of Mr. and Mrs. Richard Hunt, one of the strongholds of taste and culture."[17]

After the Civil War the private home reached a new prominence in architectural practice as the civilization movement came to justify the big house and the wealth it entailed. In 1871 New Yorker Simeon Church had equated residential "palaces" with "monuments dedicated to Art and Science" in the nineteenth-century "imperial" city. Eighteen years later, steel magnate and Fifth Avenue mansion builder Andrew Carnegie elaborated on this equivalency in his essay "Wealth."

> The contrast between the palace of the millionaire and the cottage of the laborer...measures the change which has come with civilization. This change, however, is not to be deplored, but welcomed as highly beneficial. It is well, nay, essential for the progress of the race, that the houses of some should be homes for all that is highest and best in literature and the arts, and for all the refinements of civilization, rather than that none should be so. Much better this great irregularity than universal squalor. Without wealth there can be no Mæcenas. The "good old times" were not good old times. Neither master nor servant was as well situated then as to-day.

The great financial disparity between the poor and the rich, already being debated and justified by long-lingering Calvinist values, was "beyond our power to alter," Carnegie concluded. It was simply a fact of life, to be "accepted and made the best of. It is a waste of time to criticize the inevitable," a sophistry defining civilization as a state of inequality necessary for the greater good. Where an earlier generation had found tyranny in the castle and palace, the rich now viewed their mansions as democracy at work, advancing the lives of owners and servants alike.[18]

～～～～～～

The first city residence Hunt designed as the economy recovered in the late 1870s was at the corner of Madison Avenue and Thirty-Third Street in New York's fashionable Murray Hill. It was two houses built as one, a brick block under a modified Mansard roof, a move toward articulated form without the ornaments of Virginia Osborn's double house immediately to the east (4.3, see also 3.12). The interiors by Frenchman Léon Marcotte, however, were newly historicist, elaborately finished, and richly furnished.

The house that faced the avenue was for Sara King, descendant of a New York governor, and her husband Frederic Bronson Jr. He was a Columbia-educated lawyer and heir to a real estate and insurance fortune. The other residence, entered from the side, was for his brother-in-law, widowed attorney Egerton L. Winthrop, also a Columbia College graduate

Fig. 4.3 Winthrop-Bronson house (1879), Madison Avenue, New York City, a drainpipe marking the interior divide; Winthrop's salon was at the second-floor corner; ca. 1880

and descendant of the first governor of Massachusetts. He lived in Paris on and off and introduced Edith Wharton to French furniture and décor. "[S]elf-conscious and ill at ease with insignificant people," she wrote, he "built himself a charming house.... [H]e was a discriminating collector of works of art, especially of the eighteenth century, and his house was the first in New York in which an educated taste had replaced stuffy upholstery and rubbishy 'ornaments' with objects of real beauty in a simply designed setting." However, his society life was not for serious thinkers, Wharton concluding that never have "an intelligence so distinguished and a character so admirable been combined with interests for the most part so trivial."[19]

In the 1830s archeological discoveries and romantic novels spurred a Parisian fashion for revivalist rooms conjuring up the "spectral evanescence" of memory. Alexandre du Sommerard, Hunt's inspiration, arranged his encyclopedic collections at the Hôtel de Cluny to suggest

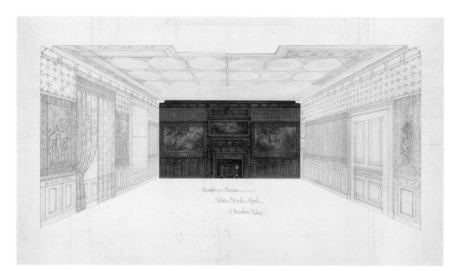

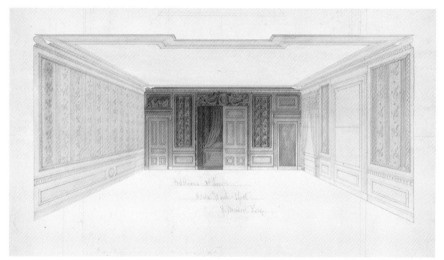

Fig. 4.4a–b Proposed period-revival reception room, top, and bedroom, bottom, for the Bronson house. L. Marcotte & Co; watercolors, ca. 1878, digitally enhanced to show rooms in three dimensions, Michael Froio and Samuel Markey, 2022

period interiors, and King Louis-Philippe reimagined palace rooms to reflect a noble royalist past. Apartments by Hector Lefuel at the Louvre and Tuileries, by Viollet-le-Duc at Pierrefonds (see 3.34, 5.38a), and by Louis Visconti at his Parisian Hôtel de Pontalba (1855) for the American baroness Micaela Almonester, exemplified the historicizing culture fostering an international market of collectors, merchants, art critics, and craftsmen well known to Hunt.[20]

In America, the interrelating of exterior and interior took hold after the Civil War, monumentally at Elm Park (1868), a Second Empire

Fig. 4.5 Louis XVI Revival drawing room, Winthrop house; the panel decoration and ceiling carvings were in papier-mâché; probably L. Marcotte & Co., ca. 1883[19]

Connecticut mansion designed and decorated by Detlef Lienau and Léon Marcotte for a speculating railroad millionaire. A decade later Hunt brought his antiquarianism to interior design. He supported American societies dedicated to establishing artisan trades and commissioned decorating studios in Paris and New York that gilded the Gilded Age. In the 1880s, as the European fashion for revivalist decoration found its ultimate expression in the reinstallation of period rooms, Hunt combined old and new paneling with furnishings in related styles.

Watercolors by L. Marcotte & Co. and photographs in *Artistic Houses* (1883), one of the illustrated publications boosting American design, presented the Bronson-Winthrop interiors as thematic by period (4.4a-b). The connoisseurship of Winthrop's Renaissance "reception-room" and Louis XVI "drawing-room" proved a "persistent determination to reproduce in all aspects the forms, color, and feeling of a particular era" (4.5). The

reign of Marie Antoinette, "the culmination of the artistic triumphs of the decorators of the French Renaissance," had been an inspiration.[21]

Completed by 1879, the Bronson-Winthrop rooms retained the superfluity, attention to craft, and internationalism of the Aesthetic interior, but Hunt and his clients had replaced the "rubbishy" eclecticism of Marcotte's Marshall Field interiors (see 3.16a) with period authenticity and decorative arts evoking the aristocratic past. This approach, combining antiques and tapestries in paneled rooms, became the foundation of Edith Wharton and Ogden Codman Jr.'s *The Decoration of Houses* (1897), its "good taste" mandates guiding upper-class imaging through the Kennedy White House years.

Catherine E. Beecher and Harriet Beecher Stowe, sisters of Hunt's client Henry Ward Beecher, wrote in their popular guide, *The American Woman's Home* (1869), that woman was "chief minister" of the family state, while professional man did the "out-door labor." Men turned to architects to build houses, but women, more ingenious, created homes through decoration. Design, the Beechers wrote, "contributes much to the education of the entire household in refinement, intellectual development, and

Fig. 4.6a–b Alva and William K. Vanderbilt; Benjamin Porter, ca. 1889. She was "quick at repartee, witty, and somewhat sarcastic…feared in society," her husband "morose" and "less popular" than his brothers, dependent on Alva's "strong character and will-power"[20]

moral sensibility," qualities core to the advancement of American culture. Fine furniture and works of art augmented the civilizing benefits of the decorated room. While not all budgets afforded "expensive" paintings and sculpture, prints of the "celebrated pictures of the world" and plaster casts, "whether of antiquity or of modern times," educated the young American musing on the imperial worlds that had enthralled Richard Hunt and his generation since the 1840s.[22]

Supported by their domestic imperative, the wives of clients shaped Hunt's residential practice after the Civil War, none being more influential than Alva Erskine Smith, who was twenty-two when she married William K. Vanderbilt in 1875 (4.6a-b). He was an heir to his grandfather Cornelius Vanderbilt's railroad fortune and a son of art collector William H. Vanderbilt. By her own telling, Alva was no arriviste, as critics later portrayed her and her class. She descended from French Huguenots and English and Scottish aristocrats, her namesake being the eighteenth-century lawyer James Erskine, Lord Alva. She belonged to a "race" of builders, "statesmen, jurists, and men of affairs" in Europe and America, inheriting their "independence of thought" and "strength of character" as the daughter of a prosperous cotton merchant in Mobile, Alabama.[23]

Among Alva's childhood recollections was consulting her father's library to design "imaginary homes" for her future family, believing that middle-class domestic life built "self-reliance" and a "sense of personal responsibility." Informed by this experience and years in Paris as a teen, she and William initiated the Vanderbilts' quarter-century association with Hunt's office, possibly on introduction from Sara and Frederic Bronson, whose patrician credentials as friends of society's reigning doyenne, Caroline Astor, were a significant endorsement. Their first commission was a house (1880) at the Connetquot River in Islip, New York, one of the fishing villages along Long Island's Great South Bay transformed from hamlet to enclave by the suburban rail. Byronically named Idle Hour, the wood mansion was a Hunt Newport cottage writ large, an empaneled continental villa.[24]

As her life would prove, Alva extended her moral obligations beyond the family home. In a gesture of noblesse oblige, she undertook the building of St. Mark's Episcopal (1880) at Islip, the first of Hunt's two Vanderbilt churches (4.7, 4.8, see also 5.41a-b). She considered the extant "house of God" and the minister's "shanty" a "disgrace to the community," and agreed to pay for the church if neighboring mansion owners funded a rectory, also to a design by Hunt. On his visit to Norway in 1867 he had sketched medieval and contemporary stave churches, proto-rationalist

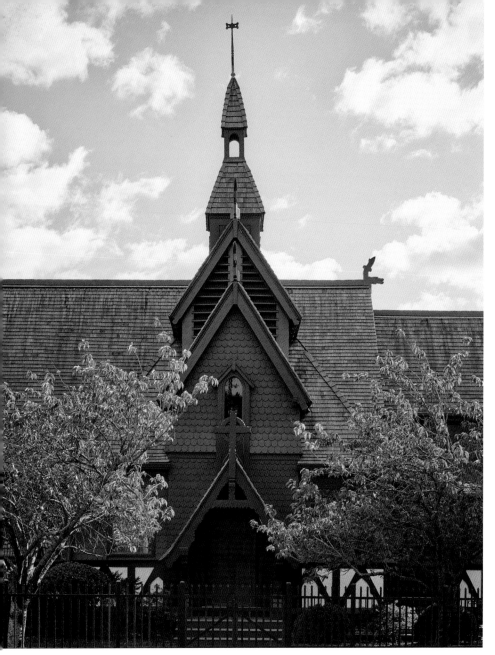

Fig. 4.7 Transept entrance, St. Mark's Episcopal Church (1880), Islip, New York, funded by Alva and William K. Vanderbilt, inspired by Norwegian wood churches; Michael Froio, 2019[21]

Fig. 4.8 St. Mark's Episcopal Church; Hunt's adaptation of open structure and high finish were evident in the hammer-beam ceiling and wood half-dome above the altar; Michael Froio, 2019

in their exposed timber construction (see SK.10). At Islip, he adapted the stepped Norwegian roof to exterior porches and installed a hammer-beam ceiling above the nave of his Latin-cross plan, a composite northern architecture for a family of Protestant and Anglican heritage.[25]

Wood and plaster were suited to country cottages and churches, but by the 1880s and 1890s industrial fortunes afforded limestone palaces, appropriate for what Europe and America considered their era's financial and cultural Renaissance, synonymous with individualism, earned wealth, and support of the arts for sociopolitical ends. Despite Hunt's affinity for French royal architecture, his clients considered themselves new Medici,

Fig. 4.9 Alva and William K. Vanderbilt house (1882), Fifth Avenue, New York City; peers lauded Hunt for introducing École rigor and limestone lightness to the city's brownstone rows; Albert H. Levy, ca. 1883

rising up from modest beginnings to rule the secular state. An exemplar of this ascendant class was Alva Vanderbilt, who wrote of her "tremendous respect" and affinity for the Florentine family.[26]

> They originated as apothecaries. Later their great wealth was used to encourage art of every kind. Florence, their native city, represents to this day the obligation they felt to endow it in every way in their power with beauty and art. So I felt about the Vanderbilt fortune, and I preached this doctrine at home and to William H. Vanderbilt....

What the Renaissance consensus yielded for the Vanderbilt clan was the mansion row William H. and his sons William K. and Cornelius II built immediately on inheriting the transformative fortune of Cornelius Vanderbilt. Only blocks apart on the west side of New York's Fifth Avenue, just south of the entrance to Central Park at Fifty-Ninth Street, these houses led the migration of wealth from Murray Hill to the Upper East Side.

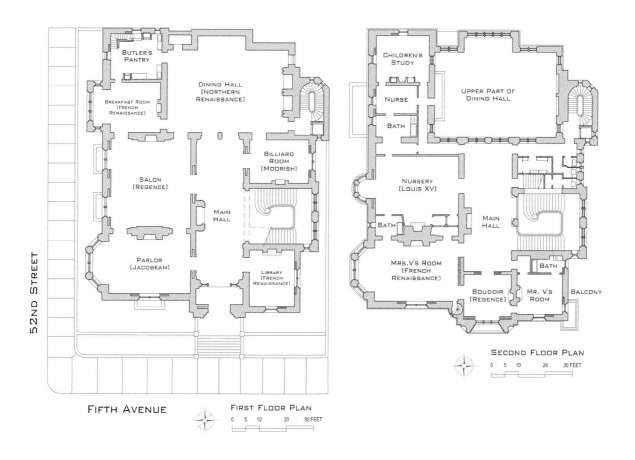

First- and second-floor plans, Alva and William K. Vanderbilt house

FIRST FLOOR PLAN (left):
- BUTLER'S PANTRY
- DINING HALL [NORTHERN RENAISSANCE]
- BREAKFAST ROOM [FRENCH RENAISSANCE]
- SALON [REGENCE]
- BILLIARD ROOM [MOORISH]
- MAIN HALL
- PARLOR [JACOBEAN]
- LIBRARY [FRENCH RENAISSANCE]
- 52ND STREET
- FIFTH AVENUE
- 0 5 10 20 30 FEET

SECOND FLOOR PLAN (right):
- CHILDREN'S STUDY
- UPPER PART OF DINING HALL
- NURSE
- BATH
- NURSERY [LOUIS XV]
- MAIN HALL
- BATH
- MRS. V'S ROOM [FRENCH RENAISSANCE]
- BATH
- BOUDOIR [REGENCE]
- MR. V'S ROOM
- BALCONY
- 0 5 10 20 30 FEET

Fig. 4.10a–b First- and second-floor plans, Alva and William K. Vanderbilt house; James B. Garrison, AutoCAD, 2021[22]

As an architectural ensemble, all three were indebted to French models and came to exemplify palace living among the Gilded Age few.

Considering New York's brownstone austerity and the city's first mansion, John Kellum's Second Empire palace for retail magnate Alexander Stewart (see 2.6), Alva and William Vanderbilt's castle at Fifty-Second Street was a rigorous orchestration of architecture, interior design, and fine furnishing that earned Hunt a generation of critical acclaim (4.9). In 1870 he had attempted his first city chateau, a Louis XIII brick and stone mansion for Brattleboro native and financier "Diamond Jim Fisk," an awkward adaptation of a suburban Parisian villa. But Hunt's recent trip to France and the rising influence of the weighty Romanesque had been determinant—the Vanderbilt mansion was all "power and massiveness," its sculpted details integral and artistic, qualities that came to characterize American architecture, markedly in Chicago where Louis Sullivan in the same years pioneered abstract ornament in service to structurally advanced civic projects. In reconciling historic forms, Montgomery Schuyler wrote, Hunt had "spanned the distance" between the "complicated modelling" of Gothic buildings and the "romantic classicism of the great châteaux of the Loire," influenced by the Hôtel de Cluny, Jacques Cœur house in Bourges, and Pierrefonds (see 2.5, 3.34). Unlike the disjointed plan for the Fisk house, never built, the Vanderbilt interior was square and ordered (4.10a-b), its axiality appealing to wealthy clients who sought a progressive hierarchy of discrete rooms, from public to private, from servants working in the basement to owners living on floors above.[27]

The year Alva's chateau was finished, the editor of a new decorating magazine pronounced it was "far better to look back to any period in which good form and artistic design and coloring are evinced, than to continue the vulgar anachronisms of design and decoration of the more modern schools of upholsterers...." The Vanderbilt interiors left behind the eclecticism of the Aesthetic movement for a veritable at-home history of European design and decorating. On the first floor was a Jacobean parlor, sometimes described as Francis I, an Anglo-Franco banquet hall by Herter Brothers, a tiled Moorish billiard room by L. Marcotte & Co., and a salon-ballroom by Parisian Jules Allard Fils (P.4), its cream and gilded paneling standard to the Régence-Louis XV revival. Above this room was Alva's Henri II-style bedroom, also by Allard. For its adjoining marble bath, artists with the Society of Decorative Art, advised by Catharine Hunt, painted blossoming cherry trees on mirrored panels.[28]

The Vanderbilt interiors were inspired by period and revivalist rooms, seen in person or in publications collected by Hunt. Popular authors were upholsterers, the era's first interior designers, whose decorations for new and old palaces throughout Europe and now America defined an international taste. A leader in this emerging field was Parisian G. Félix Lenoir (active ca. 1859-1900) who, with his competitors, displayed detailed decorating schemes at public exhibitions. His plan for a salon likely inspired, or was possibly inspired by, Hunt and Allard's Vanderbilt salon (4.11a), known from photographs taken before its gilded paneling and *rouge royale* mantle were sold at auction in 1921. Its elevations, animal skin rugs, piano, and furnishings, rearranged in the images, were all elements of Lenoir's plan that exemplified a romantic historicism.[29]

International art exhibitions and journals from the 1850s raised public awareness of art before 1800, so that by the 1870s old masters and period furniture were intrinsic to the revivalist interior, their prices bringing prestige to buyers and incredulity from the press. Though École-trained

Fig. 4.11a Salon, Alva and William K. Vanderbilt house, opposite top; at the middle of the room was a Rococo-style desk and beyond, along the wall (just visible), was Alva's prized Marie Antoinette commode under a Boucher-style tapestry, ceiling by Paul-J.-A. Baudry; ca. 1920

Fig. 4.11b Renaissance Revival dining hall, Alva and William K. Vanderbilt house, opposite bottom, English eighteenth-century portraits below the "minstrel gallery," among the early museum-quality old masters in America, ca. 1903[23]

DINING ROOM, RESIDENCE, W. K. VANDERBILT, 660 FIFTH AVE., NEW YORK.   R. M. Hunt, Architect.

architect Alexandre Sandier supplied extensive furnishings in revival styles, the pride of Alva Vanderbilt's collection were her salon's black lacquer and ormolu secretary and commode, crafted by Jean-Henri Riesener for Marie Antoinette's *grand cabinet intérieur* at Versailles. They were, wrote Alva, "of quite unequalled interest and value. Sir Joseph DeVigne [*sic*] considers them far beyond any other of that period in existence." She purchased the furniture in 1882 and her finest period paintings through the eighties, possibly guided by Hunt to finish rooms he and Allard designed. In the emerging culture of patronage, William bequeathed the furniture and paintings to the Metropolitan Museum of Art, where his brother Cornelius was both donor and trustee.[30]

Consistent with his antiquarian approach, Hunt commissioned stained-glass windows for Alva's chateau interiors. As a connoisseur of the "minor" arts, he collected preparatory gouaches for revivalist windows and befriended the Parisian maker Eugène A.S. Oudinot (see 3.1). A student of Romantic painter Eugène Delacroix and an inventor of new techniques in painted glass, he prospered when ecclesiastical restorations in France revitalized his artisan industry. He worked with Henry Richardson at Boston's Trinity Church and became in the 1880s the window maker for the international rich. Artist Émile-Antoine Bayard and Hunt's fellow student at the École, architect-designer Émile-Auguste Reiber, supplied cartoons in dynastic themes for Oudinot's windows throughout the house. The tour de force was Bayard's two-story, west-facing window in Alva's dining hall, depicting the 1520 conciliatory meeting between Henry VIII of England and Francis I of France at the Field of the Cloth of Gold near Calais (4.11b, 4.12). Promoted as a celebration of peace, the event became a competitive display of wealth between Renaissance kings. The scene was a lesson in "lofty courtesy" and "chivalrous sociability," Alva told a reporter, but it was also an allegorical spectacle of wealth, vanity, and reconciliation in a post-war marriage between a Northern capitalist and Southern hostess, unapologetic of his riches and boastful of her slave-owning, Huguenot heritage.[31]

To impress and conquer Caroline Astor's established society, Alva and William Vanderbilt held a legendary costume ball in 1883 at their Fifth Avenue chateau. In a veritable Troubadour *tableau vivant*, she was a Venetian princess to her husband's Francis I, a royal couple for their imperial present. The Hunts took their cues from the style of the building and Alva's aspirations. In a play on names, Catharine dressed in a brown velvet gown after a portrait of Catherine de' Medici, daughter-in-law of Francis I; Richard boldly arrived as Cimabue, his costume inspired

Fig. 4.12 Field of the Cloth of Gold dining hall window, Alva and William K. Vanderbilt house; photo reproduction given to Hunt by the window's maker, Eugène Oudinot, 1882[24]

by a Florentine fresco (4.13a-d). At the time, the Italian artist was revered for ushering in the Renaissance after the "dark" Middle Ages, just as Hunt was leading America from its clapboard origins into a renaissance of architecture and art.[32]

A model of social and artistic advancement, Hunt's first castle was an enviable success, "ravishingly picturesque...the suggestion of that organized, highly wrought luxury which we associate with European social life...." Even Mariana A. Griswold Van Rensselaer, biographer of Henry Richardson, made an exception to her Protestant equivalency of plainness and rectitude. Hunt had bypassed the "very showy" Second Empire style of Alexander Stewart's mansion (see 2.6) to build a house demonstrating that "the virtues and possibilities of simplicity...are not the only virtues or the finest possibilities."[33]

Fig. 4.13a Period paintings inspired costumes for Alva Vanderbilt's ball at her Fifth Avenue chateau; Catharine Hunt as French queen Catherine de' Medici, left; José Maria Mora, 1883

Fig. 4.13b Catherine de' Medici, right; unknown artist, 1547–49

Cimabue.

Hunt mastered the American chateau for the era's royalty of finance and industry seeking social entrée and acceptance. He made ashlar limestone, roof crestings, Gothic dormers, and revivalist interiors—along with central heating and electricity—standard for the upper-class home. In planning he remained true to his rationalist training, responsive to site, materials and client demands. Word traveled and soon Chicago's irascible mining millionaire William Borden was ordering what he called a modest "Vanderbilt" castle, its gold and white "Louis XV" salon by Jules C.A. Allard. In New York, financier Henry Marquand required interiors that would display his art and furnishings thematically.[34]

Descendant of a colonial Connecticut family, Marquand evolved from merchant to railroad speculator (4.14). He embodied the civilized and civilizing patron and collector, intent on building an encyclopedic museum and a house in the same spirit. He became a trustee of the Metropolitan Museum of Art in 1871 and its second president in 1889, retiring in 1902 as Hunt's Fifth Avenue entrance reached completion. He donated European and American paintings and Native American pottery to the Metropolitan, while continuing to collect for his Newport and New York houses. He was a devoted client, commissioning eight projects over fifteen years, explaining to Hunt, "I like having noisy fellows around, and you come under that head." Hunt in turn was architect and cultural advisor, acquiring works for Marquand's collection and introducing him to creative circles in Paris and

Fig. 4.14 Collector and museum president Henry Marquand holds plans, likely for Hunt's Metropolitan Museum of Art Fifth Avenue wing; John White Alexander, 1896

Fig. 4.15 Elizabeth and Henry Marquand red brick and sandstone, French Renaissance Revival mansion and adjoining houses (1884), Madison Avenue, New York City, with Central Park in the distance; ca. 1885

Rome, clarifying matters of art history as his client navigated the murky world of old master dealers and collectors.[35]

Facing south onto Sixty-Eighth Street, at the northwest corner of Madison Avenue, the Marquand mansion (1884) and nearby Charles L. Tiffany house by McKim, Mead & White (1884) were critically compared, the latter being an eclectic "pile," the former, deftly conceived in a "transition from French Gothic to French Renaissance," classical in its axial plan of rooms decorated thematically (4.15, 4.16a-b). Using materials symbolic of Marquand's international investments, Hunt designed a Japanese living room, a Tudor Revival dining room, and a Greek parlor/music room decorated by England's art stars Sir Lawrence Alma-Tadema and Sir Frederic Leighton. Beyond this Aesthetic reimagining of the ancient world was a Moorish den and conservatory, its stained-glass window a close adaptation by Oudinot of a gazebo mural at the Louvre, installed in an apartment designed by Hector Lefuel in the lavish Napoléon

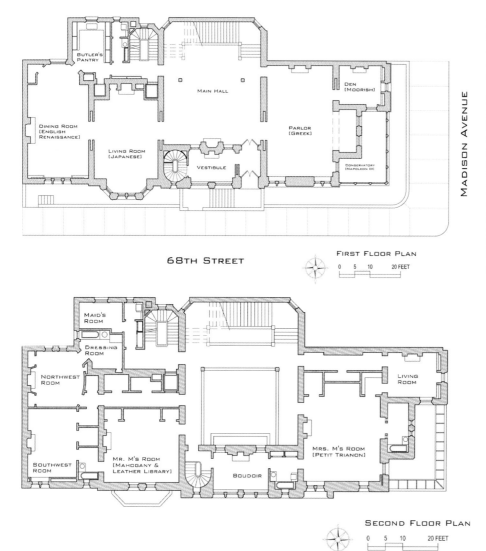

Fig. 4.16a–b First- and second-floor plans, Marquand house; James B. Garrison, AutoCAD, 2021

Fig. 4.17 Moorish-style den (ca. 1886), Marquand house, opposite; to achieve authenticity in the cabinets displaying Valencian pottery, Hunt provided decorator Léon Marcotte with castings from Spain's Moorish Alhambra; G.C. Cox, photochrom, ca. 1894[25]

FIRST FLOOR PLAN

0 5 10 20 FEET

SECOND FLOOR PLAN

0 5 10 20 FEET

III style that Hunt made his own for Vanderbilt mansions (4.17). On the second floor was Marquand's "masculine" mahogany and leather library and Elizabeth A. Marquand's "feminine" white and gold Petit Trianon bedroom.[36]

The year the Marquands' house was finished, the AIA held its annual convention in New York. There, President Thomas Walter affirmed the Institute's rejection of outright imitation and

CHAMBRE MAURESQUE
DANS L'HÔTEL DE MR H.G. MARQUAND
à New York.

affirmation of an American, interpretive eclecticism "in harmony with the acknowledged elements of good taste," taught at MIT and Columbia. Exemplary of this approach was the home of Henry Marquand, open to touring by conference participants. To Hunt's friend, but not always supportive critic, Russell Sturgis Jr., the mansion was a "comforting place to visit" for the millionaire who longed for "European wealth and abundance of sensations, and who hardly expected to find them in America." Marquand had collected like an "Italian prince of the Renaissance," and Hunt had realized "marvels of splendid variety, differing in nothing from the palace interiors which we dream of as existing in the great times of creative art." In their shared didactic connoisseurship, patron and architect had conceived a precursor to the turn-of-the-century house museum, a coming together of architecture and art for pleasure and edification, as Hunt first experienced at the Hôtel de Cluny.[37]

~~~~~~~~

The Marquand and Vanderbilt houses reflected a consensus among the nineteenth-century rich that their mansions, as well as their lives, contributed to social reform. Her family's houses, wrote Alva Vanderbilt, "represented not only wealth but knowledge and culture, desirable elements for wealth to encourage, and the public accepted them in that way." This top-down beneficence, grafting democratic ideals of education onto Gilded Age notions of wealth and its wisdom, was firmly rooted in self-interest.[38]

At the time, newspapers and popular society magazines published heart-wrenching tales of international poverty and violence, illustrated by engravings of townhouse lootings and torched public buildings (4.18a, see also 3.32). In Paris, Hunt had experienced the 1848 insurrection and seen the charred ruins of the Commune workers' rebellion. At home, when conscription, enlistment through proxy, and racism against free blacks fueled dissention among white workers during the Civil War, New Yorkers witnessed the 1863 Draft Riots (4.18b), remembered a decade later as acts of "terror" by anarchists no different from "the mobs of Paris." A Unitarian minister and journalist considered "the earlier stages of a war upon property" in the Great Railroad Strike of 1877 "a widespread revolt against civilization."[39]

As the city's population reached 1.5 million at 1890, of which forty-two percent were foreign-born, New York's response to the perceived threat of the underclasses deepened. Bound by fear of the oppressed worker and empowered by government influence, bankers, industrialists, and

Fig. 4.18a The sacking
of private houses
by rioters drove the
international rich to
promote civic order
through art and
beauty. Pillage of
the Duc de Castries
house, Paris, 1790; P.G.
Berthault, engraving,
after watercolor by
J.-L. Prieur le Jeune,
ca. 1791–1804

Fig. 4.18b Looting
during the Civil
War Draft Riots,
New York City,
1863; *The New-York
Illustrated News*, 1863,
Informative Classroom
Picture Publishers,
glass slide, 1948

merchants presented themselves from the 1880s as an aristocracy obligated to rescuing the poor from moral depravity and the rich from vengeful mayhem. Andrew Carnegie wrote that there were few millionaires "who are clear of this sin of having made beggars," a sentiment that encouraged his progressive peers to secure an incorporative future.[40]

The Yale and Union Theological Seminary graduate Charles Loring Brace founded New York's Children's Aid Society in 1853. The class threatening personal property and Christian morality, he wrote in 1884, were the "weak, lazy and sickly, the criminal and unfortunate," the "dregs" of foreign emigration.

> [T]he cheapest and most efficacious way of dealing with
> the "Dangerous Classes" of large cities, is not to punish
> them, but to prevent their growth; to so throw the influences
> of education and discipline and religion about the abandoned and
> destitute youth of our large towns; to so change their material
> circumstances, and draw them under the influence of the moral
> and fortunate classes, that they shall grow up as useful producers
> and members of society, able and inclined to aid it in its progress.

Mostly of German and Irish heritage, the "dangerous" citizens were volatile and threatening, destined to reduce American cities to "ashes and blood" if unexposed to "civilizing influences" fostered by Hunt and his "moral and fortunate" clients. Brace's Rousseauian solution for vagrant youths was rural community life. But city landowners, finding tenements good and virtuous business, made new housing a staple of architectural practice. Hunt was sympathetic to this poverty movement, criticizing architects at Philadelphia's Centennial for ignoring the "amelioration of dwelling for the laboring and industrial classes," particularly after the Paris 1867 exposition when Napoléon III received a medal for "his well-merited and successful efforts" in housing what the French considered their own "*classes dangereuses*." Citing a London construction company, Hunt noted that such buildings were not only a moral obligation, but potentially a "practical success" for the architect, given the apartments needed and ample available capital. He became an advocate for city design criteria, requiring light and air along narrow lots, and from 1872 to 1888 his office designed ten small buildings, variously called "French flats" and "apartments," or classified as second-class tenements.[41]

Multistory buildings were not the only housing need of the populous American city. When traditional at-home care no longer accommodated the era's disabled and elderly, charitable societies founded custodial institutions, some uptown in New York's Bloomingdale District, then considered therapeutic for its clean air and sunlight. Hunt competed unsuccessfully for several health service commissions, but the Association for the Relief of Respectable Aged and Indigent Females hired him around 1868 to design its second residence on twenty contiguous lots, at Tenth Avenue (later Amsterdam) between 103rd and 104th Streets, purchased from Hunt's brother-in-law, Charles H. Russell (4.19). The association board specified a private room with a fireplace for each resident, communal bathrooms, a dining room, a kitchen to serve one hundred, and a chapel for daily prayer. As with his civic work of the 1860s and early 1870s, Hunt first looked to the English Gothic, but later turned to French Renaissance architecture he made his own, substituting brick for brownstone in what was for him a simplification of form. Now, poor and aged women would live securely in a chateau of their own.[42]

Though the urban establishment considered property loss and violence priority threats, throughout the century social scientists also measured whether immigrants, shipped to American shores in "schemes of deportation" by European states alleviating their own urban poverty, were undermining beliefs foundational to the republic. After the Civil War, AIA member Rev. Samuel Osgood assessed the state of New York. He had been motivated to speak, he told the city's historical society, by:

> the strange and broad gulf between our present population and the old New Yorkers, and the almost entire absence of historical landmarks from our city, now under the sweeping tide of business and enterprise. Only a few of the ancient buildings remain, and almost all that we see before us is new. This imperial city, with its palaces and churches, rises before most of its people like Melchisedec, king of Salem, without father, without mother; and they must confess his magnificence, who cannot tell his pedigree.

The Philadelphia Centennial and subsequent Colonial Revival were outcomes of this nationalist introspection and the public drive to mark an imagined Protestant past. Opportunistically, Hunt participated in this emerging movement, designing public sculpture and family memorials embodying American values. The New England Society in the City of New York, organized in 1805, was an early philanthropic organization to "commemorate the landing of our Pilgrim Fathers on Plymouth Rock; to promote friendship, charity, and mutual assistance; and for literary

Fig. 4.19 Residence for the Association for the Relief of Respectable Aged and Indigent Females (1883), Amsterdam Avenue, New York City, opposite, for widows and genteel women after the Civil War; Michael Froio, 2020

Fig. 4.20 Pilgrim (Hunt and Ward, 1885) in Central Park, New York City, a monument to Protestant values; Michael Froio, 2019

purposes" among New Yorkers descended from Massachusetts families. A bastion of Protestant leaders in business and culture, its members were Hunt's clients and friends. During Joseph Choate's presidency, Hunt was admitted in 1868, and after thirteen years, he and John Ward were awarded the society's commission for a statue celebrating the Pilgrim landing.[43]

Sited above the Seventy-Second Street roadway through Central Park, the finished monument was dedicated in 1885 (4.20). A bronze, stolid, nine-foot-tall Pilgrim, in doublet and capotain, stood on a sixteen-foot-high base, symbolically carved from Massachusetts granite, embellished with emblems

representing Pilgrim morality, including a Bible interleaved with a sword. Ward's figure was solemn and stern, but contemporaries, seeking truth through realism, considered it vapid. Russell Sturgis Jr. scoffed that one would "enjoy getting rid of the excessive...costume part of it, and getting at the man, with the hope of finding there the kind of human nature out of which the real Mayflower Pilgrim was made, to almost the exclusion of the clothes that invested that pilgrim."[44]

The supreme monument to founding values was *Liberty Enlightening the World*, the Statue of Liberty. The French aristocrat and libertarian author Édouard René Lefèbvre de Laboulaye proposed the statue in 1865 in response to the autocracy of Napoléon III. Sculptor Frédéric-Auguste Bartholdi took hold of the project after the German Empire annexed his

Fig. 4.21 *Liberty Enlightening the World*, sculptor Frédéric Bartholdi's vision for his Liberty in New York Harbor, her tablet of law and flame of freedom signifying democracy; oil on board, signed "Bartholdi, 1876"[26]

native Colmar at the end of the Franco-Prussian War. Laboulaye and Bartholdi imagined a monument-memorial to the alliance between France and America, countries born of liberty through revolution and preserved in America by its recent war. France would pay for the sculpture and America the pedestal, the monument to rise in New York Harbor, shining the beacon of liberty.

A devoted ally of France, Hunt was ideal for Liberty's pedestal, a commission he won in December 1881, endorsed by the Union League Club of New York's Committee for the Statue of Liberty, which included Joseph Choate and Henry Marquand. Though Bartholdi found the self-assured, French-speaking Francophile "a bit boastful, full of himself," Hunt understood that Bartholdi's vision would further public acceptance of monumental sculpture, an objective he had failed to achieve with his rejected gateways to Central Park. When Hunt began his planning, Bartholdi had already conceived the pedestal in a painting he exhibited at the Philadelphia Centennial (4.21). Hunt bowed to the sculptor's approach, working through variations labelled Pharos I and Pharos II to suggest the ancient lighthouse at Alexandria in Egypt. The monument had to compete with the nearby Brooklyn Bridge without diminishing Liberty as a heroic figure and symbol (see SC.3).[45]

In late 1883, New York's National Academy of Design held a charity exhibition to fund Liberty's pedestal, slowed by public perception that the monument was a grandiose dream of the privileged few. Never losing an opportunity to advance American culture, the organizers intended to further "taste in things beautiful and refining to our homes" and to encourage "remunerative industries of interior decoration and adornment." Hunt joined banker J. Pierpont Morgan, Cornelius Vanderbilt II, and others as an honorary vice president of the event. Committees, as they had for the 1864 Metropolitan Fair, secured loans from private collections for display. Catharine lent an ecclesiastical embroidery and Richard an iron padlock from the Bastille, a symbol of liberty in the French Revolution. The lasting outcome of this educatory fundraiser was Emma Lazarus's poem, "The New Colossus" ("Give me your tired, your poor..."), included in a portfolio of letters and verse.[46]

Viollet-le-Duc and Gustave Eiffel engineered *Liberty* with a center pylon and iron and steel skeleton to support the statue's copper skin. For its pedestal, Hunt and Bartholdi settled on a modified tower, eighty-nine feet high and sixty-two feet square at the base. Its foundation was set into the colonial-era, star-shaped fortification on Bedloe's Island (Liberty Island after 1956). Though he originally conceived the pedestal in stone, Hunt

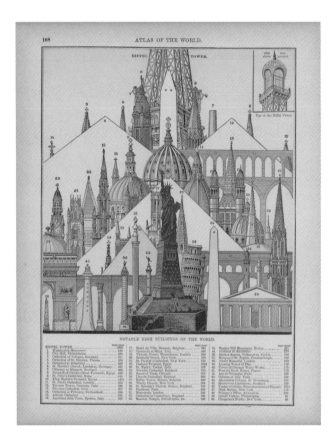

Fig. 4.22 Hunt and Bartholdi made the Statue of Liberty a world monument, bringing New York City into the canon of Western architecture; *Universal Atlas of the World*, 1896 edition

Fig. 4.23 Alliance and Victory Monument (Hunt, Ward, and Henry Van Brunt, 1884), Yorktown, Virginia; style and theme were interwoven in the Maine granite column; Michael Froio, 2019[27]

settled on concrete faced with Connecticut granite. Rondels were intended for coats of arms (never carved) of the thirty-eight states. Balconies and an observation platform overlooked the harbor. After sufficient funds were raised, leaders of the Masonic brotherhood laid the pedestal's cornerstone in 1884 at a ceremony attended by Hunt and the Vanderbilts' major domo, the omniscient Chauncey Depew. The completed monument was dedicated on Liberty Day, October 28, 1886.

Hunt's successful integration of the fortifications into the base had made the island into the plinth, the pedestal into the die, and the statue the capital of a "colossal" sculpture, wrote Montgomery Schuyler. It represented an international coming together of science and art to inspire through the sublime. At 305 feet, 28 feet above the nearby bridge, *Liberty* brought New York into the lexicon of old and new world monuments (4.22, see also SC.3), illustrated in comparative images that measured civilizations through the scale and ambition of their public art.[47]

America's own tribute to freedom at the time of the Centennial was its column commemorating the Battle of Yorktown. The Continental Congress in 1781 had resolved to memorialize the event with a "Monument to the Alliance and Victory," marking the contributions of George Washington and the Comtes de Rochambeau and de Grasse. As imagined then, a column would incorporate emblems of France and America and a narrative of General Charles Cornwallis' surrender. Finally in 1880 Congress approved $100,000 for the much-delayed memorial.[48]

The column, sited within the former British line of defense at Virginia's York River, was completed by Hunt, Ward, and Henry Van Brunt in 1884 (4.23). Ninety-eight feet high and built of Maine granite, the plinth carried a dedicatory inscription and narrative of the siege, commemorating the French alliance and peace treaty with Britain. A sculpted drum at the base incorporated thirteen classical female figures as the American colonies. The shaft was banded by laurel leaves and stars representing the thirty-eight states of the Union. A figure of Liberty reached out atop a Corinthian capital carved with the American eagle. An enclosing iron fence at the base kept "meddlesome people at a distance."[49]

The Yorktown monument was Hunt's synthesis of designs submitted for a commemorative column to the French Revolution's Constituent Assembly at Versailles, illustrated in an 1881 French journal that severely criticized the submissions as overworked. Their primary inspiration, and Hunt's own, had been the Column of July by Joseph-Louis Duc, another monument to freedom through revolution that Hunt considered as among the superior works of new French classicism. Built on the site of the Bastille in Paris, the monarchy's state prison, the monument was topped by a winged *Génie de la Liberté* to commemorate the 1830 revolution that brought Louis-Philippe to power. The source for Hunt and Ward's entwined figures of the colonies was the 1806 Fontaine du Palmier at Paris' Place du Châtelet, another site of royal prisons.[50]

By overcoming the flaws of the Versailles competition to build a column that Montgomery Schuyler found "distinctly and severely monumental," Hunt was elected a chevalier of the Légion d'Honneur in 1884. This outcome must have been particularly gratifying, for Hunt had long sustained the cause of French influence in American design, working, as he later wrote a French senator, "con amore" on both the Statue of Liberty and Yorktown memorial, the two greatest "Franco-American monuments."[51]

For cities rich from industrialization and populated by immigrant labor, the memorialization of the American military gave form to nationalism and Hunt opportunities to further Beaux-Arts design in sculpture. He and Ward competed for soldier and sailor monuments in the 1880s, their most spectacular a colossal grouping of bronze military figures for Brooklyn, abandoned because of cost. Revealingly, Hunt fell out with Ward when only the sculptor's name and photograph were published in reporting on this and other projects they shared. In the future, Hunt wrote the sculptor, he wanted his role as designer of architectural elements and the "ensemble" noted in print. With his practice dependent on reputation, Hunt was acutely aware of the press and tracked his career through clipping services. But

Fig. 4.24 President
James Garfield
memorial (Hunt
and Ward, 1887),
Washington, DC;
cover of *Harper's
Weekly*, the "Journal
of Civilization," May 14,
1887

HARPER'S WEEKLY.

JOURNAL OF CIVILIZATION.

VOL. XXXI.—No. 1586.   NEW YORK, SATURDAY, MAY 14, 1887.   TEN CENTS A COPY.

THE GARFIELD MONUMENT UNVEILED AT WASHINGTON, D.C., ON MAY 12, 1887.—J. Q. A. WARD, SCULPTOR; RICHARD M. HUNT, ARCHITECT.—[SEE PAGE 344.]

his view of reporting was not unqualified. As a potential juror for "Boss" Tweed's corruption trial in 1872, Hunt remarked contemptuously that he was "in the habit of reading the *New York Times*, and he disbelieves half he reads."[52]

Hunt knew from his time at the US Capitol the prestige of national work. He participated in two Washington, DC commissions, designing the pedestal for Franklin B. Simmons' equestrian bronze statue of General John A. Logan (1900) and a memorial to President James A. Garfield, commissioned in 1883 by the Society of the Army of the Cumberland in memory of their fellow soldier, assassinated two years earlier (4.24). Hunt's proposal included figures inspired by the Italian Renaissance and pedestals derived from an eighteenth-century French model and his own Statue of Liberty.[53]

Members of Congress, President Grover Cleveland, Supreme Court justices, and Hunt attended the Garfield dedication in 1887. The monument, to the southwest of the Capitol, was the best of what Hunt and Ward could offer, sculptural realism for a national hero whose up-from-a-cabin success resonated at a time of rapacious entrepreneurialism.

Fig. 4.25 Henry Ward Beecher memorial (Hunt and Ward, 1891), Brooklyn, New York, honoring the preacher as an abolitionist; F.E. Parshley, ca. 1891

Expressing a prevailing view that capitalist society was built on systems of distribution and production that benefited owners and workers alike, regardless of race and class, the son-in-law of William H. Vanderbilt, newspaper publisher Elliott F. Shepard, wrote in his bestselling screed *Labor and Capital Are One* (1886) that, while all men were born "in the image of the Creator," the hard work of the successful man entitled him to "make the world in which he lives," like "kings" before him.[54]

In New York, John Ward held a virtual monopoly on portrait commissions of winners in the Shepard mold. Two of his and Hunt's notable collaborations memorializing American success were bronzes of *New-York Tribune* founder Horace Greeley (1890) and preacher Henry Ward Beecher, both outspoken abolitionists. Hunt's pedestals transformed the traditional Victorian shaft of his competitors, notably Jacob Wrey Mould, into architectural space, enhancing the immediacy and realism of Ward's citizen

Fig. 4.26 August Belmont exedra (Hunt and Ward, 1891), Island Cemetery, Newport, Rhode Island. A critic wrote it was "very classic, and about Dick's best in that way"; caryatids by Bitter and Moretti; Caroline Belmont sarcophagus (1894); Michael Froio, 2019[28]

figures. The memorial to Beecher was unveiled in 1891 to fifteen thousand spectators in Brooklyn's Borough Hall Park, near the preacher's renowned Plymouth Church. The Beecher Statue Fund Committee had specified a statue at eight feet, accompanied by figures symbolizing "Beecher's character of public career." Ward used photographs and a death mask to sculpt an imposing fellow citizen on Hunt's granite pedestal as orator box (4.25). From its plinth, a young black woman, signifying Beecher's pro-abolition stance, looked up to the preacher as white children placed a memorial wreath at his feet.[55]

The Greeley and Beecher monuments honored the American cult of secular success and individualism that found its most enduring expression in the nineteenth-century cemetery, a landscaped Valhalla of marble obelisks and granite sarcophagi, many designed by Hunt following nondenominational models from antiquity (4.26). These solitary

Fig. 4.27 Vanderbilt family mausoleum, Staten Island, New York, preliminary sketch, a synthesis of past and present church architectures; Richard Hunt, ca. 1884

OFFICE OF RICHARD M. HUNT, ARCHITECT,

STUDIO BUILDING,

51 WEST TENTH STREET,

NEW YORK,_____186

monuments were joined by grand mausolea that secured the remains of power brokers and generations of their heirs after unidentified "ghouls" stole the corpse of merchant Alexander Stewart in 1878 from an early churchyard near New York's Astor Place. The threat of theft and its sensationalized reporting galvanized William H. Vanderbilt to contact Hunt and Frederick Law Olmsted in 1883 to design a family mausoleum at New Dorp, Staten Island, the Vanderbilt home since the eighteenth century. William's Protestant ancestors were buried in the town's Moravian Cemetery where, for his ancestral burial site, Vanderbilt acquired approximately twenty-two adjoining acres at the top of Todt [Death] Hill, the highest natural point in New York's five boroughs.[56]

Vanderbilt intended to live into eternity as he had in life, a model of American success at the pinnacle of wealth and power. "Every steamship and sailing craft which enters New York Harbor," boasted his biographer, "must pass in sight of this mausoleum. It will be the first prominent object seen on Staten Island by those who come from Europe to America." It was expected to "dominate the landscape he knew and loved so well," and that his father had traversed as a ferry operator, comparable in scale and ornament to the "royal tombs of Europe." But Vanderbilt's plan to loom over the harbor had competition, including the Statue of Liberty, a fact he no doubt considered when hiring its pedestal architect to establish, at minimum, a resonance between the two.[57]

Olmsted and Hunt laid out an approximately 200-foot-wide and 100-foot-deep terrace, reached through iron gates at the bottom of Todt Hill. The mausoleum overlooked the Vanderbilt family farm below and out to lower New York Bay. Hunt's initial proposal, an early sign of his coming Renaissance classicism, was a domed, free-standing tomb entered through a Gothic porch (4.27). William Vanderbilt found the design "showy" and, as he explained with false modesty, inappropriate for his "plain, quiet, unostentatious people." Though cost was a "secondary matter" and "appropriate carvings, or even statuary" acceptable, he wanted no "unnecessary fancy-work." Hunt now turned to a modified basilica plan, its entrances set into a hillock and mounted by over-door lunettes carved with biblical scenes (4.28). Bronze gates at these gray granite portals opened to a lateral foyer where monumental polished stone urns in niches framed a bronze door to the vaulted crypt. There, gated catacombs flanked a nave to a semi-circular apse. Domed lanterns at the roof illuminated the limestone interior and engineering assured air circulation against miasmas then associated with cemeteries.[58]

William H. Vanderbilt died in 1885 and Hunt finished his tomb substantially in 1886, working with William's youngest son, George W. Vanderbilt, who brought Hunt and Olmsted together at Biltmore in 1888. Once again, Hunt had orchestrated a fusion of the historical and new French, the mausoleum's plan and final aspect being Byzantine-Romanesque, the lanterns indebted to Sacré-Cœur, Montmartre's hilltop basilica begun by architect and poet Paul Abadie in 1875 when Hunt was visiting Paris.

~~~~~~

The Statue of Liberty pedestal was under construction as Hunt, accompanied by Catharine and their four youngest children, sailed for Europe in June 1885, his final, year-long respite from client demands. It had

Fig. 4.28 Vanderbilt family mausoleum (1886); the tomb and Statue of Liberty (dedicated 1886) were visible from New York Harbor, one heralding opportunity for all, the other a monument to private wealth, dueling values of the Gilded Age; Frederick Law Olmsted Jr., office photograph, 1897

been a challenging winter, after a postman poisoned the family's barking collie and the arts and literary University Club of the City of New York (founded 1865) by American graduates questioned Hunt's application for membership because he had not attended a college. Despite his international fame and work on behalf of architecture as a profession, he was still confronting the prejudice against artists he encountered at the time of his marriage in 1861.[59]

The Hunts began their trip in London where dinners and gatherings, like at home, were at the intersection of finance, society, and the arts. Their daughter Kitty was anxious to be confirmed and now, accompanied by her parents and godmother, Mrs. John J. Astor III, "Aunt Augusta," she was admitted to the Episcopal faith at a Knightsbridge church before the family traveled to the continent.[60]

When the Hunts arrived in France, their oldest son Dick was already in Paris as a student at the École des Beaux-Arts, following the path pioneered by his father forty years before. Later in the summer Esther and Herbert entered a Swiss boarding school to perfect foreign languages and Joe studied German near Frankfurt. Europe remained, possibly more than in Margaret Fuller's time, the upper-class American's "parent home." Education at continental schools and the Grand Tour, a privileged rite of passage intended to refine the American student, had become orthodoxy for children of the elite. They were groomed to continue the institutionalization of high culture begun by their parents' generation; that Hunt, a leader in the cause, should endow his own offspring with such training was inevitable.

Continuing to collect antiques and artifacts, Catharine and Richard, at times joined by Kitty, toured Switzerland and northern Italy, encountering royalty and high government officials traveling by train between countries. His passion for religious spectacle undiminished, Hunt visited Seville at the time of Holy Week, accompanied by his fellow antiquarian and realist painter, Ignacio León y Escosura. But business was always "paramount on his mind" as he sent comments and sketches to New York and met with clients William K. Vanderbilt and California banking heir Ogden Mills while taking the spa at Bad Homburg. Bartholdi asked him to review the Statue of Liberty in Paris, but to the sculptor's annoyance Hunt declined, preferring café dinners with Baron Haussmann and fellow artists to hear Charles Gounod and Jules Massenet play the piano. Some professional colleagues were also close friends, including the influential publisher of French architecture and interiors, César Daly, and stained-glass artist Oudinot, whose sons both proposed that summer to seventeen-year-old Kitty. Catharine and Richard rebuffed their offers, unable to "consent to her marriage with a Catholic," but were back in England for the September marriage of their son Dick to the Kentuckian, Pearl Carley.[61]

Hunt's entrée to all levels of French society was important to his later practice, when the rich sought to create a pan Euro-American aristocratic way of life, in manners and style. The highest prestige came from his acquaintance with a son of Louis-Philippe, Henri d'Orléans, Duc d'Aumale, living at the Chateau de Chantilly outside Paris (see P.8). His collections of rare books, old masters, gilded commodes and fauteuils in paneled interiors represented the revivalist taste Hunt was promoting to American clients. He had first met the soigné blond and blue-eyed duke, a decorated veteran of France's Algerian conquest, as a student in the 1840s. Now, at a December lunch for artists and diplomats hosted by d'Aumale at his country estate, Richard Hunt, a congressman's son from small-town Vermont, was at the apex of French society.[62]

Against this backdrop of privilege and professional success was a ceaseless battle for health, relieved by cures at German spas. Richard was besieged by crippling gout, Joseph quarantined for mumps, Herbert contracted chicken pox, and in March, uncle and brother-in-law Joseph Howland died at fifty-one in Menton, France, on the Mediterranean. Catharine, afflicted by chronic pain, traveled to Bad Schwalbach to heal and mourn her loss as Richard, his "trunk full of treasures...from Spain," sailed for America in June 1886, anxious to return after his assistant Maurice Fornachon lost the Collis Huntington commission only blocks from Alva Vanderbilt's New York chateau.[63]

Before leaving for Europe, the Hunts, with "great regret," had sold their home at West Thirty-Fifth Street. Their family had outgrown the narrow 1850s brownstone where Catharine and Richard had shared "joys and anxieties" over twenty years of a fruitful marriage (see 2.17). Once-fashionable midtown was becoming commercial, driving the Astors and Vanderbilts north to Fifth Avenue and Richard and Catharine, of colonial heritage, back to Washington Square where the Howland family had lived before Hunt launched his career at NYU's University Building (see 2.2). In November, they rented number 2 North, its airy, high-ceilinged, Greek Revival rooms facing south over the square. Nearby at University Place was relative James Renwick Jr.'s Gothic Grace Episcopal, the family church and beneficiary of Catharine's charity.[64]

Honors came to Hunt as he continued to bring his persuasive leadership and social network to a changing society. Now sixty, he was honored at the 1887 annual exhibition of the Architectural League of New York, founded in 1881 by young professionals to advance architecture and its allied arts. As a member, Hunt was on the jury for presented projects that included a watercolor from his École Algerian series (see 1.11a) and drawings for the Pavillon de la Bibliothèque, accompanied by photographs of the stained glass, bas-reliefs, tapestries, and stamped leather that he and colleagues were making integral to the American Renaissance interior. The following year, he was elected president of the AIA. In this role, he participated in the admission of women to the institute and oversaw the consolidation of it and the Western Association of Architects (WAA), acknowledging the rising importance of Chicago's architects, even as his practice continued apace, guided by ideals from France.[65]

Martin Brimmer had his lifelong friend in mind when he opined on the American architect at the 1889 opening of Wellesley College's Farnsworth Art School:

> The architect moulds the forms he has received from the past into new forms which accord with the needs of to-day. But will he mould them in subjection to the principles of good design? That depends much upon whether the public demands of him that the elevation of his building shall indicate both the construction of it and the purpose it is to serve, that the material shall befit his design, that his ornament shall be used only to soften the severity of his lines or to give accent to their beauty.[66]

Hunt had endeavored, for a quarter century to give rise, through education and design, to a discerning public who could further the movement relating form and material to function, even as he remained decidedly antiquarian. His failure to win commercial work in the 1870s sidelined him in the movement advanced by French-trained William Le Baron Jenney, who began the first steel-framed office tower, Chicago's Home Insurance Building, in 1884, a year after Alva Vanderbilt opened her limestone chateau to New York society. Hunt's preferred pier construction and picturesqueness were well suited to the demands of conservative patrons, though pragmatically he cautioned his eldest son and partner against dogmatism, advising that success came from listening to a client even if it meant building "a house upside down standing on a chimney."[67]

Hector Lefuel had introduced Hunt to the French Renaissance chateau, an architecture he considered conducive to the "comfortable" high bourgeois life, as he experienced in 1852 at the Chateau de Chenonceau. Now, as the rich person's art advisor, decorator, architect, and cultural leader, he would return to this early experience to realize a signifying theatricality in city and country mansions. Fortresses against the immigrant class and avatars of America's global ascent, they would express, unapologetically, the social and political dominance of money while encouraging architecture and art in the movement chronicled by popular *Scribners' Monthly* in its column, "Culture and Progress."

Residence for Cornelius Vanderbilt Esq. Newport
R.M. Hunt | Arch't   New York February 20. 1895. E.L.M
Bronze Candelabra for Main Hall
Scale 3/4 inch to 1 foot

Residence for Cornelius Vanderbilt Esq.
                                    Newport R.I.
R.M. Hunt Arch't Newport July
Candelabra in Bronze and Marble
      for Grand Staircase Hall
Scale 1 inch to 1 foot
New York February 20. 1895. E.L.M

Scrapbook Portfolio

Richard Hunt's grand scheme for a museum of architecture, envisioned since the 1850s on the model of French collections, included his École drawings and hundreds of published books, treatises, and journals. Of special note are scrapbooks, which formed a visual encyclopedia of the arts, that he and Catharine created from published illustrations as well as drawings by his studio and himself. When added to the photographs Richard purchased and commissioned of his built work, an inspirational panorama of old and new civilizations emerges.

The Hunt scrapbook folios are a record and a celebration of the triumphal arches and city parks, columned palaces and glass halls, opera houses and train stations, medieval streets and grand boulevards, of the chandeliers, paintings, ornaments, curtains, and consoles, and of the architects and aristocratic patrons that inspired the marbled republic Hunt imagined for America's Gilded Age.[1]

Fig. SC.1 Bronze candelabra designs for main hall of the Breakers, Alice and Cornelius Vanderbilt II house, Newport, Rhode Island; Emmanuel L. Masqueray, February 21-22, 1895.

Fig. SC.2 Dining room chandelier, the Breakers; probably France, ca. 1893

Fig. SC.3 Brooklyn Bridge compared with Statue of Liberty, New York City, to confirm how the latter was taller; on verso, "Total height of bridge 278 ft" and "Total height of torch 309 ft"; Hunt office, 1884

Fig. SC.4 Dining hall, proposed stained-glass window and dado, Alva and William K. Vanderbilt house, New York City; Hunt office, ca. 1881

Fig. SC.5 Karl Bitter's portrait rondels of Richard Hunt (left) and architect Jules Hardouin-Mansart, above a bust of Louis XIV, stair landing, Marble House, Newport, with comments by Hunt office noting Alva Vanderbilt's preference for bronze details; Jules Allard Fils or Hunt office, April 1891

Fig. SC.6 Country house planning schema, following the École des Beaux-Arts method; Richard Hunt, ca. 1853

SC.2

SC.3

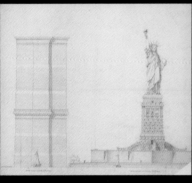

SC.4

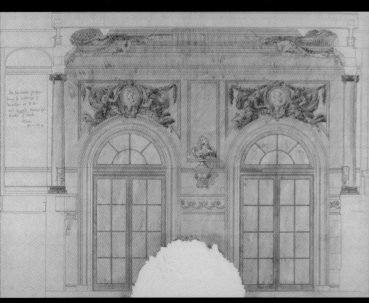

SC.5

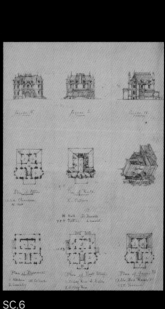

SC.6

SC.7

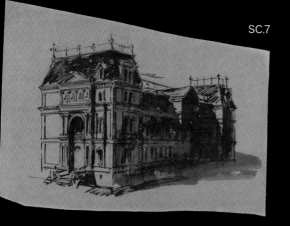

SC.8

SC.9

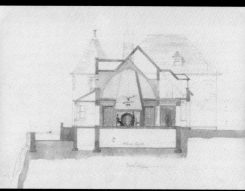

Fig. SC.7 Sketch for unbuilt New-York Historical Society Museum of History, Antiquities, and Art, Central Park, New York City; Richard Hunt, ca. 1865

Fig. SC.8 Rendering for Ogden Goelet's Pompeian-style bathroom, Ochre Court, Newport, one of several variants; Hunt office, ca. 1888[29]

Fig. SC.9 Section to main hall, Mary and Joseph Busk house, Indian Spring, Newport; Hunt office, ca. 1889[30]

Fig. SC.10 Profile, hammer beam, Sarah and William V. Lawrence house, New York City; Hunt office, ca. 1890

Fig. SC.11 Capitals, scrapbook pages

Fig. SC.12 Architects, scrapbook pages

SC.10

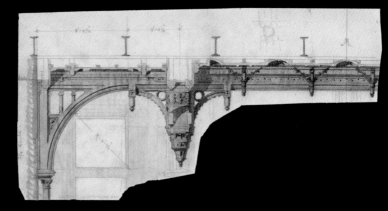

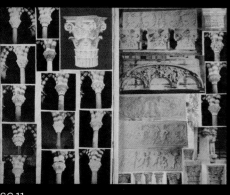

SC.11

SC.12

Chapter 5

Les Palais Hunt

In 1887 *Harper's Weekly* celebrated the strides American architecture had made since the Rev. William Furness addressed the AIA in 1870. He had lamented the greedy building trades and the public's suspicion that fine architecture was not all "high and beautiful ideals," but an indulgence of the "money-seeking classes." Now, in "this brilliant epoch of American architecture," the editors concluded, "even the public recognizes the architect as an artist of the first rank."[1]

No one was more acknowledged for this progress than Richard Hunt, who had promoted for thirty years professional architecture in American life (5.1). He was what Furness called "your true Architect," motivated by a greater purpose than "money-making," seeking "truth and grace" in "wood and iron and stone...." Despite this moral equivalency, Furness lauded the "rapidity" of rising fortunes paying for "the costliest structures, public and private." Hunt was the benefactor of this new prosperity as the rich person's preeminent architect, at once a fellow patron of new institutions and their hired hand. Given his Newport success and years with Hector Lefuel, architect for French chateaus, he was singularly qualified to be a leader in the country house revival when he could finally "surpass the palaces of Europe."[2]

In 1886 architect Bruce Price wrote that since "country mansions" were first built fifty years before the Civil War, the rich were reconceiving the "modest" house of the 1860s as a stately retreat from life in polluted cities. Along the "cliffs of Newport, the rocks of Mt. Desert...the beaches of Westchester, Connecticut, and Long Island" there were "cottages that would be mansions in England, villas in Italy, or chateaus in France." Designed by trained architects, they were an authentic American architecture founded in history:

Fig. 5.36 detail, Biltmore

Fig. 5.1 Hunt considered this bronze portrait bust, a gift from George Vanderbilt, a "picturesque" memento of their French castle tour in 1889; for Catharine Hunt it showed her husband's "stern and intellectual side;" Jean Gautherin, 1886, cast by Ferdinand Barbedienne[31]

Our country house is already a well-defined school, whether colonial, 16th and 17th century of England or France, Romanesque from the south of France, or Renaissance, the mass is American and typical in handling. The feeling may survive, but the style of the prototype has been bent to the homes we live in, and in bending yields to a new form.... So we are passing through our incipient Renaissance, copying less from the masters we studied and revere, and dropping the word style from our practice.[3]

The year of Price's precis, Levi P. Morton (see P.13) hired Hunt to design a mansion and service buildings at Ellerslie, his thousand-acre estate along the Hudson in Rhinecliff, a railroad depot for landed properties including William and Caroline Astor's Ferncliff Farm. Hunt knew the area and its mansion culture, having competed unsuccessfully for Olana, artist Frederic Church's neo-Islamic villa nearby.[4]

Fig. 5.2 Little Moreton Hall (1508), Cheshire, England, a Tudor inspiration for Ellerslie in Rhinecliff, New York; Hunt research photograph, ca. 1875

Morton was Hunt's match in entrepreneurial spirit and determination. A fellow Vermonter raised by a Congregational minister, he learned through apprenticeship and became a New York banker, marrying a descendant of the Hudson River landed establishment. Their daughter Alice married a son of Hunt's client, Lewis Morris Rutherfurd, and her sister Helen became a French duchess. These were exemplary Gilded Age marriages, one preserving the hegemony of a founding family and the other enriching an impoverished aristocracy, social alliances beneficial to Morton at the time of his political celebrity and run for New York governor. Hunt himself was both architect and friend to the financier-politician. He designed the Neo-Grec ballroom (1869) at Morton's Newport villa, Fairlawn, and a stable (1871) in New York. As minister to France, Morton provided Hunt's son Dick with the required diplomatic letter for admission to the École des Beaux-Arts; and he hosted the Hunts at his 1889 inauguration as vice president of the United States.[5]

Biographies of Levi Morton touted his ancestry in Tudor England, builders of Little Moreton Hall, a moated, half-timbered manor (1508) known to Hunt (5.2). This architectural heritage, linking Morton to the aristocratic past, determined the design of Ellerslie. On a rise overlooking the river, Hunt's only Elizabethan mansion incorporated

Fig. 5.3a–b Anna and
Levi Morton house,
Ellerslie (1887),
entrance, top, and
Hudson River façade,
below; George W.
Burger, Poughkeepsie,
New York, ca. 1890

Fig. 5.4a Levi
Morton's library,
Ellerslie, looking to
the living hall and
Anna Morton's sitting
room; George W.
Burger, Poughkeepsie,
New York, ca. 1890

Fig. 5.4b Preliminary
first-floor plan,
Ellerslie, doors and
windows aligned for
landscape views; Hunt
office, January 22,
1887

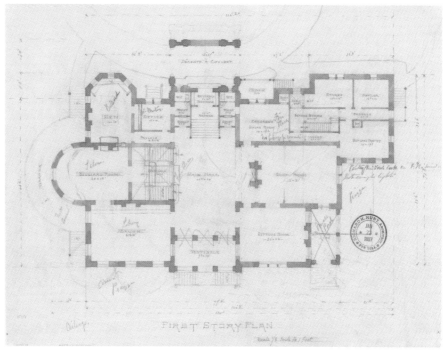

Fig. 5.5 The Hunts' Hill-Top Cottage, Newport, Rhode Island, with 1870s part-octagonal porch and two-story service and studio addition; "Hilltop," Jane M. Hunt, ca. 1880

elements of his earlier wood cottages in a new symmetry and mass characteristic of his Newport mansions that defined the American "palace" (5.3a-b, 5.4a-b). Interior spaces opened to a central hall in a squared plan, their neo-Tudor decoration in keeping with the house but without the authenticity of Hunt's New York interiors.[6]

An alternative to the country estate was a mansion in historic Newport. Near colonial clapboards and the Cushman and Appleton villas, Richard and Catharine's Hill-Top Cottage was originally a modest country house of wallpapered rooms and brown furniture. Over the decades, the Hunts transformed it into a six-bedroom homey manse, its living rooms on the first floor, family bedrooms on the second, and servants' quarters on the third, interconnected by a spiraling front staircase and service wing back stair. In the early 1870s, they built a two-story kitchen/studio wing and added a wide, part-octagonal porch to entertain what Catharine called their "piazza contingency" of society leaders and diplomats (5.5, 5.6a-b, see also 2.13). Decorated with Louis XV fauteuils and old master paintings, Hill-Top promoted not a world of Manet, Degas, and the Impressionists, but the chateau taste Hunt was selling to his palace-seeking clients.[7]

Hunt's friends and early clients were genteel artists and professionals, distinct from the ultra rich who arrived after the Civil War. They belonged to Newport's Town and Country Club, founded 1871 by author Julia Ward Howe and Colonel Thomas Higginson. Members hosted authors

Fig. 5.6a Second-floor morning room, Hill-Top Cottage, "as it was originally" when Catharine and Richard purchased the house; Richard Hunt, sketchbook watercolor, ca. 1864

Fig. 5.6b The cottage's redecorated parlor; Jane M. Hunt, ink drawing reproduction, "Newport, July 28. 1885"

who lectured on science, art, and literature in members' homes. At a Hill-Top fundraiser to send the town's Unitarian minister to Europe, one of many such trips American parishes funded to encourage clerical support of the arts, Howe read her Civil War anthem, the "Battle Hymn of the Republic," at the urging of George Bancroft. These low-key New England intellectuals were distinct from the aspirational rich living along the Atlantic. "It was not fashion that first brought people of luxurious tastes, with means for indulging them, to Newport," Frederick Law Olmsted scornfully told town managers considering public beaches. "It was a satisfaction found in its air and scenery by people of a rather reserved, unobtruding, contemplative, and healthily sentimental turn, little troubled by social ambitions. Social attractions came with them; and fashion, as is usual, followed social attractions."[8]

Newport had a coterie of local architects, but the success of his cottages placed Hunt in the lead as the town became what Parisian litterateur Paul Bourget considered a resort of "sumptuous" villas like Cannes on the French

Fig. 5.7a Hill-Top Cottage, with Hunt's ocelot sculpture and plaster casts between the windows; "R M Hunt's Studio July 12 1876," Jane L. Hunt

Fig. 5.7b Hunt office atelier, opposite, in the Hill-Top cottage carriage-house studio built in 1857 by William Morris Hunt; cast of Caspar Buberl statue of Hunt as a mason, rear right; Frank H. Child, Newport, ca. 1895

R.M.Hunt's Studio
Newport R.I.

Riviera. In the 1870s he employed German-trained architects, but by 1880 men versed in the French design now in fashion oversaw his New York and Newport studios (5.7b). Hunt pioneered the modern architect's office, his professional staff drafting plans, preparing construction documents, and painting watercolors that enticed clients into mansion projects (see 5.14, SC.4, and SC.8). Hunt sketched initial concepts, visited construction sites, and led client negotiations. He welcomed staff contributions in "council[s] of war", but there were limits. "You were not pleased with my rendering of the [banker Ogden] Mills' house façade," C. Anthony Holland wrote his boss. "I tried to follow your sketches as closely as possible—I did not see how any change would be made that was not radically a change in design."[9]

Fig. 5.8 Entrance gates,
Mary and Ogden Goelet
house, Ochre Court
(1892), Newport, Rhode
Island; Frank H. Child,
Newport, 1895

Fig. 5.9 Atlantic Ocean
façade, Ochre Court;
Michael Froio, 2019[32]

Fig. 5.8 Entrance gates,
Mary and Ogden Goelet
house, Ochre Court
(1892), Newport, Rhode
Island; Frank H. Child,
Newport, 1895

Ochre Court (1892) exemplifies the depth and scope of Hunt's
planning, his office preparing more than three hundred drawings on
tracing paper and linen, as well as blueprints of details, some in one-to-
one scale. The client was New York real estate heir and yachtsman Ogden
Goelet (see P.10). École-trained Emmanuel L. Masqueray was assistant
on the project, and watercolors attributed to him are more realized than
Hunt's own of the same period, suggesting the Frenchman's academic
skill and influence. The entrance façade was closed and imposing in
contrast to the ocean front, open and capacious, its arcaded loggia framed
by towers (5.8, 5.9). After criticism for overembellishing the exterior of Alva
Vanderbilt's New York house in the same Francis I style, Hunt dressed
Ochre Court in unornamented gray limestone blocks. As at Chateau-
sur-Mer, his French approach was a counterpoint to the neighboring
Shingle-style cottage (1883) by McKim, Mead & White for Goelet's brother
Robert. Montgomery Schuyler found Ochre Court "scholarly" and a "true
château," and though the six-acre site constrained a service wing, Hunt
had realized the "power of conforming and subordinating the immediate
surroundings to the architecture" to project the standing of his clients,
an approach he used again at Vanderbilt mansions south along the ocean.[10]

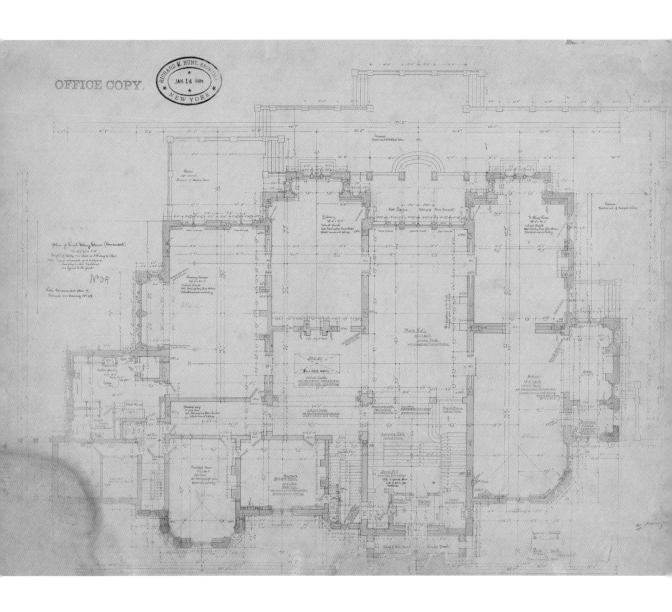

Since mid-century, landscape design had become integral to mansion architecture. Ochre Court was Hunt's third collaboration with Frederick Law Olmsted, and surviving drawings for flower parterres suggest that Hunt, possibly with American landscape architect Ernest W. Bowditch, brought a French, axial approach to the planning, as he had to the Central Park gateways in the 1860s. The Olmsted firm focused on the ocean front, writing that a retaining wall would define "the rights of the public" and give a "sense of privacy to the grounds of the house." Passersby would see Ochre Court and yet "[appear] not to be trespassers upon private property." By sharing the beauty of their domain, the Goelets would contribute to public taste, yet live securely at a distance, their house looming majestically above the rocky coast.[11]

C. Everett Clark, a Bostonian builder at Ochre Court and the Breakers, hired only "native workers," discriminating against the Italian "foreign contract labor" employed at nearby Marble House. The interiors, however, were by Paris-New York firms Jules Allard Fils, L. Marcotte & Co., and L. Alavoine Co., providing period-revival French paneling and furnishings for a client of Huguenot ancestry collecting art and furniture from the ancien régime (5.10, 5.11a-b, 5.12a-b, SC.8). Allard's reception rooms opened to a three-story court, the first floor faced in French limestone carved with royal fleur-de-lis. Above the second-floor arcaded hall, etiolated caryatids in the Fontainebleau mannerist style leaned out from a vaulted ceiling where a neo-Baroque banquet of the gods soared above. Decorations on the second, bedroom floor were Gothic and neoclassical.[12]

Hunt cultivated art collecting among his clients to complete interiors and address his expressed concern that the public museum, dependent on private donations, was easier to build than to fill with art. The first of his collectors was Henry Marquand, who acquired a French dealer's collection of ancient pottery and glass in 1881 and donated it to the Metropolitan Museum of Art that year. From the end of the decade, Goelet and his wife, Mary Wilson, whose sister Grace married Cornelius Vanderbilt III, purchased old master paintings, tapestries, and chateau furnishings of questionable vintage from European sources introduced by Jules Allard and certainly known to Hunt. Their most notable acquisition was Ochre Court's fifteenth-century German stained glass (5.11a) from the estate of Frédéric Spitzer, whose 1880s encyclopedic house-museum in Paris rivaled the Hôtel de Cluny and collection of architect and dealer Émile Gavet.[13]

Newport's carriage boulevard was leafy Bellevue Avenue, bordered by three- to thirteen-acre ocean-view lots laid out in the 1850s. Beechwood (1853), a stucco and wood "marine villa" by Andrew Jackson Downing and

Fig. 5.12b Ochre Court dining
room; Michael Froio, 2019

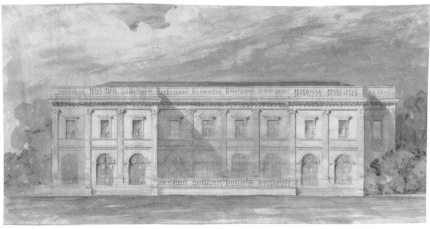

Fig. 5.13 Alva and William K. Vanderbilt's Marble House, Newport, Rhode Island, preliminary entrance elevation, a mansion as villa; Hunt office, ca. 1888

Fig. 5.14 Preliminary Atlantic Ocean elevation, Marble House as palace; Richard Hunt, ca. 1888

Calvert Vaux, was sold to William and Caroline Astor in 1880. To the south were five seaside acres, acquired in 1888 by William and Alva Vanderbilt for almost forty times their cost thirty years before. Masters of high-stakes society maneuvering, Mrs. Astor hired Hunt to plan a Louis XV ballroom addition while Alva commissioned a summer cottage that would outdo any competition, her superior culture and wealth made manifest again through architecture and decoration.[14]

The Vanderbilts rejected Hunt's initial proposal for a Second Empire mansion (5.13). What followed was a radical transformation, likely at the instigation of Alva, whose "intellect and broad grasp of architecture" Hunt acknowledged (5.14). Her chosen model was Versailles' 1768 Petit Trianon, the retreat of Marie Antoinette whose lacquered commode and secretaire she displayed in her New York chateau.[15]

Since an exhibition of the queen's collections at the Petit Trianon, organized by Empress Eugénie for the 1867 Paris Exposition, Marie Antoinette had become a martyr to art, design, fashion and wealth, believed by prosperous Americans to have been wrongly beheaded by what Alva described as the "violence of the hands of the mob." Now the queen's dramatic story was vivid in the minds of the sympathetic rich. The year before the Vanderbilts purchased their Bellevue lot, the memoir of Madame Campan, the queen's lady-in-waiting, was published in New York (5.15). An international bestseller, her account of the Reign of Terror was a romantic, cautionary tale for a society fearing its own "dangerous" classes.[16]

Fig. 5.15 Oil study for *Visite domiciliaire*, popular at the Paris Salon, 1884, from the memoir of Marie Antoinette's lady-in-waiting, Madame Campan, seen here as revolutionaries loot her eighteenth-century salon, decorated like rooms installed by Hunt in his new mansions; Victor Bachereau-Reverchon, ca. 1884

Marble House was a monumentalized Petit Trianon, sited almost midway in its narrow lot landscaped neoclassically, probably by Ernest Bowditch (5.16). Built of brick, iron, and steel faced with white American marble, its exterior sculpted reliefs were a decorative counterpoint to the massive columned entrance framed by a balustraded drive inspired by the seventeenth-century "Horseshoe Staircase" and Hermitage de la Madeleine at the Chateau de Fontainebleau (see 2.16, 5.17a-b). Hunt's famed antiquarianism was exacting and, as contemporaries alluded, at times it limited invention. When craftsmen failed to carve the columns' Corinthian capitals to his standard, Hunt purchased a cast of a capital from the Roman Forum's Temple of Castor and Pollux to guide Marble House carvers. He intended to add it to the cast collection he had donated to the Metropolitan Museum, which, like institutions throughout Europe, displayed replicas to educate the public about the classical canon.[17]

As Bruce Price observed, what made the American house American was its mass and adaptation of "prototype." Hunt's over-scaled entrance distinguished Marble House from ancient and American exemplars, yet conjured up aspects of both. Paul Bourget discerned the Temple of Bacchus at Baalbek, while national critics, in their nascent resistance to European models, saw the Federal classicism of the White House north portico. Alva herself, writing in 1932 at the time of the Colonial Revival, similarly commented that Greek classicism, long associated with democracy, had inspired her seaside palace.[18]

If a palace was the intended public impression, Marble House was an American home, its first-floor plan a Beaux-Arts elaboration of an 1850s villa interior, little different from the parlor floor of Alva's ancestral house in Mobile, a two-story, center hall, Gothic block (5.18a-b). As the mother of three children, she believed domestic life, regardless of wealth, encouraged "self-reliance, initiative, and a sense of personal responsibility," the "middle-class" values of American life. Consequently, all her houses, she wrote, "real and imaginary, reproduced certain features of the home in which I was born and where my early childhood was spent."[19]

New to Alva's "middle-class" Trianon were the scale of rooms and their Napoléon III decoration by Hunt and Jules Allard, continuing the exterior's thematic association of plutocratic America with France's royalist past. Versailles' Salon d'Hercules and Hall of Mirrors inspired the dining room and Alva's gilded "Grand Salon" (5.19). The fashion for period-revival interiors fueled an international market peddling a mélange of fake and real works of art and furniture. Alva purchased old masters as authentic, now only attributed, and in Hunt's fantastical Gothic library presented her collection

Fig. 5.16 Landscape plan for Marble House; probably Ernest Bowditch; ca. 1888

RESIDENCE

Wm K . VANDERBILT . ESQe .

NEWPORT . R . I .

BELLEVUE   AVENUE

SCALE 20 FEET TO AN INCH.

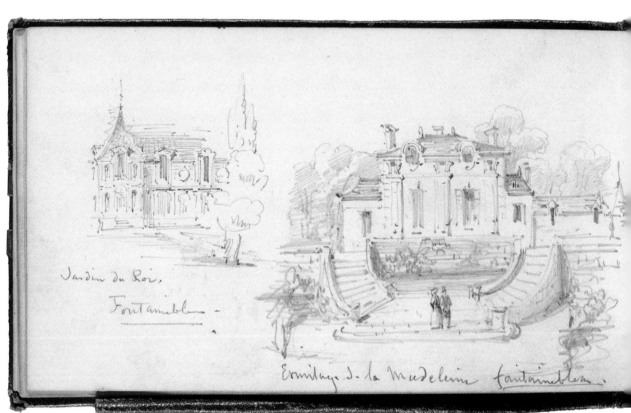

Jardin du Roi,
Fontainbleau.

Ermitage de la Madeleine Fontainebleau

Fig. 5.17a Marble House (1892) from Bellevue Avenue, opposite top, designed to awe neighbors passing by in carriages; Michael Froio, 2020

Fig. 5.17b Sketch of the seventeenth-century Hermitage de la Madeleine, Fontainebleau, France, opposite bottom, an inspiration to Hunt; Richard Hunt sketchbook, ca. 1852

Fig. 5.18a–b First- and second-floor plans, Marble House; servants discreetly circulated through "backstairs," shown next to first floor morning room; Hunt office, June 14, 1888

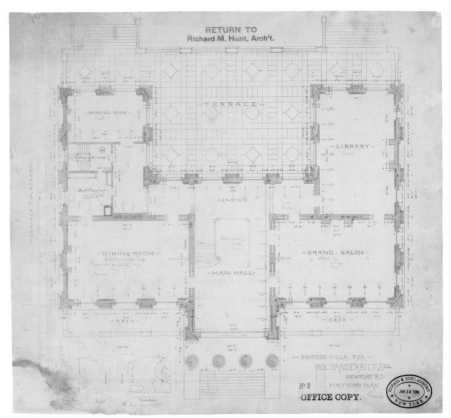

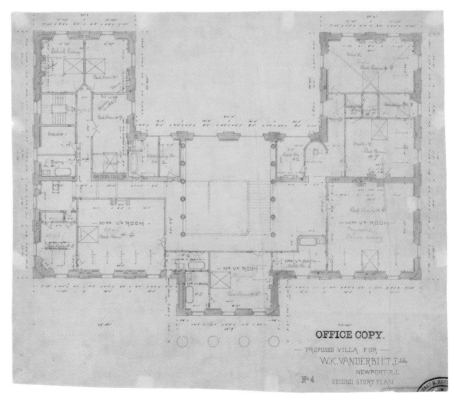

of medieval and Renaissance arts she had acquired from Émile Gavet, inspired by displays in his Paris apartment (5.20a-b). This was a unification of art, decoration, and architecture by style requiring the scholarship Hunt and French connoisseurs had cultivated since the 1840s.[20]

Alva was brazen in her aristocratic ambitions, for herself and her country. At the stair landing, she mounted a bust of Louis XIV, flanked by marble rondels of Hunt and architect Jules Hardouin-Mansart, carved by the Austrian sculptor Karl T.F. Bitter, an arrangement which Hunt viewed with "much amusement" (see SC.5). In the Louis XV Revival morning room she hung her American portrait painted in the eighteenth-century French Rococo style (see 4.6a). Presented as Venus/Diane de Poitiers, swathed in violet mousseline, the thirty-eight-year-old homemaker is a goddess of motherhood, a purveyor of art to the Gilded Age, and queen of her Trianon, an homage to the history of design from the French High Gothic to Marie Antoinette and Louis XVI, realized by her Mansart.[21]

Hunt had learned the otherworldly opulence of Marble House from 1850s interiors by Hector Lefuel and from Charles Garnier's Paris Opera House (1875) (5.21). He had toured the "Palais Garnier" accompanied by its architect in 1867, and a year after it opened he told AIA colleagues that, though imperfect, the music palace was a "remarkable edifice, so superior to

Fig. 5.19 Grand salon, Marble House, decorated by Jules Allard Fils to surpass Chateau de Versailles' Hall of Mirrors; plate-glass doors and electric lighting were advanced engineering; Michael Froio, 2020

Fig. 5.20a Marble
House's Gothic-style
library, its fireplace
after one in the
Jacques Cœur house,
Bourges, France,
top; Mattie Edwards
Hewitt, 1926

Fig. 5.20b Library
windows originally
assembled from period
and new glass; Michael
Froio, 2020

all others" because its exterior elevations clearly reflected its interior plan, and its rich and varied ornament was "so appropriate to such a monument," mandates that guided Hunt. For the Paris architect, the world was a stage: put "two or three people together and theater exists immediately, where this happens is 'the scene.'" Architecture, its structure concealed, bejeweled with colored stones and gilding, made the "palace, the court, the church, the meeting halls" settings for human drama. For the Vanderbilts, planning domestic stages to advance their international social ascent, Garnier's masterpiece, the apex of Second Empire design, was a *beau idéal*.[22]

Marble House was completed in 1892, the year William K. Vanderbilt's older brother Cornelius Vanderbilt II commissioned his own Newport mansion, the Breakers, to be built on an even more operatic scale. Privately educated, he was head of the New York Central & Hudson Railroad and a Metropolitan Museum patron and trustee (5.22). In 1885 he inherited $67 million, the largest share of his father's estate, and purchased the Breakers, an 1878 brick and shingle Queen Anne cottage at Ochre Point by Boston's Peabody & Stearns. When the house burned to the ground seven years later, Vanderbilt hired Hunt to design its limestone replacement on the property's almost thirteen acres to be landscaped by Ernest Bowditch and gardener Robert Laurie. Masqueray painted presentation watercolors of a Chambordesque chateau and a classical villa, with elements reminiscent of sixteenth-century Genoese palazzos. Cornelius and his wife, Alice C. Gwynne, whose ancestry was deep in Rhode Island's past, settled on a version of the latter for unknown reasons. Was

Fig. 5.21 Charles Garnier's Paris Opera House (1875), the culmination of Second Empire classicism and engineering; Detroit Publishing Co., photochrom, ca. 1890–1900

Fig. 5.22 Railroad executive and museum trustee Cornelius Vanderbilt II, seated before a view like one at his Newport mansion, the Breakers, holding an annual report of the Metropolitan Museum of Art; Daniel Huntington, 1895

Fig. 5.23 Limestone porte-cochère entrance, Alice and Cornelius Vanderbilt II house, the Breakers (1895), Newport, Rhode Island, landscape by Ernest Bowditch; Michael Froio, 2020[35]

it to differentiate the Breakers from Trianon Marble House and Gothic Ochre Court? Or to commemorate the quadricentennial of northern Italian Christopher Columbus?[23]

The Breakers (1895) was four times the size of Marble House for a family of eight (5.23). As at Ochre Court, the entrance elevation was formidable and closed, the ocean façade open, its loggias framed by bedroom projections. A deft rhythm of arches and orders and progression in window size differentiated the public and private rooms from servant quarters at the roof. Though familiarly Beaux-Arts in its hierarchy and U-configuration, each façade, wrote Montgomery Schuyler, was a "true architectural composition," and "the massive and monumental workmanship, so far beyond our old notions of a 'sea side cottage' [like the Astors' Beechwood] are merely the fitting presentation" of a "gentleman's mansion."[24]

Hunt's interior was balanced and unfolding (5.24a-d). Ornately decorated rooms for entertaining opened from a two-story court (5.25). At its north end, a wide stair rose to a landing and then to the family's bedroom floor. In the groined support of this marble sweep, a fountain was visible from the dining room through plate glass, its design closely adapted from Garnier's Pythia fountain at the Paris Opera. Throughout the first floor, ormolu furnishings, and paneling by Hunt and Allard, were to palazzo scale (see SC.1).[25]

Despite Cornelius Vanderbilt II's support of the Metropolitan Museum, fine art and period furnishings played a minor role in the Breakers'

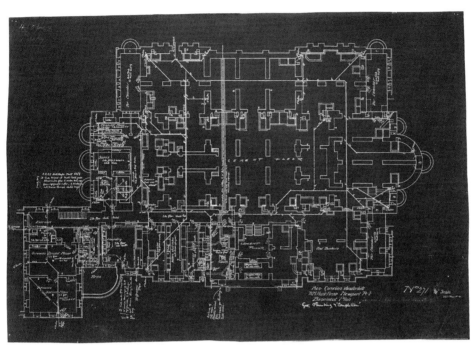

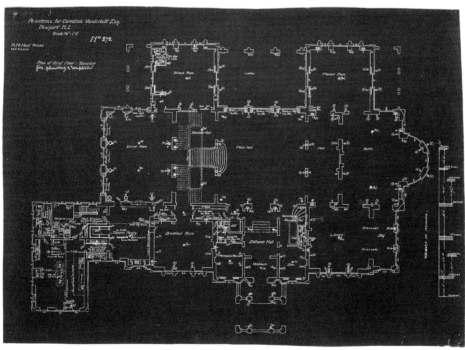

Fig. 5.24a–d Plans for the Breakers' basement, opposite top; first floor, opposite bottom; second floor, top; and third floor, bottom, showing Hunt's preferred pier-construction and services of a mansion; "Gas, Plumbing & Completion" blueprints, February 28, 1894

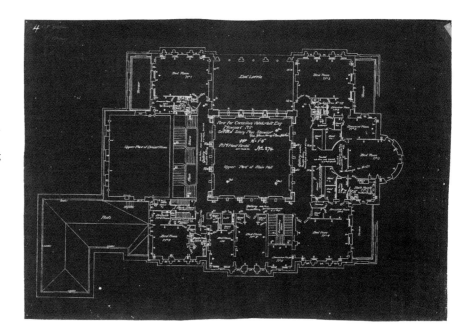

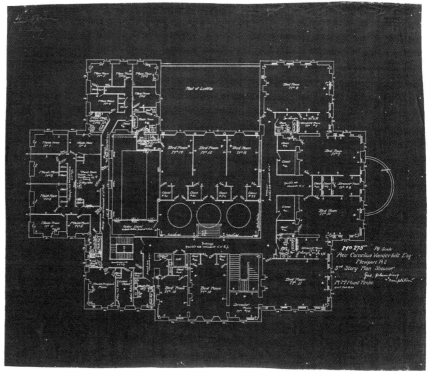

theater of domestic life. But Hunt and his client frequented Paris auctions and ateliers and followed the fashion of historic rooms after Commune fires threatened the history of French design (5.25, 5.26a-b, see also SC.2). For the reception room off the entrance, Allard supplied revivalist furnishings and reconfigured gilded and painted Louis XVI panels (5.27) from Paris' Hôtel Mégret de Sérilly, associated with Marie Antoinette and famous at the time for its much admired 1778 cabinet room, already acquired by the South Kensington Museum. Hunt again was inching the American mansion toward house-museum while making his clients aristocrats by proxy.[26]

On the second floor, Hunt orchestrated the next stage of revivalist design. Encouraged by their friend Edith Wharton and her husband,

Fig. 5.25 Main hall, the Breakers; Frank H. Child, Newport, 1895[36]

Fig. 5.26a Hunt-designed billiard room, opposite top, the Breakers, faced in imported Cipollino marble, inset with colored stones, a papal extravaganza like those that dazzled the architect when in Rome; Michael Froio, 2020

Fig. 5.26b The morning room, opposite bottom, the Breakers, a décor to impress, by Jules Allard Fils; Michael Froio, 2020

Edward, the Vanderbilts commissioned the Boston architect Ogden Codman Jr. for bedrooms in restrained Louis XVI styles. The author and arbiter of upper-class mores was promoting classicism in response to the Vanderbilts' predisposition to the baroque and their being "entrenched in a sort of Thermopylae of bad taste." Codman, her young acolyte, struggled to impose his ideas in drawings Hunt considered no more than "mere outlines," insufficient for proper construction. Furthermore, he wrote, to "servilely copy French interiors, I fear will get you into trouble." In this cryptic warning, written in the final year of his life, Hunt revealed what had guided his generation, that precedent was only a starting point for the contemporary architect seeking a modern expression.[27]

Though the past was ever present in Hunt's practice, new engineering made possible new forms and convenience. Like house builders of their generation and pressured by insurance underwriters, the Vanderbilts insisted on fireproof construction. In response, Hunt built in stone, steel and brick, and applied Guastavino tile to porch vaulting. There was telephone service, electric security, a hydraulic elevator, and central heating. To achieve his palace in three years, he employed builders from commercial construction who assured high finish and elaboration by employing the era's skilled tradesmen.[28]

The Vanderbilt stone mansions made Hunt's lasting fame and reputation, for better and then worse, at home and abroad. The French critic, the Count S.C. de Soissons, considered them and Ochre Court the town's only significant new architecture, even though Marble House appeared as a mere "fragment," a "portal of some Renaissance cathedral or immense *palàzzo*, not a *palàzzo* itself." Like American architecture overall, none were in fact original nor truly aristocratic, but it was better to give the country "tasteful buildings" than "produce architectural horrors and barbarous results," a view shared by Soissons' long-time friend, Richard Hunt. For the Frenchman, an authentic American style would come, after time and the training Hunt had promoted since the 1850s.[29]

For Alva Vanderbilt, her family's houses in Newport, New York, and North Carolina were not "merely beautiful private residences," but the "means of expression in outward and visible terms of the importance" of the Vanderbilt clan. Their lavish and costly luxury, exceeding any American precedent, had become the "Vanderbilt Style," much in the way the Europe's banking Rothschilds created *Le Style Rothschild*. Caroline Astor understood that Alva and her in-laws had raised the bar for upper-class living and responded accordingly when she moved from Thirty-Fourth Street (see 2.6) to Sixty-Fifth and Fifth to build a double house (1895) with her son, John Jacob Astor IV. Adult families living together and sharing public rooms was already known to Hunt from his Bronson-Winthrop houses on Murray Hill (see 4.3). The press reported that for several years Caroline and John had studied the "time-honored homes of the French nobility" and intended their new salons overlooking Central Park to be modeled on the Petit Trianon. John had ordered measured plans from Europe and Hunt had visited the pavilion at Versailles. Ultimately, the Astors wanted a "city palace—something that would vie, in richness and splendor, with the Vanderbilt mansions on Fifth Avenue and even excel them."[30]

The Astor limestone house was Hunt's classicizing adaptation of the Francis I style he had introduced to the city with Alva Vanderbilt's towered chateau to the south (5.28, 5.29, see also 4.9). Mother and son shared an entrance stair and gallery-ballroom, with neo-Baroque marble staircases by Karl Bitter in their respective wings (5.30a). A two-story fireplace dominated the gallery, an academic elaboration of Caroline's 1875 ballroom addition at Thirty-Fourth Street, both indebted to Second Empire decoration. For the mantle, Hunt and Bitter turned to an 1879 pattern book by a Parisian decorator and his adaptation of a French Renaissance fireplace. The paneling of the dining and reception rooms was in *Le Style Vanderbilt*, furnished by Jules Allard with paintings, tapestries, and suites of furniture then attributed to Versailles' Jean-Henri Riesener and

Fig. 5.28 Caroline Astor and her son John Jacob Astor IV double house (1895), a Fifth Avenue chateau overlooking Central Park, New York City; Detroit Publishing Co., photochrom, ca. 1900

Charles Le Brun. A journalist praised the grand salon (5.30b) as the "most perfect example of the Louis XVI decoration ever designed since the time of that splendid contemporary masterpiece of Louis Seize art, the salon of the Marquise de Sillery, lady of honor to Queen Marie Antoinette," a gossipy comparison by a reporter who certainly knew of the Breakers reception room and the rivalries between families who competed socially through Hunt's buildings and interiors.[31]

Though known for forthrightness, Richard Hunt was cautiously silent about his clients. Alva Vanderbilt, a society renegade, considered that her association with Richard was founded in friendship and shared interests, boasting that Marble House won him the Royal Institute of British Architects' (RIBA) Gold Medal in 1893, which it did not. But Catharine outspokenly recalled that her husband "chafed under [the] unconscious rudeness" of Mary Goelet and Alice Vanderbilt. No matter his class, fame, and wealth, they treated him as their architect for hire and snubbed his family. When Alice's daughter Gertrude, later founder of the Whitney Museum of American Art, befriended the Hunts' daughter Esther, Alice objected because, Gertrude

Fig. 5.29 Astor house first-floor plan; James B. Garrison, AutoCAD, 2021

FIFTH AVENUE

SAFE

SALON

DINING ROOM

RECEPTION ROOM

PANTRY

PICTURE GALLERY [BALLROOM]

RECEPTION ROOM

GRAND SALON

DINING ROOM

PANTRY

CARRIAGE HOUSE

SAFE

65TH STREET

FIRST FLOOR PLAN

0 5 10   20 FEET

imagined, she "has no bringing up." Artistic and intellectual, friends with singers and writers, the Hunts were not "quite swell enough" to be equals of the industrial plutocracy, though his renown and persistence for his profession had elevated the status of the American architect.[32]

Hunt's role as mentor, cultural guide, and designer to twenty-six-year-old George Vanderbilt at Biltmore was unlike any of his client relationships. Commissioned the same year as Ochre Court and Marble House, the North Carolina estate at Asheville was of a scale exponentially beyond the Newport villas of George's brothers, with landscaping by the Olmsted firm of commensurate scope. When asked what he thought of his ocean mansions versus Biltmore on its mountain plateau, Hunt reportedly replied that they were mere "pig sties by comparison." George Vanderbilt, however, did not begin with such ambition.[33]

Fig. 5.30a Astor house gallery-ballroom, opposite top, gilded and inlaid with green marble and jasper, emptied of its palms and damask ottoman pending sale of the house, already one of America's "white elephants"; Wurts Brothers, ca. 1926[37]

Fig. 5.30b Astor house grand salon, opposite bottom, by Jules Allard Fils; ca. 1926[38]

Fig. 5.31 George W. Vanderbilt at twenty-eight; John Singer Sargent, 1890

When railroads made the balmy South accessible to snow-bound Northerners, rural communities became destinations in what historian William Deverell calls "an age of neurasthenia" among the upper classes recovering from the Civil War. In 1888 George Vanderbilt arrived in Asheville with his ailing mother and a $10 million inheritance from his father. Taken with the soft, healing beauty of the Blue Ridge Mountains, he acquired approximately 2,000 acres of remote, timbered-out land, ultimately expanding his holdings to 125,000 acres.[34]

George was an exceptional Vanderbilt, an aesthete with his family's financial acumen. A "delicate, refined and bookish man," recalled Frederick Law Olmsted, "with considerable humor, but shrewd, sharp, exacting and resolute in matters of business." Largely self-educated and committed to the arts, beautification, and the environment, he was a civilizing American in the circle of Henry James, John Singer Sargent, Howard O. Sturgis, and Edith Wharton, each with colonial heritage and living abroad. He corresponded with Claude Monet at Giverny, commissioned portraits from Sargent and the irascible James A.M. Whistler (5.31, see also 6.1), collected engravings, and assembled an extensive library that included volumes on the arts. Meticulous, gracious, and studious, George made lists of what he read and assembled photo albums of historic buildings. A patron in the movement to educate the "masses," he funded a Hunt-designed New York public library (1888) and the Vanderbilt Gallery of the New York Fine Arts Society (1892), which exhibited new art and architecture.[35]

For Vanderbilt's barren site, Hunt and office architect Warrington G. Lawrence first proposed a modest Georgian Revival brick manor honoring the region's history. A precedent was the 1886 Commodore William Edgar house in Newport, designed by McKim, Mead & White when Lawrence was in their office. Early plans were for a bachelor's life, the first floor including a library, den, dining, music and billiard rooms, but Hunt and Vanderbilt, after several iterations, settled on a chateau, guided by Blois (see 1.12), the restored Francis I castle admired by Hunt since 1852.[36]

Development of Biltmore was well under way when Richard, Catharine, and George toured English country houses and French castles in early summer 1889, one of only two known trips by Hunt with a client, albeit one whose fortune made possible an estate of unanticipated scale. Intended as an educative tour "to see beautiful interiors and pictures," the trip yielded carpets and inspiration for furniture later ordered from European and American makers, some designed by the Hunt office. The three visited Sir Richard Wallace's London mansion before it opened to the public in 1900, its lavish layering of period furniture, old masters, and applied arts exemplifying Hunt's approach to connoisseurship and decoration. Another stop was Waddesdon, the country estate of banking heir Baron Ferdinand de Rothschild, whose biography and house building parallel Vanderbilt's own.[37]

At thirty-four, Rothschild inherited a fortune on the death of his father in 1874. That year he acquired from the Duke of Marlborough 2,700 acres of dairy fields and timbered-out land in Buckinghamshire, with resident farmers and a tenant village that he later remodeled. For his new house, where he lived with his sister, he hired Hippolyte-A.-G.-W. Destailleur, bibliophile, collector, and École student whose renovations and palaces were an antiquarian's study of Loire chateaus (5.32). For the interiors, Rothschild, a connoisseur of French decorative arts, reinstalled period paneling and competed for furnishings associated with Marie Antoinette. At the Hamilton Palace auction, an 1882 global millionaire gathering in London, he was the underbidder of the Marie Antoinette desk and chest acquired by Alva and William Vanderbilt. Four years later Rothschild hosted his auction rivals and aristocratic guests at Waddesdon, and then again in the summer of Hunt's own visit.[38]

Fig. 5.32 Baron Ferdinand de Rothschild house (Hippolyte Destailleur, 1889), Waddesdon, England, a steel-framed, Bath yellow stone chateau visited by Hunt and George Vanderbilt, summer 1889; ca. 1897

Rothschild certainly shared that he had rejected his architect's initial plan for a house substantially larger than what he built. "You will regret your decision," Destailleur cautioned the baron, "*one always builds too small.*" Drawing on the "ancient chateaux of the Valois," Destailleur conjured up a nineteenth-century Renaissance palace, placing his client in the history of French design and patronage. The interiors were in period styles, but Rothschild insisted on "ventilation, light, air, and all internal conveniences," including central heating and electricity. He had completed the mansion in 1883, but at the time of the Hunt-Vanderbilt visit, the baron was finishing a morning room addition, regretting that he had not originally included a "Central Hall" where "my friends could all meet and read and write without disturbing one another."[39]

At the end of June 1889, Hunt preceded his wife and George to Paris, where he consulted with Alva and William Vanderbilt about Marble House. On this trip they may have acquired their Émile Gavet collection of medieval-Renaissance arts, likely with Hunt's advice. The Exposition Universelle and the International Congress of Architects were on, and as a member of the professional society, Hunt addressed the École and presented awards before touring Loire castles with George. A society

Fig. 5.33 The Biltmore creative team on site, from left: purchasing agent and agricultural consultant Edward Burnett, Richard Hunt, Frederick Law Olmsted, George Vanderbilt, and Richard H. Hunt; 1892

Fig. 5.34 Entrance esplanade and façade, Biltmore, opposite top; Hunt office photo, August 27, 1895

Fig. 5.35 First-floor plan, Biltmore, a geometry of circles, squares, and axes, opposite bottom; Hunt office, initialed "J.A.J Oct. 13", 1890

highlight was lunch with statesmen and intellectuals at the Chateau de Chantilly. To its owner, the collector and bibliophile Duc d'Aumale, Hunt's military bearing and authority made him "*un general Francais* [*sic*]," more acceptable than wealthy American parvenus. Hunt's École colleague P.J. Honoré Daumet, atelier *patron* of his two oldest sons, the architects Richard and Joseph (see 1.9), had unified the chateau built over three centuries. In response to a ban on royalty leading government, d'Aumale had bequeathed his mansion and collections to the Institut de France, the society that elected Hunt a corresponding member in 1882 for his William K. Vanderbilt New York chateau. This gift, memorializing the Orléans family, made d'Aumale a forerunner of American millionaires who donated their houses and collections to the public for its edification and family ennoblement.[40]

George returned to Asheville informed of estate design and what was expected of the international rich and educated, the guardians of establishment culture (5.33). For Hunt, his client's fortune and society yearnings promised a monument to cultural progress, a 250-room chateau overlooking Olmsted's park and nature preserve created by a team of designers and artisans.[41]

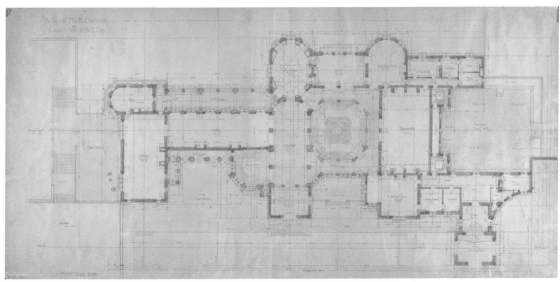

Fig. 5.36 Triumphal arch from banquet hall to winter garden, Biltmore; Karl Bitter's Joan of Arc and Saint Louis, a defender of faith and an art patron, flank the inscription, *Da Pacem, Domine, In Diebus Nostris*, "Give Peace, O Lord, in Our Time," resonant in a nation healing from the Civil War; Michael Froio, 2020

Fig. 5.37a Walnut-paneled library, opposite top, Karl Bitter mantle, Biltmore, at the time of George Vanderbilt; ca. 1905

Fig. 5.37b George Vanderbilt's bedroom, Biltmore, opposite bottom, in a Tudor Revival style inspired by English country houses visited by client and architect in 1889; Michael Froio, 2020

The completed mansion appeared from a distance as a Francis I chateau, but up close, its massing, spans of limestone blocks and deep window enframements made the house thoroughly American, exemplary of Mariana Griswold Van Rensselaer's "simplicity" with decoration (5.34). A defining element was the spiraling interior stair, distinctive for its diagonal windows at the entrance façade (see page 274). It was Hunt's reimagining, wrote Montgomery Schuyler, of a "motive" (i.e., a motif) from Blois (see page 274), not unlike the stair at Waddesdon inspired by one at Chateau de Chambord.[42]

On the interior, the continental fashion for non-rectangular interiors, seen in Hunt's houses since the 1860s, was evident again, their oval, part-octagonal, and squared plans in an axial grid giving variety to exterior elevations (5.35). A tapestry gallery, Biltmore's "Central Hall," extended south to a two-story, paneled library. Hunt's integration of the classical and Gothic and his time with Eugène Viollet-le-Duc were evident in the medieval-style banquet hall and gallery, both indebted to Pierrefonds in scale and decoration (5.36, 5.37a-b, 5.38b). For up-to-date convenience, Hunt specified a servant call system, telephone, hot water, heating, and refrigerators.

As the outline of Biltmore emerged, Richard wrote Catharine with master-builder hubris and humor, that the mountains were finally "just the right size and scale for the chateau!" From years of monument building and the recent Statue of Liberty, Hunt knew the challenges of scale in the vast American landscape. He and Olmsted had sited the mansion between an entrance esplanade and a steep escarpment reforested with native trees and flowering shrubs that were part of Vanderbilt's conservation program. At its base Olmsted laid out a meandering lagoon to reflect the mansion above, as water features did at chateaus in the Loire River valley (5.39). In his reconciliation of the manmade and nature, wrote Montgomery Schuyler, Hunt had made Biltmore without "limitations, not alone in cost," the true country "seat" for another American aristocrat. The house and its landscape, viewed from afar, appeared as a living engraving, evoking illustrations in chateau histories and romance novels that Hunt and his generation collected.[43]

The quaint workers' hamlet was an appurtenance of the aristocratic estate (5.40). Hunt's buildings for Vanderbilt's Biltmore Village (1900) included All Souls Episcopal Church (the Cathedral of All Souls from 1995) and parish house (1896). Using brick, pebble dash, and red tile, Hunt looked again to the Norwegian stave church tradition for All Souls'

Fig. 5.38a A. Maurice-A.-G. Ouradou, Knights of the Round Table fireplace, above left, in the bedroom of Emperor Napoléon III, Chateau de Pierrefonds, France, 1883; Colombe Clier, n.d.[39]

Fig. 5.38b Tapestry gallery fireplace, above right, Biltmore; Michael Froio, 2020

Fig. 5.39 View to Biltmore chateau, opposite, reflected in the estate's landscaped lagoon; Michael Froio, 2020

Fig. 5.40 Biltmore Village below the estate chateau, with worker cottages and Hunt's All Souls Episcopal Church (1896); V.G. Schreck, ca. 1899

entrance and to the modified cruciform plan he championed for Protestant worship (5.41a-b). In England, Hunt and Vanderbilt would have seen parish churches by revivalist architects that inspired All Souls' vaulting and deep Romanesque arches supporting a crossing tower.[44]

At Biltmore, Hunt and Olmsted availed themselves of the wealth and aesthetic sensibilities of a willing client to reconcile English and French design traditions they failed to broker during the Central Park gates debacle. For all their later cooperation and Hunt's admiration of Olmsted's Biltmore work, the New York project still loomed as unfinished business. After New York City commissioners returned in 1893 to the possibility of a monumental entrance at Fifth Avenue and Fifty-Ninth Street, Hunt saw his opening. In May the following year, when he and Olmsted would be at Biltmore together, Hunt intended to discuss "an old proposition of his as to building in Central Park...a very sore subject...," Olmsted wrote his business partner Charles Eliot, son of Harvard's president. Olmsted would have to "simply try to bring him to some compromise. I suppose you know something of his tempestuous, self-willed way of carrying on such discussion and perhaps you know that I am liable to be provoked to such a point that temper breaks...." As Olmsted suspected, Hunt had already submitted a plan for a triumphal arch to the park, but died before he could push his case to mutual agreement.[45]

The Vanderbilt houses confounded critical reception. The press played to the public's ambivalence toward big money, the morally corrupting

Fig. 5.41a All Souls
Episcopal Church,
Biltmore Village;
Michael Froio, 2020

Fig. 5.41b View from
altar to narthex;
Michael Froio, 2020

outcome of praiseworthy achievement. Professional critics and *flâneurs* found the Newport mansions over-scaled for their sites, a discord Hunt had consciously used to project his clients' social ascent. But George, like his sister-in-law Alva, also contributed to American life. Neither "a visionary Socialist nor a luxurious sybarite," wrote a New York journalist, George had improved society through "object lessons in art, architecture, agriculture, forestry, viticulture, dairying, road making, and other useful sciences...." Levi Morton, then governor of New York, concurred after a visit to North Carolina in 1896, adding that "no palaces in Europe can equal Mr. Vanderbilt's for elegance, comfort, and convenience."[46]

A guest who experienced George Vanderbilt ensconced at his seat was Henry James. In February 1905, besieged by an arctic "fury of the elements" and stricken with gout, the author wrote Edith Wharton that he was at glacial Biltmore as a guest with Richard Hunt's "little pleasant squinting" married daughter Kitty, whom he called, with mock Florentine endearment, the "Huntita." They were "two *drearissime* days from Richmond," in the "strange, colossal heartbreaking house...so gigantic & elaborate a monument to all that *isn't* socially possible" in North Carolina. Nonetheless, Biltmore seemed to be a "phenomenon (of brute *achievement*)." For the English critic Sir Edmund Gosse, James described his visit as one of "polar rigour" at a house of "high Rothschild manner, but of a size to contain two or three Mentmores or Waddesdons, the *gageure* (wager) of an imperfectly aesthetic young billionaire." As intended, George had joined the international, estate-owning class and Hunt had advanced his reputation as an architect for civilization, even if James, a denizen of the English manor and Île-de-France chateau, saw no potential for one in the war-torn South.[47]

The recognition Hunt sought for himself and his profession was acknowledged by wealthy clients. His profile in relief was at Marble House, and Alva Vanderbilt mounted Caspar Buberl's sculpture of Richard as a stone mason at the roof pinnacle of her New York chateau (see 4.9, SC.5, and 5.7b); Cornelius Vanderbilt II included Hunt's acclaimed Chicago Administration Building in an interior over-door relief at the Breakers; and for Biltmore, George Vanderbilt commissioned full-length portraits of Hunt and Olmsted by John Sargent (see 6.1), each with attributes of their profession in the tradition of old master portraiture.[48]

In a scale below the Vanderbilt palaces were Hunt's country houses for businessmen in the Romanesque style popularized by Henry Richardson, who died at forty-seven in 1886. The finest was Indian Spring (1891) in Newport, built for Englishman Joseph R. Busk, heir to a wool trade fortune

and a winner of the America's Cup (5.42, SC.9) on an ocean-view lot purchased from the estate of Hunt's brother-in-law, Charles Russell.[49]

Indian Spring exemplified Hunt's historicist method, the adaptation of another architect's work, whether period or contemporary, through Beaux-Arts planning. Anchored by tourelles framing a veranda, the arcing, rough-stone *manoir* was set into the ridge of the hill. Without the scale of Biltmore, Hunt had again responded to a dramatic site, integrating the house into a rocky landscape naturalized with native plantings by the Olmsted firm. Montgomery Schuyler praised Hunt for this integration, writing that he had achieved "Richardsonian simplicity without the Richardsonian exaggeration."[50]

~~~~~~

Hunt turned again to the Romanesque, an architecture of fortifications, for work at the US Military Academy at West Point. Since the 1870s he and his AIA colleagues had promoted independent architects to improve federal buildings and Hunt, as the Institute's president, had put his national reputation behind the Tarsney Act, signed into law in 1893. It opened federal commissions to private firms in limited competitions,

juried by independent architects, at the discretion of the office
of the Supervising Architect of the US Treasury, which had controlled
federal design since 1852.[51]

In early 1889 Congress, in response to the unrelenting criticism
of government design, elected Hunt to build a gym (1893) and an academic
hall (1895) at West Point, coordinated with existing neo-Gothic granite
buildings (5.43). The twin-towered Romanesque east façade and
buttressed sides of Hunt's gym, supporting an iron and glass skylight over
a central exercise room, was related to George Post's acclaimed 1869 gym
at Princeton. West Academic Hall (later Pershing Barracks), in contrast, was
a fortress, its symmetrical masses relieved by a machicolated cornice and
clock tower. The west façade, reached through a central passage, formed

Fig. 5.43 West
Academic Hall (1895),
fortress architecture
for the US Military
Academy, West Point,
New York; Michael
Froio, 2019

a side of the academy quadrangle dominated by the crenelated Central Barracks (ca. 1851).[52]

The success of these projects earned the Hunt firm a library renovation and guardhouse at West Point, finished posthumously. Hunt's only government building commission in Washington, DC itself was the US Naval Observatory (1893) on the grounds of the vice president's house (5.44). Hunt and his assistant Maurice Fornachon struggled with bureaucrats and contractors over program and budget. Defined by equatorial instruments, an electric generator, and transit circles, the completed row followed the arrangement of the 1844 observatory in Washington's Foggy Bottom. Rational in their functional aesthetic, the linked structures were an assemblage of severe classical forms in dressed and battered marble, the telescope block detailed with Egyptian motifs referencing Claudius Ptolemy.[53]

The observatory represented a new phase in American architecture as the nation, in response to immigration and the Colonial Revival, embraced republican classicism. In 1870 the United States was a nation of family farms and towns, with under a quarter of its thirty-eight million citizens living in cities, powered by immigrant labor and new technologies creating a prosperous middle class and the industrial millionaire. That percentage nearly doubled before World War I, as the population rose two-fold. This rocket growth made America an international economic power, but urban centers, of rundown tenements along treeless streets, prone to catastrophic fire and riots, had not kept pace with Europe. Now the nascent movement for art and architecture civilizing American life took a civic turn, when Chicago's 1893 World's Columbian Exposition of classical buildings launched the City Beautiful movement.[54]

In 1886 George Bancroft and a committee of the American Historical Association lobbied Congress for an international celebration of the upcoming four-hundredth anniversary of the "discovery of America" by Christopher Columbus. That year Senator George F. Hoar of Massachusetts proposed a world's fair for 1892, setting America as the North Star of world commerce, a role played by Britain and France at fairs before the Civil War. Hunt and Frederick Law Olmsted joined the effort to secure the celebration for New York, but ultimately the House of Representatives awarded the exposition to Chicago, believing the city would help keep politics out of the event.[55]

Olmsted was lead planner for the fair's 690 acres on the Windy City's south side. Crippled by gout, Hunt hesitated to assume a managing role, but on coaxing from his competitor and former student George Post,

U.S. Naval Observatory from South East.

reluctantly agreed to become president of the Board of Architects, grimly joking that the demands were likely to "kill" him with pain. Promoting the celebration, Hunt told the AIA that national conditions for monuments refining American culture, like those in Europe, were improving due to "large fortunes; to the great variety of building materials; to the excellency of our mechanics, etc.," all developments benefiting Hunt's own practice. Consequently, the fair's objective would be a temporary White City, an incarnation of modern antiquities affirming the nation's political foundation in Greece and Rome, and a demonstration of what professional architects and engineers could achieve empowered by big money and public faith in the arts.[56]

Fig. 5.44 US Naval Observatory (1893), Washington, DC; ca. 1895

Despite encouraging new architecture, Hunt sustained his belief that the classical canon was foundational. Not surprisingly given his mission to educate and inform, he had supported the founding in 1888 of MIT's *Technology Architectural Review*, a folio of student Beaux-Arts-style drawings. He advised its editor to "emphasize the resources of classical architecture, and its influence as a basis for all design." At century's close, it was "questionable whether too much had not been already sacrificed of late to picturesqueness in architecture, and whether the frivolity with which such effects may be secured, does not encourage distaste for the more serious study of the highest form of art." Hunt was foreseeing the decline of Romantic architecture and the rise of academicism, in part due to the training he had promoted. But hemmed in by client expectations and decades of École planning and representation, he continued his eclectic practice.[57]

Hunt's contribution to the Chicago fair was the visitors' Administration Building sited between the train depot and Court of Honor, a harmony in Renaissance geometry, its dome visible throughout the fairgrounds (5.45, 5.46a-b, and page 4). Four square pavilions projected from an octagonal gathering hall, ornamented with soaring allegorical figures to the arts and sciences sculpted by Karl Bitter. It was Hunt's response to the Palais Garnier and a Prix de Rome mausoleum (1854) by Hunt's École classmate, J.-A.-Émile Vaudremer. The young muralist William de Leftwich Dodge painted the interior of the dome, 315 feet in circumference, a neo-Baroque *Glorification of the Arts and Sciences* inspired by murals at the Paris Opera.[58]

Rising above the fair's lagoon, a reimagining of Venice's Santa Maria della Salute and St. Peter's in Rome, the Administration Building was the "gem and crown" of an American agora, the culmination of Hunt's thirty-year support of architecture and its allied arts. S.C. de Soissons found no originality at all, the fair exhibiting none of the genius of Paris' 1889 exposition. But Alfred Bloor boasted of American ingenuity. "Ho! Johnny Crapaud [toad, i.e. frog, slang for the French], you *Ecole* fellows think that we in this new country are still barbarians or, worse, babies in the Fine Arts. But just look at our faultless Renaissance—at our Court of Honor and all the rest where, fifty years ago, there was only a desert swamp, tenanted by skunks and prairie dogs." Montgomery Schuyler considered Hunt's temple to American utility and function "classic only in letter," not "in spirit.... An alert and bristling pyramid...as characteristically Parisian of the second Empire, as Mr. Garnier's Opera-house itself." The similarities were not just architectural. Hunt had integrated his secular basilica into

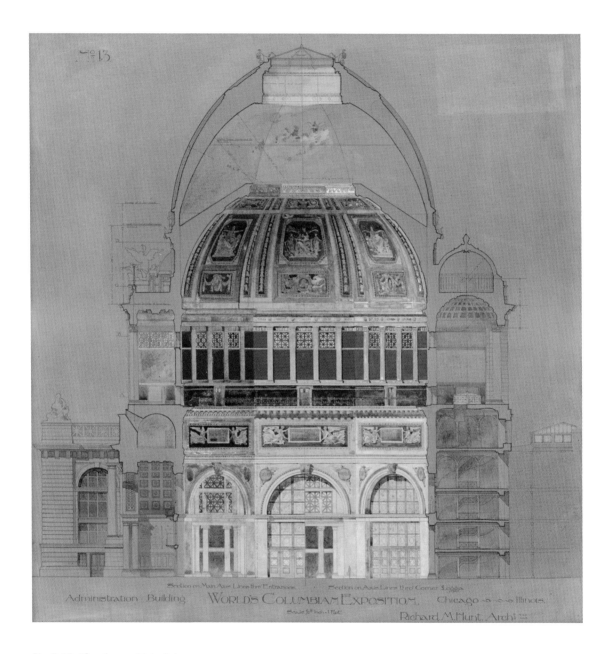

Fig. 5.45 "Section on Main Axis
Lines thro' Entrances; Section on
Axis Lines thr' Corner Loggia,"
Administration Building; Hunt
office, ca. 1892

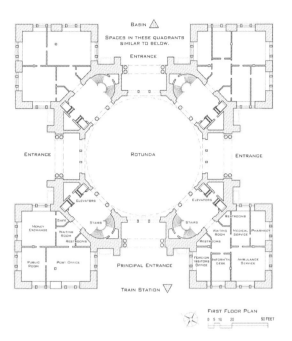

Fig. 5.46a Administration Building plan, above left; James B. Garrison, AutoCAD, 2022

Fig. 5.46b Administration Building, oil modello, above right, for dome's interior mural, *Glorification of the Arts and Sciences*; William de Leftwich Dodge, 1892

an urban plan, maximizing circulation at the fair's entrance while anchoring the axis of the Grand Basin, as the Paris Opera, surrounded on three sides, rises at the end of its avenue.[59]

Hobbled by gout and fatigue, Hunt traveled with Catharine by private rail car in October 1892 for the fair's dedication. Labor unrest in Chicago slums was endemic to the industrial city, and demonstrators, assumed by their appearance, wrote Catharine, to be "Russian and Polish Jews," delayed their ride to the hotel. The Hunts had each contributed to the fair's success in ways exemplary of their shared commitment to the arts. Richard served on the honorary committee of the architecture exhibit in the Fine Arts Building and Catharine lent decorative arts to the New York State pavilion, joining Elizabeth [Mrs. Henry] Marquand and Jules Allard Fils. "Mrs. Vanderbilt" loaned an embroidery made for Marie Antoinette, displayed in a case of its own.[60]

The exposition, founded in the moral philosophy that classical beauty inspires, launched the American City Beautiful movement and galvanized authorization of the Tarsney Act. "Modern civic art," wrote urbanist Charles Mulford Robinson, "desires the beauty of towns and cities not for beauty's sake, but for the greater happiness, health, and comfort of the citizens." Energized by Chicago's white spectacle, civic leaders returned home to organize building campaigns for cleaner, safer cities. Their new columned courthouses, municipal offices, capitols, and libraries in Beaux-Arts classicism embodied the beauty of a civilized and civilizing America. To the annoyance of Louis Sullivan and others moving architecture away from European precedents, classicism put what Hunt first described to Ralph Waldo Emerson as "Greek grandeurs" within national reach. A technological, agricultural, and manufacturing powerhouse, the United States would now join history as a great republic dedicated to the arts.[61]

~~~~~~~

Europe, once again, took note of Hunt's achievement. In recognition of his long career and Administration Building, RIBA awarded him their Royal Gold Medal, won in prior years by publisher César Daly and Charles Garnier, whose ceremony Hunt attended in 1886. Together with Catharine, Richard crossed the Atlantic in June 1893 for the Institute's honors. Garnier and Honoré Daumet were unable to attend, but the latter's praises were read at the dinner. Without commenting on his works, they noted Hunt's association with Hector Lefuel and suggested that American *and* French architecture were being honored. Attendees commended the "Brunelleschi of the United States" for his William K. Vanderbilt house, the pedestal of the Statue of Liberty, and the Lenox Library, all monuments to American progress indebted to French design. But the introductory remarks by the Institute's president laid bare the envy Hunt and his generation faced as they surpassed the "parent home."[62]

> The art of a new country is necessarily devoid of the native inspiration and guidance to be found in the history of centuries and in ancient monuments, which are the glory of older countries. In the case of America, the possession of boundless resources and of illimitable wealth—the rapid development of which almost appalls us—without the accompaniment of the experience of the past to guide lavish indulgence, presents a condition which, in respect of art, is beset with temptation and pregnant with danger, for without the restraining curb of necessity broad and easy is the road from luxury to extravagance, from liberty to license.

To his British peers, Hunt's achievement had been to "define or limit the influence...[of] the early masters of the arts" in New World design. Under his guidance, America was now determining, at a judicious pace, an architecture appropriate to its youth while still acknowledging the invaluable artistic leadership and "glory" of Europe's past.[63]

Hunt's acceptance speech was digressive and long-winded, grounded in themes of his career—the adaptation of the classical canon, the necessity of new materials, the need for monuments signifying progress, and the poor quality of federal buildings. Reflecting the difficulties architects faced when adapting precedents for new design, he noted that he and Lefuel had made the Ionic order too "slim" for the three-story façade of the Pavillon de la Bibliothèque; and that though "iron construction, glass and tiles" permitted the "monumental look" required of world fairs, only in Chicago had this effect been achieved. As for his own Administration Building, it was an "object-lesson for the United States Government."[64]

After London, Catharine and Richard traveled to Paris to deal with "demands" by Ogden Goelet and Cornelius Vanderbilt II, and to meet with dealers selling "boiserie" for client commissions. When gout hindered his mobility again, they sailed home in late July. Hunt was now exemplary of the individual achievement still possible in a young democracy, despite the oppressive inequities of the Gilded Age. When "a man is singled out as the 'most worthy exponent of his profession,'" wrote New York's *Sun*, "and receive[s] a medal won by his own unaided abilities and acquirements, all who associated with him, by ties of kindred or country must feel that they, too, are honored in the tribute paid to him...."[65]

In the 1850s and 1860s, Hunt had practiced professional architecture and shaped its future through new institutions. He approached the City Beautiful similarly, as architect and consultant for private and state commissions, gathering end-of-career accolades. He was an architect for the Columbia College campus at 115th Street, ultimately an amalgam of several plans (1893), and Charles F. McKim (see P.12) enlisted him as "pioneer, missionary and general slugger" when they launched the American School of Architecture in Rome (the American Academy from 1897) for a graduate program on par with France's Prix de Rome.[66]

Lifelong proponents for integration of the arts, Hunt and his generation founded societies dedicated to bringing murals, stained glass, stone, and iron work to civic commissions, the Chicago fair furthering their efforts. In 1887 Hunt was elected to the Architectural League of New York, founded by young architects in 1881, and in 1893 became a founder and first president of the city's Municipal Art Society, open to men and women, dedicated to urban beautification through "adequate sculptural and pictorial decorations for the public buildings and parks in the City of New York." The same year, he and John Ward, with Augustus

Saint-Gaudens and Daniel Chester French, founded the related National Sculpture Society.[67]

Since childhood, Hunt had known the Brahmin world of Charles Eliot, Boston Latin graduate and transformative president of Harvard. In 1892 the educator awarded Richard an honorary LL.D. degree. Catharine sat devotedly with artist and William Morris Hunt student Sarah Wyman Whitman and Marianne Brimmer listening to her husband's acceptance speech, appropriately given at Gothic-style Memorial Hall (1874), designed by his students William Ware and Henry Van Brunt. Before the young governor of Massachusetts, William E. Russell, and seven hundred alumni, Richard began peevishly, noting that architecture did not need a degree to "dignify" it as a profession. He touted the upcoming Chicago fair and its application of new materials and engineering, superior to prior efforts by Europe, notwithstanding America's "simply abominable" national architecture. He concluded by supporting increased remuneration to government architects as a "desideratum for better public buildings."[68]

A year after the award that had no doubt helped secure the commission, President Eliott asked Hunt to design the William Hayes Fogg Museum of Harvard College (1895), funded by the merchant's widow in 1892. The building committee included Martin Brimmer, then president of Boston's Museum of Fine Arts. The Fogg collection was educational, consisting mainly of casts and photographs of master works. Private donors were encouraged, but with the caveat that donated collections might be exhibited elsewhere. Brimmer considered the city's museum, with superior space and collections, a Harvard institution sharing a mission to educate.[69]

The Fogg at Harvard Yard faced Cambridge Street, north of Gothic-style Appleton Chapel (1858) (5.47). From the outset, Hunt warned that lack of funding doomed the ambitious project. The outcome was a classical marble block with a semi-circular auditorium at the rear. After Hunt's death, the critical response was sharp. Cousin of Harvard's president and its first professor of art history (appointed 1874), the Ruskinian Charles Eliot Norton spoke to undergraduates on civilization in America, including the Fogg in his review. The museum was "beneath contempt" and another sign that "architecture was not an art" at Harvard. Acoustical flaws rendered his lectures inaudible and structural elements were neither truthful nor "real," made of iron, but "covered with a false covering." Overall, the museum and other eclectic university buildings reflected "a low state of intellectual development."[70]

Hunt's Harvard museum and Washington observatory were indebted to the German classicism he had commended in the 1870s, but their

Fig. 5.47 William Hayes Fogg Museum (1895), Harvard University, Cambridge, Massachusetts, an art gallery and lecture hall; ca. 1895[41]

Fig. 5.48 The Metropolitan Museum of Art (1902), New York City; Hunt's neoclassical Fifth Avenue wing overwhelmed the museum's first building, a Gothic Revival gallery (1880); Irving Underhill, photochrom postcard (detail), ca. 1902

spareness did not realize the promise the world had experienced in his heralded Administration Building. In 1894 Henry Marquand, as board president of the Metropolitan Museum, made this achievement possible. He appointed Hunt head of the museum's building committee and commissioned a master plan for the Metropolitan's expansion. Its first project would be a Fifth Avenue entrance wing, funded in part by a million dollars from New York, authorized by Governor Levi Morton, certainly with Hunt's encouragement. The completed museum would become a neoclassical temple in the City Beautiful, along with the Brooklyn

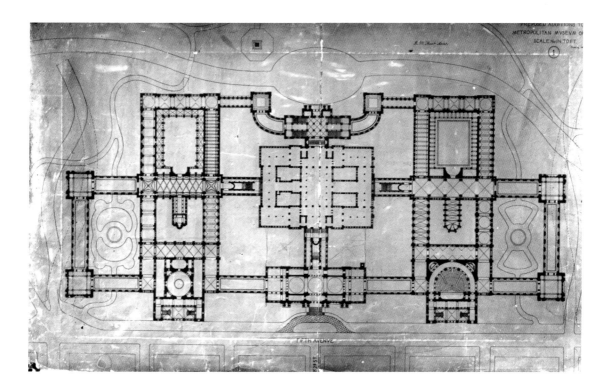

Museum of Fine Arts (1897) and the Art Institute of Chicago (built for the exposition).[71]

The long-serving museum director Colonel Luigi Palma di Cesnola, considered by Hunt the wealthy patron's "toady," recalled that the architect intended the entrance to be his lasting "monument." Hunt had waited two decades for this recognition, as a museum founder, board member, and donor. Though never the Metropolitan's architect through expansion years, he had served on the review committee of its reviled 1872 gallery, his objections going unheeded. "I alone formally protested [Calvert Vaux's plan] & it was not until the building was well-nigh completed that the Board recognized that I was right," he wrote museum president and collector John Johnston in 1884.[72]

Hunt presented the Metropolitan's Executive Committee plans and sketches in April 1895 (5.49b). Returning to the Renaissance geometry of his Chicago pavilion, he imagined four wings to engulf Vaux's brick and granite museum. A triumph of the neoclassical over the Gothic, the new entrance along Fifth, when finished, was American in its undecorated limestone blocks and window pediments, its pairs of two-story columns and never-built heroic sculptures by Karl Bitter showing the long reach of the Louvre in Hunt's work (see 1.17). Inside, three saucer domes were high above arches on engaged piers, linked by column screens, a plan derived from antiquity's tepidarium architecture, an established source for eclectic civic buildings, its scale ennobling public space (5.49a). Hunt knew the Baths of Caracalla since his first trip to Rome in 1844 and from the work by many in his Parisian circle and Italy's celebrity archaeologist Rodolfo Lanciani, married to a Rhode Islander. Not surprisingly, in light of Hunt's attention to museum architecture, the classical proposal by Karl Friedrich Schinkel for Berlin's Friedrichswerder Church (1824) was an inspiration.[73]

The Metropolitan Museum, the Chicago Exposition, and the Vanderbilt and Astor projects took a toll on their architect, Catharine finding Richard's "wonderful vitality" now diminished. In recent years, he had traveled to Boston, Newport, Asheville, West Point, and to oil-rich Cleveland where the Flora Stone Mather College for Women built his Queen Anne academic hall. Only Esther was still living at home while her brother Herbert struggled through Connecticut's Pomfret boarding school. Dick was an architect in his father's office, and Joseph, after graduating from Harvard in 1892 and attending architecture classes at Columbia, entered the École in 1895. Kitty was living in Washington, DC with her husband, a paymaster in the US Navy.

Hunt's obligations to clients and colleagues continued unabated in the spring of 1895. In March he attended the opening of Boston's public library by Charles McKim, an American Renaissance landmark indebted to Henri Labrouste's Bibliothèque Sainte-Geneviève that had influenced Hunt's design of New York's Lenox Library twenty-five years before. By May Hunt was back at Biltmore, sitting for his Sargent portrait (6.1), and in early June, at the insistence of Alva Vanderbilt, he attended the wedding of her niece in Massachusetts. Always anxious to make a train, he rode on a carriage box in the rain so that by the time he reached Newport the following day, a chill had laid him prostrate with gout.

Over the following weeks Richard convalesced in Hill-Top's second-floor morning room (see 5.6a), overseeing his thriving practice and insisting that Catharine, as a dutiful parent, attend Herbert's graduation. A specialist in Philadelphia came north, and after examination, predicted that America's architect had years ahead. But at the end of July, Catharine summoned her oldest son from New York. The day after his arrival, July 31, 1895, Richard Morris Hunt died at home of what *The New York Times* reported as "a complication of diseases."[74]

A widow after thirty-four years of marriage, Catharine held Richard's memorial service on August 3 at Newport's white-steepled Episcopal

Trinity Church, down the hill from Hill-Top Cottage. There Alva, George, and Cornelius Vanderbilt II joined family and friends. Buttresses of his life—attorney Joseph Choate and studio assistant Maurice Fornachon, collectors/clients Martin Brimmer and Henry Marquand, and architects Charles McKim and George Post—were pallbearers at the family plot in Island Cemetery, the town's Gilded Age burial place with monuments and mausoleums by Richard Hunt (see 4.26). At his grave, the Hunt family laid a massive ledger stone in polished black granite, similar to the one Richard designed for his brother William. On its face was inscribed: "Richard Morris Hunt / born Oct 31 1827 / died July 31 1895 / *Laborare est Orare* ["to Work is to Pray"]. This aphorism from the Rule of St. Benedict is a motto of Freemasonry, the mystic order that set the cornerstone of the Statue of Liberty, and was known to Americans through Thomas Carlyle's influential *Past and Present* (1843). Its sentiment succinctly expressed Hunt's prodigious life, grounded in work on behalf of community and the greater good.[75]

Afterword

Richard Morris Hunt lived by expectations of his class and civic-minded family to lead America toward civilization (6.1). Sustaining a protean momentum through war, riots, financial boom and bust, poor health and family tragedy, he enlisted friends and patrons to found institutions to "refine" America with education and classical beauty. Personally, every contact, job, trip, and speech led to more of the same, establishing his authority as architect, decorator, collector, and art advisor contributing to an American renaissance.

On news of his death, obituaries of the nation's dean of architecture ran across the Western world. They were remarkable for their shared perception of Hunt's long and varied career, lauding his dedication to advancing French design and enumerating his famous works, without actually commending any. Germany considered only Henry Richardson comparable in stature among the "New World" architects. For France, all roads led back to Paris. Over forty years, Hunt had, through "his professorship, his works, and his high social standing," made the École "methods" and "trends" in French art dominant in American social and artistic circles. At home, the editorial board of *The New York Times* considered he had "discharged the duty which every man is said to owe to his profession, not only by his constant labors for its welfare...but also by endeavoring to impart at home the professional knowledge which he had acquired abroad...." He believed that a cadre of trained artists and an educated public would build the enlightened democracy hard won by his ancestors a generation before.[1]

Architects concurred with the *Times*, having to reconcile Hunt's celebrity with his architectural practice of uneven success, not unexpected considering he had navigated in a world of transition, from merchant wealth to industrial dominance, from Protestant colonialism to immigrant diversity, from the Classical/Gothic divide into eclecticism and its implications. The Griswold house, the Lenox Library, and Alva Vanderbilt's New York castle foregrounded structure and rational planning on American soil. The Tenth Street Studio building, Tribune tower, and Stuyvesant apartments contributed to architectural types of the modern city. This ranging practice and his institutional engagements made Richard Hunt, in the words of a critic, the most "renowned" and "conspicuous" architect at "home and abroad...," though not a "representative architect of America

Fig. 6.1 Portrait of Richard Hunt at Biltmore's entrance terrace, shortly before his death, commissioned by George Vanderbilt; John Singer Sargent, 1895

in the originality of his genius." Hunt had promoted and incorporated new technologies to achieve light, air, and convenience. But he had been too "refined and scholarly in his habits of thought," too devoted to "European culture," too adhering to precedent and his training to develop a language of his own. Never "novel or inventive," wrote architect Peter Wight in 1895, Hunt could "not be compared to John W. Root, or even to H.H. Richardson, and several men now living." In conversation with French architecture throughout his career, Hunt "never laid claim to originality," believing no "modern work" could surpass the ancient world.[2]

Despite their origins in European history and the work of his contemporaries, Hunt's buildings were individualistic, reflecting his generation's faith in architecture to convey meaning through association. This Romanticism contributed to Hunt's reputational decline when national classicism, representing American democracy and progress, superseded the "servile imitation" and "eccentric originality" of eclectic design.[3]

If Hunt's exteriors and interiors were too romantic and indebted to precedent for the next generation, in the realm of spectacle his work transcended. He admired "the great monuments of all great periods of art," and had learned that a Renaissance integration of architecture and decoration, of sculpture and painting, could signify global status. He brought this understanding and his sensibility for the ornamented and theatrical to the American city and countryside, from his Metropolitan Museum entrance to the Statue of Liberty pedestal, Yorktown column, and chateaus that kept French architecture at the forefront of American design for forty years. Through this colossal work Hunt gave expression to the pursuit of achievement in accumulated riches, to the simultaneous devotion to private wellbeing and public betterment, and to the moral right to unbridled self-expression that make his monuments a defining architecture of the Gilded Age. In their daring and scale, they were inspirational and American—to students and architects, to clients seeking to elaborate their lives, to Booker T. Washington lifting his world from the ravages of the Civil War, and to George Vanderbilt, wrestling from the nation's hard-won peace the potentialities for art, preservation, and husbandry in a rural utopia.[4]

Determinant in Hunt's privileged and aspirational world were the salt-of-the-earth tradesmen who realized and then maintained the stone buildings he designed (6.2). In a moment rare for the qualities expressed and the risk articulating them entailed, the "Biltmore Chateau" bricklayers, carpenters, plumbers, stone cutters, and wood carvers broke their customary silence in a memorial statement they wrote for Catharine Hunt. It spoke to their lives among the privileged few and gratitude for

Fig. 6.2 Biltmore laborers on temporary railroad spur to the chateau's construction site; 1890

her husband's "generosity, sympathy, and services in behalf of the worthy laboring man of all classes...," his "great fame" and "wealth" never leading him "to be forgetful, indifferent, or careless of the rights and feelings of his fellow men and laborers...." To Hunt they owed "the elevation of their trades and arts to the position which they now hold in the ranks of the great army of skilled workmen."[5]

Women too were integral to Richard Hunt's success, and though known through diaries and memoirs, their contributions to the careers of sons, brothers, and husbands remain in the shadows. As the family's standard bearer for public engagement, Jane Leavitt Hunt brought her Unitarian faith and courage to the lives of her children. While grooming her daughter for the role of dutiful sister and wife, she gave her sons a European education, its breadth and liberality preparing them to compete in an industrializing world.

Alva Vanderbilt was singular in Hunt's practice for her vocal support of design as both a societal benefit and totem of family standing. Persevering in a male-dominated world, her life became a paradox: a leader of the super rich who divorced her husband in 1895 when divorce was a scandal, she embraced "middle-class" values promoting home and family. She championed independence and self-sufficiency for women through the suffrage movement, but in her unrelenting reach for social inclusion sold her only daughter into a loveless marriage with England's impoverished Duke of Marlborough. Alva was idiosyncratic for her choice of French architectural landmarks which Hunt transformed into American buildings. Her Gothic Hôtel de Cluny on Fifth Avenue initiated Hunt's chateau practice, its massing and integrated decoration being harbingers of American style. Her Trianon *Atlantique* a decade later brought him into the coming fashion for academic classicism practiced by a generation of École-trained architects. Through her support of interior design and fine arts at home, Alva extended the domestic prerogatives of women into the professional realm, leading the way for Isabella Stewart Gardner and Arabella D. Huntington as collectors and institutional founders in Boston and Los Angeles.[6]

Catharine Hunt, whose early years are unrecorded, had wealth and social position that might have confined her to motherhood and spousal duty grounded in faith. She and Richard were attentive parents, raising their children in the Eurocentric world foundational to the American culture they were fostering. They focused on their three sons' educations, sending all to boarding schools and Dick and Joseph to Ivy League colleges and the École, while preparing Kitty and Esther for marriage. But at a time when women sought independence, Catharine was also a public figure in concert with her husband. As Richard's collections contributed to his practice and reputation, so too did Catharine's collecting of antique textiles, fans, and jewelry deepen her engagement as a patron of the arts. Together, they were a model of private interests furthering civic good through the era's philanthropy movements.[7]

Living on in failing health after Richard's death, Catharine died of pneumonia while touring Luxor, Egypt in 1909, receiving her own obituary in *The New York Times* with a tribute by the Hunts' long-time attorney, Joseph Choate. She had been "a refined and noble character, of a most pleasing personality, of a truly sympathetic nature," her "placid, serene, and gentle" temperament the "complement of [Richard's] fiery and exuberant nature," making them "a simply perfect couple." Her life of "good works," of "fun, but free from frivolities," was a "splendid example to the educated women of New York." She was buried next to her husband at Newport's Island Cemetery, her grave marked by a polished granite slab matching his own, its inscription capturing her welcoming spirit, "Thou Shalt Love Thy Neighbour as Thyself" (Matthew 22:39). Though finding religion "impersonal" later in life, she had continued to work on behalf of the Episcopal Church and the Society of Decorative Art, but her enduring legacy was the memorialization of Richard's life.[8]

In its notice of his death, *The New York Times* reported that "Mr. Hunt possessed the finest architectural library in America, and had a peerless collection of casts, drawings, and photographs. These, it is believed, are willed to a public institution." Catharine devotedly assembled Richard's print collections and hired a book restorer who, over fifteen years as secretary, conservationist, and cataloger, preserved his books and thousands of drawings, photographs, and clippings. Catharine donated these materials to the AIA, retaining his art and remaining cast collection for family inheritance (see 2.3). From this fifty-year archive and letters and reminiscences, Catharine wrote her unpublished biography, one among several produced at century's end to secure the reputations of artist relatives whose moralizing paintings and sculpture faced oblivion as art-for-art's-sake took hold.[9]

Catharine and Richard's oldest sons were architects and contributors to the professional societies founded and promoted by their father. Dick was president of the Architectural League of New York and the New York chapter of the AIA. Joseph was elected president of the Municipal Art Society, dying in 1924, followed by Dick in 1931. Esther Hunt Woolsey died in 1901 at twenty-six in London, her mother donating a stained-glass window in her memory to Grace Episcopal Church at New York's University Place. The youngest child, Herbert, died in France in 1960, and Kitty Hunt lived until 1963. They were heirs to their parents' arts collections, which subsequent generations have been selling in private and public sales.

Dick continued his father's firm until 1901 when he and Joseph, also an École attendee, renamed it Hunt & Hunt, a partnership no doubt encouraged by their father who had known the dynastic enterprises of French architects, some of whom worked in America. Until the dissolution of the firm at Joseph's death, they practiced a ponderous revivalism for their father's clients and their descendants, competing with École-trained architects at Delano & Aldrich (founded 1903) and Warren & Wetmore (founded 1898), a firm joined by Emmanuel Masqueray after Richard's death. Dick oversaw the completion of Biltmore and the Fogg, but his singular contribution to his father's legacy was realizing the Metropolitan Museum's new entrance. Plans were incomplete in 1895 when trustees questioned Dick's ability to carry through the transformative project. Anticipating controversy and in control of her husband's estate, Catharine wrote to museum president Henry Marquand in 1896. She assured him of her husband's confidence in their oldest son and politely insisted that the Metropolitan's new building was not only merited for a museum founder, but as a "memorial to his genius." In 1898, three years after Hunt's initial presentation, the project was finally under construction. [10]

When the Metropolitan Fifth Avenue wing opened in December 1902, critics praised its columned façade and domed hall for their "proportions and massive simplicity" (see 5.48, 5.49a-b). At the reception, Mayor Seth Low spoke on themes that had shaped American culture. The museum had become an institution bridging the past and present, the outcome of work by dedicated citizen-patrons inspired by Old World Paris and London, its republican incarnation due to the late Richard Hunt and Henry Marquand, who had died in February the year of the unveiling. [11]

As the Metropolitan plans were in development, the valorizing of Richard Morris Hunt took a public turn. In the closing months of 1895, Catharine and Dick curated exhibitions of his work as the Municipal Art Society of New York spearheaded a memorial to add their founder and first president to the city's collection of honorary statues, several of which Hunt and John Ward had designed. The selection of sculptor Daniel Chester French and architect Bruce Price was uncontentious, but the choice of site stirred debate. City Hall Park, the site of Hunt's Tribune building, was far downtown. Along Fifth Avenue were his first and last city mansions, the Alva Vanderbilt and Caroline Astor houses. At Eighty-First Street was the Metropolitan Museum, his final civic work. Between these houses and the museum was the architect's Lenox Library. Despite controversy that Central Park had no memorial to its own architects—Frederick Law Olmsted and Calvert Vaux—the selected site was the park's perimeter wall at East Seventieth Street, on axis with the library. [12]

The memorial, funded by a committee of Hunt's clients and colleagues, underwent the Beaux-Arts planning he had introduced to America forty years before. Designs that various architects had submitted to an 1874 Institut de France competition for a monument to composer Gioachino Rossini provided inspiration for the Hunt memorial. The Municipal Art Society settled on a granite exedra, its bench below a screen of columns, anchored into the wall of Central Park and facing the Lenox Library (6.3). Panels above the seat were inscribed with the names of eleven donor

Fig. 6.3 Richard Hunt memorial by Daniel Chester French and Bruce Price, Central Park, New York City; dedication day, October 31, 1898

institutions, including ones Hunt had founded, joined, and managed over forty years.

Above this roster of the art establishment, French mounted his bronze bust of Hunt as America's diplomat for culture. On its pedestal the Municipal Art Society engraved: "To Richard Morris Hunt / October 31, 1828 / July 31, 1895 / in recognition / of his services to / the cause of art / in America / this memorial was erected 1898 by / the Art Societies / of New York." In 1901, French finally installed bronze muses on piers terminating the exedra. "Art" held a painter's palette, sculptor's mallet, and the torso of Dionysus from the Parthenon; "Architecture" to the north embraced a model of Hunt's Administration Building at the Chicago Exposition. At a time of the City Beautiful movement, the art establishment had reduced Hunt's forty-year, eclectic practice to a career advancing the classical canon.[13]

The Central Park memorial asserted the Municipal Art Society's authority as cultural arbiter and deftly conveyed what its funding committee considered relevant about Richard Hunt. Beginning the year of his death, the society's secretary, architect Edward H. Bell, solicited

Fig. 6.4 Laurel leaf from wreath laid at the Hunt memorial, sent by Catharine Hunt to George Vanderbilt, October 31, 1898

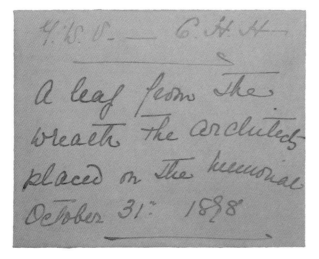

donations cloaked in a nuanced appeal. "Hunt's pre-eminence in the movement which he may be said to have started forty years ago for the elevation of architecture and the union of it with the sister arts of sculpture and painting, and which he carried forward unweariedly until his death," was worthy of their money. In paying tribute to the "services of a fellow laborer," Bell concluded, "we shall be doing ourselves honor." In this, Hunt as architect/artist receded and Hunt as a "general slugger" for the Society's mission to unite the visual arts in civic commissions emerged.[14]

On the seventy-first anniversary of Hunt's putative birth, October 31, 1898, power brokers and cultural illuminati gathered along Fifth Avenue to dedicate the Hunt memorial, while Catharine and her daughters watched the ceremony from the balcony of the Lenox Library. She had witnessed her husband's critical success in the library's design and his humiliation over the gateways to Central Park. As she looked out to the yellowing leaves of that fall afternoon, George Post presented the Richard Hunt memorial to the city while members of the Art Artisans and AIA placed laurel wreaths at the plinth of the bronze bust. Catharine commended the modest dignity of the proceedings and the architectural ensemble as "heroic." At close of day, she mailed George Vanderbilt a laurel leaf from the dedication as a memento of their friendship (6.4), writing later that "next to his sons [Richard] loved you and for that as much as other reasons you will always be very near & dear to me." In turn, Vanderbilt, Hunt's student and fellow civilizer, honored Catharine with a tower window in Biltmore's All Souls Episcopal Church (see 5.41a). For its transept he commissioned a stained-glass panel in memory of Richard, paired with one to his collaborator and sometimes nemesis, Frederick Law Olmsted.[15]

As modern architecture pushed the primacy of structure and technology over precedent and representation, Hunt the architect vanished into footnote obscurity. Historicist buildings were now mere farragoes of style and eclecticism, a practice devoid of imagination. An exception to this techno-centricity was historian Henry-Russell Hitchcock Jr., who reassessed Hunt as creatively venturesome for his earliest cottages, unromantic in their structural articulation. With an irony befitting the vicissitudes of fashion, this work made Hunt the predecessor to Richardson as the progenitor of architecture that was expressive of its time through form and structure. Now the Breakers was not "merely a local monument," but the "acme of its style and of its age." Its architect, wrote Hitchcock, "seems to have known that he was creating a prime symbol of a plutocratic way of life," of "fantastic and useless expense," of the "glamour of Hollywood with that of the Riviera and Palm Beach...."[16]

Progressive views of the Gilded Age furthered the implosion of Hunt's reputation, some believing his over-civilized society drained the existential from daily life while others condemned his storied mansions as displays of "conspicuous consumption." Denying Alva Vanderbilt's assurance that public reception of her family's houses was submissive gratitude, this moralizing condemnation had been decades in the making. In 1878, the year Hunt began her Fifth Avenue chateau, *The Atlantic Monthly* reported that the lower classes were threatening society's acceptance of fine architecture. They saw "works of art and instruments of high culture, with all the possessions and surroundings of people of wealth and refinement, as causes and symbols of the laborer's poverty and degradation, and therefore as things to be hated."[17]

Wealth responded to this proletarian descent through new institutions. After Hunt secured state funds to cover expenses, the Metropolitan Museum, following years of resistance by "wealthy, influential, learned people," opened on a Sunday for the first time, May 31, 1891, to accommodate the American worker. Director Luigi Palma di

Cesnola reported to the museum's board, including Richard Hunt, that the public arrived imagining collections as "specimens to be seen in the Dime Museums on the Bowery" and "fully expecting to see freaks and monstrosities similar to those found there. Many visitors took the liberty of handling every object within reach; some went to the length of marring, scratching, and breaking articles unprotected by glass; a few proved to be pickpockets." Consequently, a donor rescinded a bequest as the museum was now "burdened" with more visitors without a compensating increase in revenue. But the Metropolitan soon returned to the established premise that art brought social enlightenment, concluding that the visitors' character markedly improved after a few months, becoming "respectable, law abiding, and intelligent." By 1903 the deferential museum-goer could experience the private "possessions and surroundings of people of wealth" by visiting the jade collection of investor Heber R. Bishop, installed in a reproduction of his Louis XV-style Fifth Avenue ballroom, designed in 1894 by Hunt and Allard and compared with rooms at Versailles and Sanssouci in Potsdam. Seemingly, Hunt and his generation had achieved their goal: the museum had regally institutionalized the taste of wealth for the edification of the underclass.[18]

Hunt's reputational decline had enduring consequences. In 1911 steel magnate Henry Clay Frick, dismissed as an "iconoclast" by Catharine, razed the Lenox Library to build his house-museum (today The Frick Collection). This outcome was the result of New York State permitting trustees to break the trust agreements of the Lenox and Astor libraries to combine their collections at the 1911 Forty-Second Street New York Public Library, a fact already known to insiders who attended the dedication of the Hunt memorial. The fate of the Lenox was followed by the demolition of the Tenth Street Studio building, the Stuyvesant apartments, the Tribune tower, and Hunt's most enduring critical success, the Alva and William K. Vanderbilt house on Fifth Avenue. Hunt's architectural legacy was victim to the very idea he had himself sanctioned, the leveling of the past for the sake of future progress.[19]

Liberated from the moral verities of the Victorian era, architectural historians in the 1980s reassessed Hunt's aesthetic and technological range. Their writings contributed to the preservation of his remaining legacy, with surviving buildings repurposed or preserved as museums. After years of the antidemocratic clubbiness that some in his generation had always feared, organizations he founded or supported—the AIA, the Municipal Art Society, and others—now respond to twenty-first-century demands unimaginable to Hunt and his society. The Metropolitan Museum of Art remains a force for world culture, welcoming millions of global visitors, but its founding legacies came under scrutiny as the "cancel culture" movement took hold after the COVID-19 pandemic, the murder of George Floyd, and an insurrection at the US Capitol unleashed a national questioning of the very institutions Hunt and his generation had built to realize the American dream.[20]

Reflecting the tenor of the times, New York's Museum of Modern Art opened its 2021 exhibition dedicated to "architecture and blackness" in America.

> We take up the question of what architecture can be—not a tool for imperialism and subjugation, not a means for aggrandizing the self, but a vehicle for liberation and joy. The discipline of architecture has consistently and deliberately avoided participation in this endeavor, operating in complicity with repressive aspects of the current system. That ends now. We commit ourselves to annihilating the willful blinders that have enabled architecture to continue to profess its Eurocentrism as a virtue and claim apolitical ends.[21]

Hunt can be, and variously has been, accused of such oppressions. There is no denying that his monuments and what Henry Van Brunt derided as the "superb privacies" of the Astors and Vanderbilts, glorified their white leaders in an immigrant and race-oppressive society. But Hunt was not authoritarian, nor his clients singular in their self-aggrandizement, supporting cultural enterprises that in the early twenty-first century began to cross race and class divides. As architecture, Hunt's work embedded America in Eurocentric traditions that he and his generation institutionalized at new museums and universities. The eclecticism of his era, embracing world traditions, can be viewed as more reflective of the American experiment than the national classicism of the City Beautiful.[22]

Most important, Hunt was aspirational for the arts when they struggled for recognition in an America dedicated to the pragmatic needs of a new nation. The year of his apotheosis in architecture, painting, and sculpture at the Chicago fair he told New York's Architectural League that, "if this country doesn't take up art, we'll make it, we'll educate it, we'll show it what a great and glorious thing it is." Richard Morris Hunt, a son of privilege and duty, an institutionalist and architect, dedicated his life to this ideal.[23]

Acknowledgments

This book owes its existence to individuals and institutions, forces rallied by Richard Hunt to build a culture of civilization. At the Library of Congress, in the Prints and Photographs Division, Mari Nakahara, a Virgil through the confounding Richard Morris Hunt archive, the ever-supportive Helena Zinkham, C. Ford Peatross, Elisabeth Parker who cataloged Hunt's library, and the digital conversion and cataloging team who have overseen the thousands of Hunt images available online; members of the Conservation Division who brought life to century-old materials; and in the Publishing Office, Becky Clark, Aimee Hess, Zachary Klitzman, and editor extraordinaire, Susan Reyburn: I am indebted to all for their sharp minds, humor, and generous collaboration. To the Madison Council, for their exceptional support, goes my deepest appreciation.

Generous and dedicated patrons of American architecture, Marc Appleton and Edward Bass, made possible a twenty-first-century appreciation of Hunt's legacy through the photography of Michael Froio, whose evident talent was only matched by his perseverance under fraught circumstances, with the assistance of Samuel Markey; complementary to Michael's new images are James B. Garrison's elegant new plans.

Ken Soehner and librarians of the Thomas J. Watson Library at The Metropolitan Museum of Art, in ways Richard Hunt and his fellow museum trustees could never have imagined, made this book possible through the library's collections and, toward the end, soldiered me through the COVID-19 pandemic.

Paul Carnahan, Callie Raspuzzi, and Jeanne Walsh brought Vermont to my doorstep at critical junctures.

Ben Bowery, Trudy Coxe, Genna Duplisea, Katherine Garrett-Cox, Leslie Jones, Lauren Landi, Théo Lourenço, and Carola Schueller at the Preservation Society of Newport County; and Kaela Bleho, Bert Lippincott, Ingrid Peters, and Ruth Taylor at the Newport Historical Society; Lorna Condon, Arlene Pringle, and Judith Tankard in Boston; Joseph Patzner, Jeff Richman, and Adrianna Slaughter in New York; Shelly Burke and Nancy Hadley in Washington, DC; Michael J. Lewis and Richard White; librarians at Duke, Harvard, Princeton and Yale; archivists at the Ryerson and Burnham Archives, the National Portrait Gallery, and Hampton University were essential.

Hunt had no better advocates than William Alexander, Laura M. Cope, Rev. Todd M. Donatelli, Jill Hawkins, Hannah Parks, and Darren Poupore at Biltmore; Cheryl Boujnida, Bernard Kohn, Rev. Rick Simon, Alfred G. Vanderbilt, and Craig Wolf in New York; Mary E. Edwards, Hillary Fortin, and Zachary Russell in Newport.

Blois-style stairs, George Vanderbilt house, Biltmore, Asheville, North Carolina; Michael Froio, 2020

Melanie Apsley, Valeria Carullo, Mathieu Deldicque, Jean-François Dontenwill, Nicole Garnier, Andrea Gilbert, Catherine Taylor, and Fabien Trichet made Richard Hunt in England and France come alive.

Samoan Barish, Lee Bartlett, Matthew Cornell, Michele Daniel, Barbara Davilman, William Deverell and Jennifer Watts, Ulysses Dietz, Carla and Lisa Ellern, Erika Esau, Judith and Walter Flamenbaum, Shannon Hughes, Patrice Marandel and John Willenbecher, Barry Miller and Victor Sotos, Jeanne and Alexander Sloane, Chris P. Thompson, John Tompkins, and exceptionally, Judith Ginsburg and Paul LeClerc, were hand-holding friends, chefs, commentators, grammarians, provocateurs, and cheerleaders along the way.

And finally to William Davis and David Rodes, to Peter Mason, to *mon cher ami* Paul Micio, to Valeska and Alice, I owe the life force, scholarly and familial, that sustained me through the storm, held by the memory of David Eidenberg to whom I dedicate this book.

San Francisco, 2024

Sources and Abbreviations

This book is integral to the Hunt Project, an initiative to catalog, restore, and research the historic Richard Morris Hunt Collection at the Library of Congress. The collection comprises rare books, drawings, sketches, photographs, and personal items, many searchable on the Library's website.

Sources for the history of Richard Hunt are diverse and often of limited scope. For overviews, see: Paul R. Baker, *Richard Morris Hunt* (Cambridge, MA: The MIT Press, 1980); *The Architecture of Richard Morris Hunt*, ed. Susan R. Stein (Chicago: University of Chicago Press, 1986); *Exploration, Vision & Influence: The Art World of Brattleboro's Hunt Family* (Bennington, VT: The Bennington Museum, 2005); *Very Simple Charm: The Early Life and Work of Richard Morris Hunt in Newport, 1858-1878* (Newport, RI: Newport Art Museum, 2014).

For the Hunt Family Papers (HFP), consult the archives of Biltmore, Asheville, North Carolina.

For additional resources and expanded author notes, see the Richard Morris Hunt Collection at https://guides.loc.gov/richard-morris-hunt.

AIA   American Institute of Architects

Baker   Paul R. Baker, *Richard Morris Hunt* (Cambridge, MA: The MIT Press, 1980)

CHH   Catharine (Clinton) Howland Hunt, wife of Richard Morris Hunt

CHHB   Catharine Howland Hunt typescript biography, in HLOC: LC-DIG-ppmsca -35141, -35155, -35156, -35157, -89827, -89828, Library of Congress, Washington, DC

HFP   Hunt Family Papers, 1758-1908, Vermont Historical Society Library, Barre, Vermont

HLOC   Richard Morris Hunt Collection, Library of Congress, Washington, DC

JHD   Diaries of Jane Hunt, sister of Richard Morris Hunt, in HFP

JHJ   "The Journals of Jane Hunt," the travel logs and memoirs of Richard Morris Hunt's sister, 1822-1903, in HFP

JLH   Jane (Maria) Leavitt Hunt, mother of Richard Morris Hunt

LOC   Library of Congress, Washington, DC

LXNY   Lenox Library Records, New York Public Library, New York

META   Office of the Secretary Records, 1870 to the present, The Metropolitan Museum of Art Archives, New York

RHH   Richard Howland Hunt, eldest son of Richard Morris Hunt and Catharine Hunt

RIBA   Royal Institute of British Architects, London

RMH   Richard Morris Hunt

RMHJ   Richard Morris Hunt journal, 1844-48, in HFP, photocopy in HLOC

RMHS   Richard Morris Hunt sketchbook, forty-six in total, 1844-95, with multiple years covered in individual volumes, in HLOC

TWP   Theodore Winthrop Papers, New York Public Library, New York, NY

VHS   Vermont Historical Society Leahy Library, Barre, Vermont

Notes

Introduction

1. Typescript list of awards, HLOC.
2. Roberta Smith, "The Philip Guston Hoard: A Boon or Overkill," *The New York Times*, January 25, 2023; Abraham Lincoln, "First Inaugural Address, March 4, 1861," in *Abraham Lincoln: Speeches and Writings, 1859-1865* (New York: The Library of America, 1980), 219.
3. Peter B. Wight, "Richard Morris Hunt," *The Inland Architect and News Record* 26, no. 1 (August 1895): 2.
4. Michael Holroyd, "Our Friends the Dead," *The Guardian*, May 31, 2002; CHHB, 7; see also CHH on Charlotte Cushman, CHHB, 128.
5. CHHB, 339; John B. Gass, "American Architecture and Architects, with special reference to the works of the late Richard Morris Hunt and Henry Hobson Richardson," *The Architectural Journal* 3, Third Series (1896): 231, reprinted from the *Journal of the Royal Institute of British Architects* (November 1895– October 1896): 231; Wight, *Richard Morris Hunt*, 2.
6. RMH sat for the portrait on June 6, 12, and 17, 1852, RMHS. For the portrait hung at the home of Joseph H. Hunt, see De Witt H. Fessenden, "Two Architects and Their Homes," *The International Studio* 62, no. 247 (September 1917): LXXI; RMH to JLH, March 15, 1855, Folder 5, HFP.

Chapter 1
No Small Potatoes

1. Jasper Adams, "The Relation of Christianity to Civil Government in the United States: A Sermon Preached in St. Michael's Church, Charleston, February 13th, 1833, before the Convention of the Protestant Episcopal Church of the Diocese of South-Carolina."
2. Mary Rogers Cabot, *Annals of Brattleboro, 1681-1895* (Brattleboro, VT: E.L. Hildreth, 1921), 1:288-90; Ellen Hunt to JLH, April 18, 1834, Folder 1, HFP; Ellen, in turn, named one of her sons Gouverneur Morris.
3. *The Encyclopedia of New England*, ed. Burt Feintuch and David H. Watters (New Haven, CT, and London: Yale University Press, 2005), 714-15; Cabot, 498.
4. Jane Hunt wrote that her parents moved into the new house in July 1822, Folder 9, JHJ; Cabot, 289, 319, 405.
5. Ralph Waldo Emerson, *Journals of Ralph Waldo Emerson, 1820-1872*, ed. Edward Waldo Emerson and Waldo Emerson Forbes (Cambridge, MA: Riverside Press, 1912), 7:12; Daniel Walker Howe, *The Political Culture of the American Whigs* (Chicago: University of Chicago Press, 1979), 11-23, 69-96; as quoted in *Documents in the City of Boston* (Boston: J.H. Eastburn, 1852), 2:2, 53.
6. CHHB, 3, 7-9, 17; Cabot, 289; Robert V. Remini, *Daniel Webster: The Man and His Time* (New York: W.W. Norton, 1997), 201, over river rights between New Jersey and New York, in 1843; Daniel Webster, *The Works of Daniel Webster*, 7th ed. (Boston: Little, Brown, 1853), 1:187, 190. This speech was reprinted through the period and cited in contemporary commentary on early views of architecture.
7. Webster, 190.
8. Cabot, 337, 340, 345-46; William Wells, *Some observations, taken in part from an address delivered in the new meetinghouse in Brattleborough, July 7th, 1816. "Being the First Christian Communion Held in that Place,"* np.
9. "Oration of the Fourth of July, 1812," Folder 43, HFP; Lawrence A. Cremin, *American Education: The National Experience 1783-1876* (New York: Harper & Row, 1980), 103.
10. CHHB, 10-11.
11. CHHB, 11-14; *Life and Letters of Catharine M. Sedgwick*, ed. Mary E. Dewey (New York: Harper & Brothers, 1872), 223; letter from de Castillia to JLH, New York, June 12, 1837, Foresti to JLH, December 26, 1837, Folder 1-1, HFP; Sally Webster, *William Morris Hunt, 1824-1879* (Cambridge and New York: Cambridge University Press, 1991), 8; CHHB, 12-14; Folder 11, JHJ.
12. Folder 11, JHJ; CHHB, 16-17; "Notable Alumni," Boston Latin School, www.bls.org (accessed May 5, 2020); CHHB, 20; CHHB, 1; "My Resolutions, 1843," Folder 13, JHJ.
13. For JLH's society, see CHHB, 4, 8, 17; Paul R. Sweet, *Wilhelm von Humboldt: A Biography* (Columbus: Ohio State University Press, 1980), 2:530-56; David B. Tyack, *George Ticknor and the Boston Brahmin* (Cambridge, MA: Harvard University Press, 1967), 82.

14. Paul Revere Frothingham, *Edward Everett: Orator and Statesman* (Boston: Houghton Mifflin, 1925), 138; Everett was behind the admission of Jonathan Hunt to Harvard, see attestation to his admittance, Folder 11, HFP; Ralph Waldo Emerson, *The Conduct of Life* (Boston: Ticknor and Fields, 1864), 218.

15. Elizabeth Parker to JLH, September 15, 1843 and Samuel and Elizabeth Parker to JLH, September 15, 1843, Folder 1-1, HFP; Webster to JLH, October 2, 1843, Folder 3, HFP; Webster to JLH, October 2, 1843, CHHB; as first noted by Baker, note 17, 477-78; Helen M. Knowlton, "William Morris Hunt," *New England Magazine* 10 (August 1894): 687-88 and variant in the author's *Art-Life of William Morris Hunt* (Boston: Little, Brown, 1899), 3.

16. As quoted from Ticknor April 3, 1817, Journal IV in Tyack, *George Ticknor*, 64; letter from George Bancroft to President John T. Kirkland, president of Harvard, August 17, 1821, in Mark A. DeWolfe Howe, *The Life and Letters of George Bancroft* (New York: Charles Scribner's Sons, 1908), 1:117.

17. Margaret Fuller Ossoli, *At Home and Abroad; or Things and Thoughts in America and Europe*, 3rd ed. (Boston: Crosby, Nichols, 1856), 250-52.

18. William Cullen Bryant, *Letters of a Traveller; or Notes of Things Seen in Europe and America*, 3rd ed. (New York: George P. Putnam, 1851), 9; October 9-October 29, 1843, Folder 5, JHJ; CHHB, 21-22; 25.

19. Henry William Moulton, *Moulton Annals, 1909*, reprint (London: Forgotten Books, 2013), 144-45.

20. March 3-5, 1844, RMHJ; CHHB, 23; William L. Vance et al., *America's Rome: Artists in the Eternal City, 1800-1900* (Cooperstown, NY: Fenimore Art Museum, 2009), 9.

21. Avis Berman, "Sketch Club of American Artists at Rome," *Archives of American Art Journal* 40, no. 1/2 (2000): 2-3.

22. For these travels in Italy, see March 4-April 31, 1844, RMHJ; CHHB, 23.

23. For days leading up to Geneva, see Folder 6, JHD; May 9, 15-16, 17-26, 1843, RMHJ; CHHB, 18; Sally Webster, *William Morris Hunt*, 10. Arnold J. Heidenheimer, *Disparate Ladders: Why School and University Policies Differ in Germany, Japan, and Switzerland* (Piscataway, NJ: Transaction Publishers, 1997), 14-20.

24. "Notes sur les voies romaines de la Haute-Savoie," *La Revue Savoisienne* (1926; 1st semester): 125. The Newport merchant was Charles Dabney, a cousin of Henry Chauncey, whose sons attended the school in 1839; Joseph C. Abdo, *On the Edge of History* (privately printed, 2005), 187. The Briquet family owned Briquet et Fils, and Alphonse Briquet, contributing member of the Société des Amis de la Bibliothèque nationale et des grandes bibliothèques de France in the 1870s, was the teacher of his nephew, the historian of Renaissance paper and watermarks, Charles-Moïse Briquet; Liliane Mottu-Weber, "Briquet," *Dictionnaire historique de la Suisse* (Hauterive, Switzerland: Editions Gilles Attinger, 2003), 324.

25. RMH to JLH, January 3, 1845, a typed transcription by a Hunt family member is in HLOC (the original is not at HFP); RMH to JLH, May 5, 1845, Folder 2, HFP.

26. James L. Morrison Jr., *The Best School in the World: West Point, 1833-1866* (Kent, OH: The Kent State University Press, 1998), passim; Ticknor to Lydia Ticknor, June 12, 1826, *Life, Letters and Journals of George Ticknor* (Boston: James R. Osgood, 1876), 1:375.

27. *Les Monuments d'Art et d'Histoire du Canton de Genève*, ed. Philippe Broillet (Berne, Switzerland: La Société d'Histoire de l'Art en Suisse, 1997), 1:330; Anita Frei, *Samuel Darier, Architecte à Genève (1808-1884)* (Geneva: Editions Passé Présent, 1999), 30, 81-85.

28. Jane Hunt to JLH, July 30, 1845, and RMH to JLH, July 28, 30, 1845, Folder 2, HFP.

29. George Weisz, *The Emergence of Modern Universities in France, 1863-1914* (Princeton, NJ: Princeton University Press, 2014), 33.

30. Richard Chaffee, "Hunt in Paris," in *The Architecture of Richard Morris Hunt*, ed. Susan R. Stein (Chicago: The University of Chicago Press, 1986), 14-17; undated [1846], RMHJ.

31. Charles Garnier, *Le Théâtre* (Paris: Hachette et Cie, 1871), 405.

32. Richard Chaffee, "The Teaching of Architecture at the École des Beaux-Arts," in *The Architecture of the École des Beaux-Arts*, ed. Arthur Drexler (New York: The Museum of Modern Art, 1977), 83-86; for awards, see Chaffee, "Hunt in Paris," 37-42.

33. Barry Bergdoll, "The Ideal of the Gothic Cathedral in 1852," *A.W.N Pugin: Master of the Gothic Revival* (New York:

The Bard Graduate Center for the Studies of the Decorative Arts, 1995), 114; Corinne Bélier, "Affinities and Posterity: The French Heritage," in Corinne Bélier, Barry Bergdoll, and Marc Le Cœur, *Henri Labrouste: Structure Brought to Light* (New York: The Museum of Modern Art, 2013), 227.

34. See notes online for these texts, all in HLOC. For a list of Hunt's assignments, see Chaffee, "Hunt in Paris," 37–42.

35. See notes online for text of the assignment, in HLOC; Ben Kiernan, *Blood and Soil: A World History of Genocide and Extermination from Sparta to Darfur* (New Haven, CT: Yale University Press, 2007), 374; for the exhibition, *Catalogue of the Third Annual Exhibition of the Architectural League of New York* (1887): 19, where *maison hospitalière* is translated as "Station in an oasis;" Chaffee, "Hunt in Paris," 39, translates it as "hostel." For Hunt's side elevation of the hostel, see HLOC: LC-DIG-ppmsca-57936.

36. "*Des archives pour la cour des comptes, Concours d'émulation, 2 Mars, 1852*" (*projet rendu*), HLOC.

37. Hunt ended his studies before students could be considered "graduates," which required a thesis or "*diplôme*," the first being awarded in 1895. Isabelle Gournay and Marie-Laure Crosnier Leconte, "American Architecture Students in Belle Epoque Paris: Scholastic Strategies and Achievements at the Ecole des Beaux-Arts," *The Journal of the Gilded Age and Progressive Era* 12, no. 2 (April 2013): 158, 196; August 8 and 28, 1846, RMHJ; June 13–October 8, 1848, JHD.

38. 1851 RMHS. For RMH's photographs of the Crystal Palace by Louis-Émile Durandelle, see HLOC: LC-DIG-ppmsca-57032, and the Egyptian exhibit, -57022.

39. 1852 RMHS; see letter from RMH to H.M. Lefuel, June 28, 1852, where Hunt requests help in securing permission to visit chateaus, noting that all he was missing "to conclude his studies" was to visit "monuments built by the great masters ("*pour terminer mes études...les monuments construits par les grands maîtres*"), family archive of Hector Lefuel, as quoted in Barbara Korn Silvergold, "*Richard Morris Hunt and the Importation of Beaux-Art Architecture to the United States*" (PhD dissertation, University of California, Berkeley, 1974), 51; see 1855 RMHS for July 1852 part of this trip.

40. David R. Hanlon, *While the Sun Shines: The Lives and Pioneering Photographs of Leavitt Hunt and Nathan Flint Baker* (David R. Hanlon, 2001); 1855 RMHS; for Duban, *Mémoire Descriptif des Études*, October 1847, HLOC; Richard Wittman, "Félix Duban's Didactic Restoration of the Château de Blois: A History of France in Stone," *Journal of the Society of Architectural Historians* 55, no. 4 (December 1996): 412; Henry Van Brunt, *Greek Lines and Other Architectural Essays* (Boston and New York: Houghton Mifflin, 1893), 164.

41. Travel companions were Daniel S. Elliott and George H. Timmins; CHHB, 52–94, particularly 40, 54, 62; February 5, 14, May 6, June 22–28, 1853, RMHS; for

native costume from Hunt's 1852-53 sketchbook, see HLOC: LC-DIG-ppmsca-57991.

42. Theodore Winthrop to his mother, November 2, 1849, TWP; Gogol, 1831, as quoted by Stephane Kirkland, *Paris Reborn: Napoléon III, Baron Haussmann, and the Quest to Build a Modern City* (New York: St. Martin's Press, 2013), 22; Folder 9, JHJ; July 3, 1846, RMHJ; CHHB, 25–27; Baker, 40; Kathleen D. McCarthy, *Women's Culture: American Philanthropy and Art, 1830–1930* (Chicago: University of Chicago Press, 1991), 8.

43. John Harley Warner, *Against the Spirit of System: The French Impulse in Nineteenth-Century American Medicine* (Baltimore and London: The Johns Hopkins University Press, 1998), 3; Sally Webster, *William Morris Hunt*, 11.

44. Margaret A. Nash, "A Means of Honorable Support: Art and Music in Women's Education in the Mid-Nineteenth Century," *History of Education Quarterly* 53, no. 1 (February 2013): 45–48.

45. "*comme à l'ordinaire*," January 25, 1846, June 7, 1846, RMHJ; CHHB, 26; for a discussion of Hunt's architectural readings, see Silvergold, *Richard Morris Hunt*, 54–56; February 23, 1848, RMHJ.

46. Translates as "Renewed City." Allison Unruh, *Aspiring to la Vie Galante: Reincarnations of Rococo in Second Empire France*, PhD dissertation (Institute of Fine Arts, New York, 2008), 212; Matthew Truesdell, *Spectacular Politics: Louis-Napoleon Bonaparte and the Fête Impériale, 1849-1870* (Oxford and New York: Oxford

University Press, 1997), 97; Georges-Eugène Haussmann, *Mémoires du Baron Haussmann, Grands Travaux de Paris* (Paris: Victor-Havard, 1893), 3:351.

47. Emmanuel Jacquin, *Archives de l'Agence d'architecture du Louvre et des Tuileries, XIXe–XXe siècles* (Paris: Centre historique des Archives nationales, 2006), Introduction.

48. "*le cher Dick*," Lefuel to CHH, April 28, 1867, CHHB, 97. For one of RMH's Louvre drawings, see HLOC: LC-DIG-ppmsca-51626. The only photograph of the pavilion in Hunt's collection is of an oblique view, by Édouard Baldus, HLOC: LC-DIG-ppmsca-58051; for Baldus view of the Louvre under construction, see HLOC: LC-DIG-ppmsca-57606.

49. As quoted in CHHB, 98.

50. Letter from Winthrop to his mother, November 2, 1849, TWP; Rossiter to William J. Stillman and John Durand, November 21, 1855, Thomas Prichard Rossiter and Rossiter Family Papers, 1840–1961, Archives of American Art, Washington, DC.

51. Rev. Joseph S. Buckminster to Arthur Walter, December 20, 1806–January 10, 1807, Dartmouth College Library, New Hampshire, as quoted in Tyack, *George Ticknor*, 63; RMH to JLH, January 14, 1855, Folder 5, HFP; CHHB, 27.

52. RMH to JLH, March 15, 1855, Folder 5, HFP; CHHB 97; Sally Webster, *William Morris Hunt*, 36. For date of return, see "Important Trial: Compensation of Architects," *Architect's and Mechanic's Journal* 3 (March 9, 1861): 224.

53. Van Buren to Upjohn, February 5, 1854, Upjohn Collection, New York Public Library, New York.

Chapter 2
Soldier of the Crayon

1. Sven Beckert, *The Monied Metropolis: New York City and the Consolidation of the American Bourgeoisie, 1850–1896* (Cambridge: Cambridge University Press, 2001), 17–19, and passim.

2. "Great Cities," *Putnam's Monthly Magazine* 5, no. 27 (March 1855): 255–56. This distinction was well known to American Whigs through Scottish philosopher Adam Furgeson (1723–1816).

3. The estate of Jonathan Hunt Jr., apportioned between his wife and five children, was valued at $107,500 on November 2, 1831, see his will, Folder 17, HFP.

4. Theodore Winthrop, *Cecil Dreeme* (Boston: Ticknor and Fields, 1861), 34–51; *The Collection of Richard Howland Hunt, American and Italian Furniture, Tapestries, Textiles, and Needlework, Pictures, Pewter, Japanese Armor, Etc. Including Many Heirlooms of the Hunt Family Removed from "The Studio" at Portchester, New York to be Sold by Mr. Hunt's Order*, Anderson Galleries, March 26, 1927; for the Hunt brother interiors, see Fessenden, "Two Architects and Their Homes," with photographs by Frances Benjamin Johnston, originals of which are in the HLOC and LOC's Johnston collection. For Johnston's view of the RHH "Studio" gallery, with RMH's sculpture of an ocelot, see LC-DIG-ppmsca-56271.

5. James Wynne, *Private Libraries of New York* (New York: E. French, 1860), 269, compiled from Wynne's column "Private Libraries of New York," published serially in the *New-York Evening Post*, 1856–57.

6. The title of the Hunt library was given by CHH when she had the collection cataloged after RMH's death: for this, see here Afterword, online note 9; *Architecture françoise, ou, Recueil des plans, élévations, coupes et profils des églises, maisons royales, palais, hôtels & édifices les plus considérables de Paris, ainsi que des châteaux & maisons de plaisance situés aux environs de cette ville, ou en d'autres endroits de la France*, 4 vols. (Paris: Charles Antoine Jombert, 1752–56).

7. Wynne, *Private Libraries*, 278–79.

8. Ibid., 279.

9. For Reiber, see here chapter 4; for Gavet, see chapter 5; Wynne, *Private Libraries*, 270–71, 279; Anca I. Lasc, *Interior Decorating in Nineteenth-Century France: The Visual Culture of a New Profession* (Manchester, UK: Manchester University Press, 2018), 17.

10. As quoted in Charles Lockwood, *Bricks & Brownstone* (New York: McGraw Hill, 1972), 139; "Important Trial: Compensation of Architects," *Architect's and Mechanic's Journal* 3 (March 9, 1861): 222; Edith Rossiter Bevan, *Thomas Pritchard Rossiter, 1818–1871* (1957), typescript, Thomas J. Watson Library, The Metropolitan Museum of Art, New York.

11. For an intended exterior, see HLOC: LC-DIG-ds-13986.

For Hunt's Rossiter second and third floor plans, see HLOC: LC-DIG-ppmsca-56364 and -56365.

12. Montgomery Schuyler, "Works of the Late Richard M. Hunt," *The Architectural Record* 5, no. 2 (October–December 1895): 99. For a photograph of the street when the Rossiter house was just finished, see HLOC: LC-DIG-ppmsca-64850. At the Parmly trial, the contractor stated that after completing the house he built "two houses" adjoining the Rossiter house, which suggests that Parmly, after criticizing Hunt for his excessive expense, may have capitalized on Hunt's forward-looking design. There are no city records for ownership. "Important Trial: Compensation of Architects," *Architect's and Mechanic's Journal* 3 (March 23, 1861): 242.

13. The trial was reported over five issues of *Architect's and Mechanic's Journal*, on March 9, 16, 23, 30 and April 6, 1861. For cost, see March 23: 245. For RMH pencil sketch of the bookcase, see HLOC: LC-DIG-ppmsca-56362.

14. Ibid., March 16: 222–24.

15. Ibid., March 9: 222–24.

16. Ibid., March 16: 233.

17. Ibid., April 6: 1–9; also see comment by AIA on the importance of the trial in establishing the rights of architects, March 9: 224.

18. Ibid., March 9: 222; Walter to RMH, March 6, 1856, and June 5, 1856, Thomas Ustick Walter Papers, 1829–1887, Archives of American Art, Washington, DC.

19. "The Studio Building," *The Crayon* 5 (January 1858): 56, stating studios ranged between fifteen by twenty and twenty by thirty feet; Sarah Bradford Landau, "Richard Morris Hunt: Architectural Innovator and Father of a 'Distinctive' American School," in *The Architecture of Richard Morris Hunt*, ed. Stein, 49-50.

20. Annette Blaugrund, "The Tenth Street Studio Building: A Roster, 1857–1895," *The American Art Journal* 14, no. 2: 67–71.

21. Mary Woods, "The First American Architectural Journals: The Profession's Voice," *Journal of the Society of Architectural Historians* 48, no. 2 (June 1989): 117–18; *The Century: 1847–1946* (New York: The Century Association, 1947), 385, 396.

22. CHH wrote "My impression is that his first New York work was a picture gallery for Mr. Wright," CHHB, 102; Anne McNair Bolin, "Art and Domestic Culture: The Residential Art Gallery in New York City, 1850–1870" (PhD dissertation, Emory University, 2000), 78n164; also 77–83; "Visitors Book," 1865–1881, and undated pages (ca. 1867–1871), John Taylor Johnston Collection, Institutional Archives, META.

23. Helen Mary Knowlton, *Art-Life of William Morris Hunt* (Boston: Little, Brown, 1899), 125; Martha A.S. Shannon, *Boston Days of William Morris Hunt* (Boston: Marshall Jones, 1923), 94–95; Baker, 100, 102.

24. "An Address Delivered before the Art-Union of Philadelphia in the Academy of Fine Arts on Thursday Evening, October 12th, 1848" (Philadelphia, 1848), 3, 22. Frank Furness, "What I remember of Mr. Richard M. Hunt during the time when it was my privilege to be under his care and guidance in the study of architecture," 1895, private collection. The author thanks Michael J. Lewis for a copy of this reminiscence.

25. Hunt was responding to William Ware's approach to architectural education. *Proceedings of the Third Annual Convention of the American Institute of Architects* (1869): 171; CHHB, 340; Furness, np. For student work in the HLOC, see online note.

26. Henry Van Brunt, "Richard Morris Hunt," *Proceedings of the Twenty-Ninth Annual Convention of the American Institute of Architects* (1895): 76; Furness, np.

27. Burton J. Bledstein, *The Culture of Professionalism* (New York: W.W. Norton, 1978), 86-87; letter from Ware to Frank Furness, 1898, in the Furness family archive, as quoted in James F. O'Gorman, *The Architecture of Frank Furness* (Philadelphia: Philadelphia Museum of Art, 1973), 24.

28. "Address of 22 February 1858, AIA," *The Crayon* 5 (April 1858): 111.

29. For the library committee's recommended books, with Hunt's handwritten additions, see *Catalogue of Books on Architecture* (1867), bound with RMH's collection of AIA Proceedings, still at the AIA library, Washington, DC.

30. *Minutes of the Annual Convention of the American Institute of Architects* (December 1858): 44; "Honorary Deceased Members," and "Corresponding Members," *Proceedings of the Thirty-Seventh Annual Convention of the American Institute of Architects* (1903): 189-90; 192-93.

31. Alfred J. Bloor, *The Architectural and Other Art Societies of Europe; Some Account of Their Origin, Processes of Formation and Methods of Administration, with Suggestions as to Some of the Conditions Necessary for the Maximum Success of a National American Architectural-Art Society. With its Local Dependencies, Read before the Regular Meeting of the AIA, New York Chapter, February 16, 1869* (New York: AIA Committee on Library and Publications, 1869), 109, published when RMH was chair of the committee.

32. J. Coleman Hart, "Unity in Architecture," *The Crayon* 6 (February 1859): 86, 88.

33. *The Crayon* 5 (January 1858): 5; *The New American Cyclopedia: A Popular Dictionary of General Knowledge*, ed. George Ripley and Charles A. Dana (New York and London: D. Appleton, 1859), 2:33, 45-46.

34. Henry G. Marquand, William H. Aspinwall, and Alexander Van Rensselaer contributed as lifetime members. *Proceedings of the Fourth Annual Convention of the American Institute of Architects* (1870): 225-26, 227.

35. "Boston Metropolitan Area: Population from 1790," Demographia, http://www.demographia.com/db-bos1790.htm (accessed June 4, 2018); Stephen Puleo, *A City So Grand: The Rise of an American Metropolis, Boston, 1850-1900* (Boston: Beacon Press, 2010), 85-90; Arthur Gilman to the Back Bay Commissioners, November 1856, as quoted in Puleo, 89. For a long view of the Morland houses, see HLOC: LC-DIG-ppmsca-64862.

36. Sally Webster, *William Morris Hunt*, 39, 43.

37. "Sketchings," *The Crayon* 5 (September 1858): 268; Baker, 122, 487, note 9.

38. CHHB, 127; James L. Yarnall, *John La Farge: A Biographical and Critical Study* (London and New York: Routledge, 2016), 49; Henry James, *Notes of a Son and Brother* (London: Macmillan, 1914), 63; Sally Webster, *William Morris Hunt*, 58-59.

39. CHHB, 126-27; Baker, 71; Col. Duncan S. Somerville, *The Aspinwall Empire* (Mystic, CT: Mystic Seaport Museum, 1983), 1-3, 43-65; Samuel Howland left each of his children $225,000; the declared value of the estate was $11,176,112, as quoted from Final Accounting of William H. Aspinwall, John L. Aspinwall, & Charles H. Risse of Samuel S. Howland, filed January 29, 1855, as quoted in Thavolia Glymph, *The Women's Fight: The Civil War's Battles for Home, Freedom, and Nation* (Chapel Hill: The University of North Carolina Press, 2020), 156, 301n117; "The Collection of William H. Aspinwall," *The American Art Journal* 6, no. 7 (February 16, 1867): 265-66.

40. George Templeton Strong, *The Diary of George Templeton Strong: Post-War Years, 1865-1875*, ed. Allan Nevins and Milton Halsey Thomas (New York: Octagon Books, 1974), 4:274; July 14, 1861, Part II, Folder 8, JHJ, the entry being exceptional in her family memoir for its sharpness; Van Brunt, "Richard Morris Hunt," 80.

41. CHHB, 127-29; James as quoted from *The Literary World* 7 (February 1, 1851): 94 by Neil Harris, *The Artist in American Society, The Formative Years* (Chicago: University of Chicago Press, 1966), 258.

42. CHHB, 143-44; Diary of Jane Maria Leavitt Hunt, June 29-July 20, 1820, HFP; reflecting changing attitudes, Catharine deleted the fact of service by proxy in revisions to her biography, CHHB, 144.

43. CHHB, 145; Part II, JHJ. For RMH watercolor of composite view from their first Paris hotel, see RMH's sketchbook watercolor HLOC: LC-DIG-ppmsca-57983.

44. 1861-62 RMHS and RMH date diary, 1861 at the VHS; CHHB, 145-47. For Dana and CHH drawing, in sketches by RMH, see HLOC: LC-DIG-ppmsca-57973 and -57975.

45. Jardin des Plantes, CHHB, 145, 150, 146, 151-55; Sally Webster, *William Morris Hunt*, 29; Charles de Kay, *Life and Works of Antoine-Louis Barye, Sculptor* (New York: Barye Monument Association, 1889), 65, 95, 152; *Catalogue of the Works of Antoine-Louis Barye* (New York: American Art Association, 1889), 49. For RMH watercolor of Biarritz, see HLOC: LC-DIG-ppmsca-73181.

46. 1862 RMHS; CHHB, 155, 156-57, 242, 263, 271, 316-17.

47. Richard Howland Hunt (1862-1931), Catharine Howland Hunt Livingston (1868-1963), Joseph Howland Hunt (1870-1924), Esther Morris Hunt Woolsey (1875-1901), and Herbert Leavitt Hunt (1877-1960); Choate, "Choate Pays Tribute to Mrs. Hunt's Life," *The New York Times*, March 6, 1909; CHHB, 173a, 240; *The American Architect and Building News* 27, no. 732 (January 4, 1890): 1.

48. CHHB, 165-66. War losses are now debated, but the historic baseline quoted

here for military dead from battle, disease, and wounds was published in RMH's lifetime; William F. Fox and Thomas Leonard Livermore, *Regimental Losses in the American Civil War* (Albany, NY: Albany Publishing, 1889); https://www.ncbi.nlm.nih.gov/pmc/articles/PMC4790547/ (accessed: May 14, 2014).

49. *A Record of the Metropolitan Fair in Aid of the United States Sanitary Commission, Held at New York, in April, 1864* (New York: Hurd and Houghton, 1867), 241, 243-44, 12; for annex and main building plans showing the astonishing array of displays, see from 18; Russell Sturgis, *The Artist's Way of Working in the Various Handicrafts and Arts of Design* (New York: Dodd, Mead, 1910), 2:605-6, "the most effective flag display known to the present writer," also in Baker, 143.

50. *A Record*, 34, 82, 77, 98. For the art gallery and Leutze's painting, see LC-DIG-stereo-1s08405.

51. CHHB, 166; Henry T. Tuckerman, *Book of the Artists: American Artist Life, Comprising Biographical and Critical Sketches of American Artists: Preceded by an Historical Account of the Rise and Progress of Art in America*, reprint of first edition, 1867, fifth printing 1870 (New York: James F. Carr, 1967), 11.

52. Frederick Law Olmsted to Professor Oliver W. Gibbs, founder of the Union League Club movement, November 5, 1862, in *Historical Sketch of the Union League Club* (New York: Union League Club, 1879), 11-12.

53. Beckert, *Monied Metropolis*, 125-35; CHHB, 169.

54. For RMH's National Academy of Design submission, see HLOC: LC-DIG-ppmsca-59725.

55. Olmsted, "Passages in the Life of an Unpractical Man," ca. 1877, as quoted in David M. Scobey, *Empire City: The Making and Meaning of the New York City Landscape* (Philadelphia: Temple University Press, 2002), 159.

56. Robert Minturn Jr., *Memoir of Robert Bowne Minturn* (privately printed, 1871), 65-146; George W. Curtis, "Editor's Easy Chair," *Harper's New Monthly* 11, no. 61 (June 1855): 125, both quoted in Roy Rosenzweig and Elizabeth Blackmar, *The Park and the People: A History of Central Park* (Ithaca, NY: Cornell University Press, 1992), 14-15, 23.

57. Baker, 146-47; Vaux to Olmsted, May 22, 1865, *The Papers of Frederick Law Olmsted: The California Frontier, 1863-1865*, ed. Victoria Post Ranney (Baltimore: The Johns Hopkins University Press, 1990), 5:378.

58. Richard M. Hunt, *Designs for the Gateways of the Southern Entrances to the Central Park* (New York: D. Van Nostrand, 1866), 6.

59. Ibid., 23, 20. For a sepia of the Gate of Peace, see HLOC: LC-DIG-ppmsca-57950. For Hudson column and Washington grotto, see LC-DIG-ppmsca-57959.

60. Ibid., 19-20.

61. Baker, 154. Hunt proved remarkably prescient about the direction the entrances should take, as later seen in the development of the Fifty-Ninth Street Grand Army Plaza and Columbus Circle during the City Beautiful movement.

62. Sarah Bradford Landau, "Richard Morris Hunt, the Continental Picturesque, and the Stick Style," *Journal of the Society of Architectural Historians* 42, no. 3 (October 1983): 272-89; Margery Deane, "Letter from Newport," *American Society*, May 2, 1871, in Deane Scrapbook, Newport Historical Society, cited in Landau, 287; Schuyler, "Works," 101.

63. Exterior framing of the Charlotte Cushman, Elizabeth Coles, and related Newport projects was certainly not structural. "The John Griswold House, National Historic Landmark Nomination," nd, 4, https://npgallery.nps.gov/NRHP/GetAsset/NHLS/71000023_text (accessed March 5, 2020). For Coles house, see HLOC: LC-DIG-ppmsca-57613; for view of the Griswold carriage house, also by Hunt and only attached to the main house later, see HLOC: LC-DIG-ppmsca-55253.

64. David Van Zanten, *The Architectural Polychromy of the 1830s* (New York and London: Garland Publishing 1977), passim. Richard Upjohn, "President's Address," *Proceedings of the First Annual Convention of the American Institute of Architects* (1867): 71; "The John Griswold House," 5.

65. CHHB, 179; 1867 RMHS; CHHB, 174, 181.

66. *Reports of the United States Commissioners to the Paris Exposition Universal Exposition*, ed. William P. Blake (Washington, DC: Government Printing Office, 1870), 1:3-4; *Exposition Universelle de 1867 à Paris, Catalogue général publié par la Commission impériale. Histoire du Travail et Monuments Historiques* (Paris: E. Dentu, and London:

J.M. Johnson & Sons, 1867), 3, 5; *L'Exposition Universelle de 1867 Illustrée*, ed. François Ducuing (Paris: Administration Publication Internationale Autorisée par la Commission Impériale, 1867), 242, 119–23, for the United States, see 194 and 396. For an image of the fair, see LC-DIG-pga-00497.

67. 1867 RMHS for lists; *Reports*, 116; CHHB, 181–83; Knowlton, *Art-Life*, 27–28; *The Journal of the Proceedings of the Royal Institute of British Architects* 9, no. 11 (March 16, 1893): 233.

68. CHHB, 182–92; for von Klenze and lists of purchases and trunks, see 1867 RMHS.

69. James to Thomas Sergeant Perry, September 20, 1867, *Henry James Letters*, ed. Leon Edel (Cambridge, MA: Harvard University Press, 1974), 1:77; for influence, see Landau, "Continental," 287–89, and Landau, *George B. Post, Architect: Picturesque Designer and Determined Realist* (New York: The Monacelli Press, 1998), passim; Michael J. Lewis, *Frank Furness: Architecture and the Violent Mind* (New York: W.W. Norton, 2001), 107 and passim; for impact of the Neo-Grec on Van Brunt, see his *Greek Lines and Other Architectural Essays*, which he sent to CHH in 1903 as she was writing her husband's biography, suggesting that if she had "patience to look it over [she] may discover some recognizable features of the inspiration which I gained as a pupil of Mr. Hunt's many years ago," CHHB, 374.

Sketchbook Portfolio

1. Quoting from Frank Furness, "What I Remember," np; CHH dated Richard's sketchbooks after his death, and though she gave each a single year, noting some as undated, research reveals that RMH used individual books over several years.

Chapter 3
A Robust and Vivacious Temperament

1. Delivered July 18, 1867, Ralph Waldo Emerson, *The Complete Works* (Boston and New York: Houghton, Mifflin, 1904), 8:212, 229; Carlos Baker, *Emerson Among the Eccentrics: A Group Portrait* (New York: Viking, 1995), 471–72.

2. Ralph Waldo Emerson, *The Journals and Miscellaneous Notebooks of Ralph Waldo Emerson*, ed. Ronald A. Bosco and Glen M. Johnson (Cambridge, MA, and London: The Belknap Press of Harvard University Press, 1982), 16:139, 144, 188. "My Men" is undated. A striking example of the architecture envisioned is *The Architect's Dream*, 1840, by Thomas Cole, Toledo Museum of Art, Ohio. See Hunt's Johann Joachim Winckelmann, *Histoire de l'art chez les anciens*, vols. 1 and 2 (Paris: E. Gide, 1801–3), HLOC: N5330 .W8, suggesting Hunt read them while a student in Paris; also Wynne, *Private Libraries*, 270–71.

3. The top ten percent rose from owning fifty-eight percent of the national wealth at the turn of the century to eighty percent by 1910, Thomas Piketty, *Capital in*

the Twenty-First Century, trans. Arthur Goldhammer (Cambridge, MA, and London: The Belknap Press of Harvard University Press, 2017), 348; George M. Fredrickson, *The Inner Civil War: Northern Intellectuals and the Crisis of the Union* (New York: Harper & Row, 1965), 183; Scobey, 25; Edwin G. Burrows and Mike Wallace, *Gotham: A History of New York City to 1898* (Oxford: Oxford University Press, 1999), 939–40.

4. "Table-talk," *Appleton's Journal: A Magazine of General Literature* 8, no. 140 (December 2, 1871): 638, as quoted in Richard Plunz, *A History of Housing in New York City* (New York: Columbia University Press, 2016), xxxvi; Winthrop, letter to "Bre," dated August 12, 1857, Folder 15, TWP.

5. For Borden, see letters to and from the Hunt office, HLOC; CHHB, 300–1.

6. Surviving correspondence, much expurgated, is in the archives at Biltmore, North Carolina.

7. Though RMH assembled scrapbooks, after his death CHH created the majority of the albums, from files he maintained throughout his professional life, and which she then left to the AIA, CHHB, 315, 334.

8. "a picturesque figure," Royal Cortissoz, *Art and Common Sense* (New York: Charles Scribner's Sons, 1913), 391; George Post, "Richard Morris Hunt," *Proceedings of the Twenty-Ninth Annual Convention of the American Institute of Architects* (1895): 88; CHHB, 126A; Louis H. Sullivan, *The Autobiography of An Idea* (New York: Press

of the American Institute of Architects, 1924), 190.

9. RMH, "Architecture," in *The American Cyclopedia*, ed. George Ripley and Charles A. Dana (New York: D. Appleton, 1873), 1:652.

10. *Cyclopedia* (1873), 1:666; with Viennese architect Friedrich von Schmidt, Hunt visited Théodore Ballu's restored medieval Tour Saint-Jacques; also the neo-Romanesque Saint-Ambroise, and Renaissance Sainte-Trinité. He toured Joseph-Louis Duc's Palais de Justice and the unfinished Paris Opera house, with its architect Charles Garnier, 1867 RMHS.

11. Hunt may have won the hospital in competition with George Post as a competitor, see Landau, *George B. Post*, 15. For Seventieth Street elevation by the Hunt office, see HLOC: LC-DIG-ppmsca-54512; for plans, see -71425 and -74004.

12. "Correspondence," *The American Architect and Building News* 1 (April 1, 1876): 111; Schuyler, "Works," 104.

13. Sarah Bradford Landau and Carl W. Condit, *Rise of the New York Skyscraper: 1865-1913* (New Haven, CT: Yale University Press, 1996), 17; Landau, "Architectural Innovator," 62; *New-York Tribune*, November 4, 1869; for an overview, see Plunz, *History of Housing*, 62-63; for Wooster, see "The New Homes of New York," *Scribners' Monthly* 8, no. 1 (May 1874): 67; for a contemporary view of the Stuyvesant's impact on apartment planning, see Charles H. Israels, "New York Apartment Houses," *Architectural Record* 11, no. 1 (July 1901): 477-508.

14. Hermione Lee, *Edith Wharton* (New York: Alfred A. Knopf, 2007), 60-61; "In the Superior Court of the City of New York, Richard M. Hunt against Marietta R. Stevens, Executrix, & C. and others" (New York: Evening-Post Stram Presses, 1878), as quoted in Theron G. Strong, *Joseph H. Choate* (New York: Dodd, Mead, 1917), 187. For exterior view of Stevens House, see HLOC: LC-DIG-ppmsca-55256.

15. For an insightful analysis of Hunt's commercial work and contributions to structure, see Landau, "Architectural Innovator," 55-60. For Phelps building, see HLOC: LC-DIG-ppmsca-74916.

16. "Cast Iron and Architecture," *The Crayon* 6 (January 1859): 24.

17. For Hunt's Equitable submission, see HLOC: LC-DIG-ppmsca-59731.

18. As quoted in Lee E. Gray, "Type and Building Type," in *The American Skyscraper*, ed. Roberta Moudry (New York: Columbia University Press, 2005), 87-89. Reid was brother-in-law of Hunt client Ogden Mills. For a competing submission by architect J. Cleveland Cady, see HLOC: LC-DIG-ppmsca-53805. For an early view of the Tribune tower, see HLOC: LC-DIG-ppmsca-53806. For Delaware and Hudson Canal Co. building, see LC-DIG-ppmsca-74006.

19. Jeremy C. Wells, "History of Structural Hollow Clay Tile in the United States," *Construction History* 22 (2007): 27-46; Landau, "Architectural Innovator," 57-58.

20. Landau, "Architectural Innovator," 58.

21. "The New Tribune," *New-York Tribune*, April 10, 1875, including a laudatory description of the building overall; despite his public satisfaction, Reid was unhappy with supervision by Hunt architect Edward Raht and refused to pay Hunt's fees, a matter settled by Joseph Choate, CHHB, 242-43; "The Tribune Mausoleum," *The Sun*, May 2, 1875. For Hunt's Western Union Telegraph, see HLOC: LC-DIG-ppmsca-58352.

22. Address of Simeon Church, reprinted in West Side Association, *Processing of Six Public Meetings* (1871): 55, also cited in Scobey, 158.

23. Fr. Saule, "The Lenox Collection," *The Aldine* 8, no. 10 (1877): 318.

24. Henry N. Stevens, *Recollections of James Lenox and the Formation of His Library* (London: H. Stevens & Sons, 1887), 141-42; CHHB, 195-96; 221-22; an exceptional gift from Hunt to Lenox was a ca. 1510 Italian copper globe, given as a birthday present to Lenox and held in the New York Public Library. See Hunt to Lenox, August 19, 1871, Correspondence, LXNY.

25. *Annual Report for the Year 1870 of the Trustees of the Lenox Library of the City of New York* (Albany, NY: Argus, 1871), 9; Lenox, "Building Fund" note, 1875, Correspondence, LXNY.

26. For the library's design, see David Van Zanten, "The Lenox Library: What Hunt Did and Did Not Learn in France," in *The Architecture of Richard Morris Hunt*, ed. Stein, 91-106.

27. "The Lenox Library, New York, NY," *The American Architect and Building News* 2, no. 88 (September 1, 1877): 280-81;

for contemporary commentary on the library breaking the convention of a central stair, see Silvergold, *Richard Morris Hunt*, 20. For a view of the northwest corner of the library, see HLOC: LC-DIG-ppmsca-57608. For published drawings of the library, LC-DIG-ppmsca-71421 and -71422; and plan, HLOC: LC-DIG-ds-10071.

28. Fornachon to George H. Moore, January 20, 1877, Lenox Library Correspondence, LXNY; "Iron and Stone Buildings," *The New York Times*, July 5, 1873; Schuyler, "Works," 112.

29. Hunt to Lenox, February 24, 1874, Correspondence, LXNY.

30. Lenox to Tweed, December 22, 1869; Papers of Incorporation, 1870, see these and articles in Corporation Papers and Clippings, LXNY. "Public" had many meanings in the nineteenth century as commissioners and trustees sought to define the use and intent of public spaces and institutions. For an introduction, see Rosenzweig and Blackmar, *Park and the People*, 4-7.

31. *A Metropolitan Art-Museum in the City of New York* (New York: Union League Club, 1869), 4; in this see "Mr. Bryant's Address," 8-9; "Remarks of Rev. Dr. [Joseph P.] Thompson," 20-21, and "Remarks of Richard M. Hunt," 17-18.

32. *A Metropolitan Art-Museum*, 151; *New York Herald*, March 15, 1871; donors included William Aspinwall, Alexander Van Rensselaer, James Pinchot, and Levi Morton.

33. Rosenzweig and Blackmar, 350-51; Winifred E. Howe, *A History of the Metropolitan Museum of Art, with a Chapter on the Early

Institutions of Art in New York (New York: Metropolitan Museum of Art, 1913), 1:176. For variants of Hunt's historical society museum, see HLOC: LC-DIG-ppmsca-57598; for his American Museum of Natural History, see HLOC: LC-DIG-ppmsca-59729.

34. As quoted in Howe, *Metropolitan*, 198.

35. "National Academy of Design, Forty First Annual Exhibition," *The Evening Post*, April 28, 1866; Knowlton, *Art-Life*, 43. For RMH's inscribed copy of his brother's book, see HLOC: LC-DIG-ppmsca-57961 and -57962.

36. Howe, *Metropolitan*, 200, 202-3; invitation to April 20, 1880, exhibition of student work and invitation from Arthur L. Tuckerman to Hunt, April 25, 1888, HLOC: Metropolitan Museum scrapbook; loan to Metropolitan Museum of Art, letter from H.G. Hutchins to Hunt, August 18, 1874, HLOC, including loan of a fan belonging to CHH released for the first annual exhibition of the Society of Decorative Art.

37. McCarthy, 38, 40; Amelia Peck and Carol Irish, *Candace Wheeler: The Art and Enterprise of American Design, 1875-1900* (New York: Metropolitan Museum of Art, 2001), 11, 17-18, 22-23; CHHB, 256, states that Hunt rented space to the Society from 1879 to 1895, the lease likely terminated when Richard Howland Hunt moved his office there. See *Eighth Annual Report of the Society of Decorative Art of the City of New York* (New York: 1885); Hunt to William Hand, April 17, 1894, HLOC. *Catalogue of the Loan Exhibition in Aid

of the Society of Decorative Art (New York: Society of Decorative Art, 1877), 1, and the catalogue of the same name for 1878.

38. The Osborns' children exemplified the continuity of their generation's upper-class cultural interests. Henry F. Osborn became the influential president of New York's American Museum of Natural History (1908-33) and William C. Osborn was president of the board of the Metropolitan Museum of Art (1941-47).

39. *Egypt, Three Essays on the History, Religion, and Art of Ancient Egypt* (Cambridge, MA: The Riverside Press, 1892); John Jay Chapman, *Memories and Milestones* (New York: Moffat, Yard, 1915), 88.

40. Martin Brimmer, *Address Delivered at Wellesley College Upon the Opening of the Farnsworth Art School, October 23, 1889* (Boston and New York: Houghton, Mifflin, 1889), 27-28, 18.

41. Schuyler, "Works," 104; "New Residence of Hon. Martin Brimmer," *Boston Traveler*, nd [ca. 1877], clipping scrapbook, HLOC; Chapman, 91, 89.

42. The illustration "Details from Martin Brimmer's Houses," signed J.M. [Joseph Morrill] Wells suggests he may have been an assistant architect on the project, *The American Architect and Building News* 2 (January 27, 1877): np; *Boston Traveler*, nd [ca. 1877], clipping scrapbook. HLOC; Brimmer to RMH, April 19, 1889, HLOC.

43. Elaine Harrington, "International Influences on Henry Hobson Richardson's Glessner House," in *Chicago Architecture, 1872-1922: Birth of A Metropolis*, ed. John

Zukowsky (Munich, London, and New York: Prestel, 1987), 192–93. For a photograph of the Field house library, see LC-DIG-ppmsca-56275.

44. "Correspondence," *The American Architect and Building News* 1 (April 1, 1876): 111.

45. For decorating, see invoice from Pottier & Stymus to Ward, July 10, 1869, John Quincy Adams Ward Papers, Miscellaneous Manuscripts Collection, Manuscript Division, LOC. For a photograph of the first house, see HLOC: LC-DIG-ppmsca-58064; for floor plans of the 1869 and 1882 houses, see HLOC: LC-DIG-ppmsca-94077, -94078, -94079.

46. CHHB, 277.

47. "The Perry Statue," *New-York Tribune*, October 14, 1868. The dedicating minister was the Rev. Dr. Francis Vinton, married to a niece of the commodore.

48. *Walt Whitman's Civil War*, ed. Walter Lowenfels (New York: Alfred A. Knopf, 1960), introduction passim; William Dean Howells, "The Question of Monuments," *The Atlantic* 17, no. 103 (May 1866): 646–49.

49. Lewis, *Frank Furness*, 54–55; CHHB, 143; letter from Olmsted and Vaux to Ward, nd, American Institute of History and Art, Albany, New York, as quoted in Lewis I. Sharp, *John Quincy Adams Ward: Dean of American Sculpture* (Wilmington: University of Delaware Press, 1985), 51; Thomas J. Brown, *Civil War Monuments and the Militarization of America* (Chapel Hill: The University of North Carolina Press, 2019), 50–55; unidentified scrapbook clipping in J.Q.A. Ward Papers,

New-York Historical Society, as quoted in Brown, 51. For color rendering of Drayton, see HLOC: LC-DIG-ppmsca-59726; for early sketches by Hunt, see "Early No Date" RMHS.

50. Alan Trachtenberg, *The Incorporation of America: Culture and Society in the Gilded Age* (New York: Hill and Wang, 2007), 143.

51. Horace Bushnell, *Building Eras in Religion* (New York: Charles Scribner's Sons, 1903), 9, from his 1868 *Hours at Home* v. VII.

52. RMH, "Architecture" (1873), 661–62. For Hunt's early conception for the society, see HLOC: LC-DIG-ds-03990.

53. Hunt, quoted in the Executive Committee of the Society of Alumni, "Supplement" to "Yale College in 1870," June 1, 1870: 4, 13–14; Catherine Lynn, "Building Yale and Razing it from the Civil War to the Great Depression," in *Yale in New Haven: Architecture and Urbanism*, ed. Vincent Scully et al. (New Haven, CT: Yale University Press, 2004), 121. For early site plan, see HLOC: LC-DIG-ppmsca-73177; for a photograph of the hall before the Marquand chapel, see HLOC: LC-DIG-ppmsca-57605; chapel plan and interior view, HLOC: LC-DIG-ppmsca-74001.

54. Lynn, "Building Yale," 176.

55. CHHB, 165–66.

56. Thelma Robins Brown, "Memorial Chapel: The Culmination of the Development of the Campus of Hampton Institute, Hampton, Virginia, 1867–1887" (Master's thesis, Faculty of the School of Architecture, University of Virginia, May 1971), 1–15; Helen W. Ludlow, "The Hampton Normal and Agricultural Institute," *Harper's New*

Monthly Magazine 47, no. 281 (October 1873): 674, 676. For the first Academic Hall, see HLOC: LC-DIG-ppmsca-56360.

57. Booker T. Washington, *Up from Slavery* (New York: A.L. Burt, 1901), 58. For an illustration of the first Academic Hall, see LC-DIG-ppmsca-68593.

58. Brown, "Memorial Chapel," 12; Montgomery Schuyler, "Modern Architecture" (1894), in *American Architecture and Other Writings*, ed. William H. Jordy and Ralph Coe (Cambridge, MA: Belknap Press of Harvard University Press, 1961), 1:113. For period long view of the second Academy building, by Frances Benjamin Johnston, see LC-DIG-ppmsca-17491.

59. A university precedent for Hunt and Armstrong was Deane and Woodward's High Gothic, Oxford University Museum of Natural History (1860); "Virginia Hall," unidentified clipping [ca. 1875], scrapbook, HLOC.

60. See Eliza Woolsey Howland, *Letters of a Family* (New Haven, CT: Tuttle, Morehouse & Taylor, 1899).

61. Elijah M. Haines, *The American Indian (Uh-Nish-In-Na-Ba)* (Chicago: The Mas-Sin-Na'-Gan Company, 1888), 788; Francis R. Kowsky, *The Architecture of Frederick Clarke Withers* (Middletown, CT: Wesleyan University Press, 1980), 35; Howland, 34–35; Henry Winthrop Sargent, *Skeleton Tours through England, Scotland, Ireland, Wales, Denmark, Norway, Sweden, Russia, Poland, and Spain* (New York: D. Appleton, 1870); "Tioronda," National Register of Historic Places, December 20, 2021, https://parks.ny.gov/ documents/shpo/

national-register/Tioronda Estate Craig HouseHistoric District BeaconDutchess County.pdf (accessed June 19, 2023). For exterior of music room, see LC-DIG-ppbd-01327. For Tioronda long-view stereo card, see HLOC: LC-DIG-ppmsca-57031.

62. For the Presbyterian church, see HLOC: LC-DIG-ppmsca-58061. For plan and elevation of Howland library, see HLOC: LC-DIG-ppmsca-73174; for a corner view of the exterior, see HLOC: LC-DIG-ppmsca-57617.

63. Thomas Wentworth Higginson, "Old Newport Days," *The Outlook* 91 (April 17, 1909): 878; [Martha J. Lamb] "The Homes of America," *The Art Journal* 2 (October 1876): 291–92; color as suggested by Landau, "Continental," 286, quoting from *Boston Journal*, April 18, 1870, Margery Deane scrapbook, 2, Newport Historical Society. For Hunt's photograph of Chillon, see HLOC: LC-DIG-ppmsca-57025; for the Colford chalet, see HLOC: LC-DIG-ppmsca-64847; for 1852 sketch of a Swiss chalet by Hunt, see HLOC: LC-DIG-ppmsca-57972; for a possible inspiration in France, see chalet of the romantic author Alphonse de Lamartine, Passy, France, HLOC: LC-DIG-ppmsca-57954.

64. Landau, "Continental," 286–88. For the Appleton cottage, see HLOC: LC-DIG-ds-05286 and HLOC: LC-DIG-ppmsca-56359; for Marquand, see HLOC: LC-DIG-ppmsca-74928 and HLOC: LC-DIG-ds-05284 and -05285. For Linden Gate German inspiration, see LC-DIG-ppmsca-74914, a revelatory comparison

first cited by Landau in "Continental," 288.

65. Winslow Ames, "The Transformation of Chateau-sur-Mer," *Journal of the Society of Architectural Historians* 29 (December 1970): 291–306; Nicole Nicas Rovner, "The Neo-Renaissance Style and the Victorian Interior: The Expression of Identity in the Library at Chateau-sur-Mer, Newport, Rhode Island," a paper for the Preservation Society of Newport County, June 20, 2010, and revised, January 2014, https://www.newportmansions.org/documents/learn/luigi%20frullini%20paper.pdf (accessed June 5, 2020); Paul F. Miller, "The Pure Newport Time," in *Very Simple Charm: The Early Life and Work of Richard Morris Hunt* (Newport, RI: The Newport Art Museum, 2014), 37; CHH recalled that in 1874 or 1875, Hunt shipped "mantels and carvings from Florence and Paris" for the Wetmores' chateau, CHHB, 234. For Hunt's shadow study of Chateau-sur-Mer, see HLOC: LC-DIG-ppmsca-94080.

66. See, for instance, Chester, England, HLOC: LC-DIG-ppmsca-57956 and -74925. Another likely inspiration was Colmar, France.

67. Jonathan Hunt to JLH, June 3, 1871, Folder 4, HFP; CHHB, 225–26.

68. Hunt purchased a vault in Père Lachaise for Jonathan and his family, and left the design of a "monument" to a colleague from Hector Lefuel's office, CHHB, 236–38.

69. 1867 RMHS; CHHB, 238; for Hunt's books by Viollet-le-Duc, see HLOC catalogue by Elisabeth Parker; Henry Van Brunt, *Discourses on Architecture* (vol. 1, 1875,

vol. 2, 1881). For Hunt's sketch of Pierrefonds, see HLOC: LC-DIG-ppmsca-57982.

70. Post, 88; CHHB, Beecher to CHH, April 4, 1874; and 129.

Chapter 4
Desirable Elements
for Wealth

1. As quoted in CHHB, 245; *International Exhibition. 1876 Official Catalogue, Part II, Art Gallery, Annexes, and Outdoor Works of Art: Department IV—Art*, rev. ed. (Philadelphia: Centennial Catalogue Company, 1876), 33–35; "Lettres de Philadelphie," *Revue générale de l'architecture et des travaux publics*, 4th series: 4:234. For one of the park drawings exhibited, see HLOC: LC-DIG-ppmsca-57950.

2. "Paper on the Architectural Exhibit of the Centennial Exhibition," *Proceedings of the Tenth Annual Convention of the American Institute of Architects* (1876): 35.

3. Ibid., 35–37.

4. "Correspondence," *The American Architect and Building News* 2, no. 98 (November 10, 1877): 361.

5. Hunt, "The Church Architecture That We Need," *The American Architect and Building News* 2, no. 100 (November 24, 1877): 374–75, and no. 101 (December 1, 1877): 384–85; see also 2, no. 98 (November 10, 1877): 1.

6. "Marquand, Allan, Class of 1874," Princetoniana Museum, https://www.princetonianamuseum.org/artifact/5e779c7f-b8ac-434b-a53e-0923d76935a7 (accessed April 27, 2023); Allan to Henry Marquand, November

25, 1879, Historical Subject Files, Grounds and Buildings, Series A, Princeton University Archives, as quoted in Sara E. Bush and P.C. Kemeny, "The Princeton University Chapels: An Architectural and Religious History," *The Princeton University Library Chronicle* 60, no. 3 (Spring 1999): 330.

7. Bush and Kemeny, "Chapels," 330, quoting from Allan to Henry Marquand, November 25, 1879; Michael J. Paulus, "Beyond 'Pabulum for the Undergraduates': The Development of the Princeton Theological Seminary Library in the Nineteenth Century," *Libraries & the Cultural Record* 42, no. 3 (2007): 251, including an interior photograph of the Lenox Library. For the library's plan, see HLOC: LC-DIG-ppmsca-73175; for the exterior, HLOC: LC-DIG-ppmsca-57604.

8. Bush and Kemeny, "Chapels," 329-31; CHHB, 271. For view of the altar, see HLOC: LC-DIG-ppmsca-57044.

9. CHHB, 372; as quoted from *The Princetonian*, October 21, 1881, in Bush and Kemeny, "Chapels," 335; Schuyler, "Works," 120.

10. Bush and Kemeny, "Chapels," 330, quoting from Allan to Henry Marquand, November 25, 1879.

11. For Hunt's Trinity submission, see *The New York Sketchbook of Architecture* (March 1879). Hunt was persistent in his prosaic approach; his ca. 1876 submission for Holy-Trinity Church in New York, HLOC: LC-DIG-ppmsca-59730, was remarkably similar to his earlier Boston Trinity plans. For RMH National Academy of Design submission, see HLOC: LC-DIG-ppmsca-59725.

12. For the obituary letter he wrote to *The American Architect and Building News* in 1886, see CHHB, 309-10, including Hunt's visit to the dying Richardson.

13. Mariana Griswold Van Rensselaer, *Henry Hobson Richardson and His Works* (New York: Houghton, Mifflin, 1888), 74-75, recounts these positions. For Hunt's copy of this book, see HLOC: NA737. RV3c.2 fol. "'The Remonstrance of the Architects,'" *The American Architect and Building News* 1, no. 3 (April 22, 1876): 135, and RMH et al., "The Experts and the New York Capitol," 2, no. 56 (March 17, 1877): 85.

14. CHHB, 255.

15. Sally Webster, *William Morris Hunt*, 185-86; Marian Hooper Adams, *The Letters of Mrs. Henry Adams* (Boston: Little, Brown, 1936), 181; Baker, 157; CHHB, 268. William Morris Hunt's gravestone is in Prospect Hill Cemetery on a ridge overlooking the Connecticut River, and matches his father's, suggesting Hunt designed both, possibly at the same time. I am grateful to Paul Carnahan for searching out the Brattleboro site during the COVID-19 lockdown.

16. A proposed solution to Leavitt Hunt's financial troubles was to sell his "Chardin" to Martin Brimmer; January 17, 1872, August 26, 1874, and passim, part 2, Folder 8, JHJ, suggesting all the Hunt brothers were collectors. July 26, 1873, part 2, folder 8, JHJ; Jane Hunt's watercolors of California's Spanish missions are now in the Pasadena Public Library, Pasadena, California.

17. CHHB, 215-16, recalls that, in a performance of the opera, the star bit Victor Capoul singing Faust, for "taking advantage of the situation." M.E.W. Sherwood, "New York in the Seventies," *Lippincott's Monthly Magazine* 62, no. 26 (July-December 1898): 393-98.

18. Carnegie first published his essay "Wealth" in *North American Review*, June 1889, and then in his *The Gospel of Wealth*, see https://www.carnegie.org/about/our-history/gospelofwealth/ (accessed June 18, 2020).

19. Edith Wharton, *A Backward Glance* (New York: Charles Scribner's Sons, 1933), 92-93.

20. Martin Bressani, "Revivalism," in *Nineteenth-Century Architecture*, ed. Bressani and Christina Contandriopoulos, vol. 3, part I (Chichester: Wiley-Blackwell, 2017), section 1; Lasc, *Interior Decorating*, 17, and passim for an illuminating history of the period room.

21. RMH to house contractor William Hand, October 20, 1879, William Hand Collection, Prints and Photographs Division, LOC; that Marcotte did the Winthrop interiors is supported by elevations for the Winthrop interiors in the same hand as the Bronson renderings, see HLOC: LC-DIG-ppmsca-57958. For Winthrop's reception room, see LC-DIG-ppmsca-56273; George Sheldon, *Artistic Houses*, vol. 1, part 2 (New York: D. Appleton, 1883), 135-37; for Bronson Marcotte interiors. See HLOC: LC-DIG-ppmsca-64989, -64990, -64991, -64992, -65169, -65170.

22. Catherine E. Beecher and Harriet Beecher Stowe, *The American Woman's Home* (New York: J.B. Ford, 1869), 143, 19, 84, 93-94; for the culture of home, see Louise

L. Stevenson, *The Victorian Homefront: American Thought and Culture, 1860–1880* (Ithaca, NY, and London: Cornell University Press, 1991), 1–29, and passim.

23. Alva Vanderbilt Belmont, unpublished memoir, 1932, Matilda Young Papers, Special Collections, William R. Perkins Library, Duke University, Durham, North Carolina, 1-6.

24. Ibid., 10–11; Alva's daughter, Consuelo Vanderbilt Balsan, attended a school for six girls in the Bronson house, see her *The Glitter and the Gold*, reprint ed. (New York: Harper, 1952; London: Hodder and Stoughton, 2011), 17; the Bronsons were on Caroline Astor's list of 400 acceptable New Yorkers. For a photograph of Idle Hour, see HLOC: LC-DIG-ds-11203.

25. "History of St. Mark's Episcopal Church," Historical Society of Islip Hamlet, https://www.isliphamlethistory.org/historic_markers.html?select=%22episcopal_church.html%22 (accessed June 14, 2019); Belmont, memoir, 99-101.

26. Belmont, memoir, 111, 25.

27. For the French Villa Saint-Maur, by Pierre Manguin (1852), clearly known to Hunt through Hector Lefuel, see Marek Zgórniak, "Le château de Świerklaniec, oeuvre oubliée d'Hector Lefuel," *La revue du Louvre et des Musées de France* 1 (1989): 46–52; Montgomery Schuyler, "The Vanderbilt Houses," in *American Architecture and Other Writings*, ed. William H. Jordy and Ralph Coe, first published in *Harper's Weekly* 1882 (Cambridge, MA: Belknap Press, 1861), 489-99. For Fisk drawings, see HLOC: LC-DIG-ppmsca-94081, -94082, -94083.

28. "Art Applied to Decoration and Furniture of Modern Houses," *The Decorator and Furnisher* 1, no. 2 (October 1882): 8. The room decorators are identified in John V. Van Pelt, *A Monograph of the William K. Vanderbilt House* (New York: privately printed, 1924), 16, and by plans in the HLOC; for descriptions of the rooms, see "The Vanderbilt House," *The Decorator and Furnisher* 2, no. 2 (May 1883): 44; also Belmont, memoir, 105-7; the two mirror artists were "Misses Ely," CHHB, 271. For sketch of the bathroom, see HLOC: LC-DIG-ds-10878; for view of the Vanderbilt hall interior, see LC-DIG-ppmsca-65044; for the main stair and its stained glass, see LC-DIG-ppmsca-64797.

29. Allard hired outside architects, decorators, and upholsterers to create the furnished interiors he supplied to American clients. The plan was first published in G. Félix Lenoir, *Traité théorique et pratique du tapissier : principes de la décoration* (Paris: Librairie artistique, industrielle et littéraire de Ch. Juliot, 1885), LOC: NK2115.5.F3 L46, but could easily date to the time of the Vanderbilt salon, having been drawn and seen by Allard and Hunt before publication, possibly at a salon; for Lenoir plan, see LC-DIG-ppmsca-74207.

30. Francis Haskell, *The Ephemeral Museum: Old Master Paintings and the Rise of the Art Exhibition* (New Haven, CT: Yale University Press, 2000), 22–25, 83–84; the published cost of Sandier's furnishings was some 10 million French francs, *Le Petit Journal* (December 5, 1902): 1, as quoted in Amélie Duntze-Ouvry, "Eugène Stanislas Oudinot de la Faverie artiste peintre-verrier (1827–1889) et le renouveau du vitrail civil au XIXe siècle" (PhD thesis, Université Blaise Pascal, Clermont-Ferrand, 2016), 317; Belmont, memoir, 107, Sir Joseph "Duveen"; for provenance, see https://www.metmuseum.org/art/collection/search?q=William+K.+Vanderbilt (accessed September 3, 2021).

31. The ceiling of the Vanderbilt dining hall was twenty-eight feet high. For Oudinot's private clients, including Henry Marquand and August Belmont, and window artists, see Duntze-Ouvry, 346-55; and window artists, 319, 354; "Mrs. Vanderbilt's Window," *Truth* 11, no. 274 (March 30, 1882): 445; CHHB, 334. Status of the window is unknown. For armorial windows in the grand stair, see LC-DIG-ppmsca-57019.

32. "All Society in Costume," *The New York Times*, March 27, 1883, for interiors, guests, and CHH. Already in 1852 Hunt had considered the painting in Santa Maria Novella (illustrated here) a "very fine fresco," 1852 RMHS.

33. Cortissoz, *Art and Common Sense*, 395; Mariana Van Rensselaer, "Recent Architecture in America," *Century* 31, no. 9 (1899): 162.

34. C. Anthony Holland to RMH, June 8, 1886, Misc. Letters, HLOC; for the leaden outcome due to Borden's wrangling with the Hunt office, see the finished house, HLOC: LC-DIG-ppmsca-57021; for the related Josephine Schmid, Elbridge T. Gerry, and

William V. Lawrence New York chateaus, see HLOC: LC-DIG-ppmsca-65046, -53812, and -64870. See here SC.10.

35. Marquand to RMH, October 7 [1885], Allan Marquand Papers, Princeton University Library, Special Collections, Princeton, New Jersey; and in the same papers, letters from Marquand in Europe that reveal Hunt's engagement in the collecting and decorating of the house. The sale catalogue of the Henry Marquand collection noted that a Louis XVI clock had been "bought for Mr. Marquand by the late Richard M. Hunt." *Illustrated Catalogue of the Art and Literary Property Collected by the Late Henry G. Marquand* (New York: American Art Association/Anderson Galleries, 1903), lot 1205.

36. For the interrelationship between Marquand's investments and the house's wood and stone, an interpretation that could be extended to Vanderbilt houses, see Melody Barnett Deusner, "Building a Reputation: Henry Gurdon Marquand's New York Mansion," in *Orchestrating Elegance: Alma-Tadema and the Marquand Music Room*, ed. Kathleen M. Morris and Alexis Goodin (New Haven, CT: Yale University Press, 2017), 45-49; "New York Houses," *Harper's Weekly* 30, no. 1535 (May 22, 1886): 331; *Catalogue of the Marquand Residence Auction Sale Held Thursday April 27, 1905* (New York: De Vinne Press, 1905), 3-9. For Marquand interiors, see HLOC: LC-DIG-ppmsca-57601, -57602, and -57603. The referenced mural, by Alphonse Forestier and C. Héron, is in the breakfast room of the Louvre's extant

Napoléon III apartments, created by Lefuel 1854-61.

37. *The Inland Architect and News Record* 8, no. 9 (December 1886), 90-91; Russell Sturgis, "Introductory," *Illustrated Catalogue of the Art and Literary Property Collected by the Late Henry G. Marquand*, ed. Thomas E. Kirby (New York: American Art Association, 1903), np.

38. Belmont, memoir, 111.

39. J.T. Headley, *The Great Riots of New York, 1712–1873, Including a Full and Complete Account of the Four Days' Draft Riot of 1863* (New York: E.B. Treat, 1873), 19, as quoted in Beckert, *Monied Metropolis*, 141; Jonathan Baxter Harrison, "Certain Dangerous Tendencies in American Life," *Atlantic Monthly* 42, no. 252 (1878): 392-93, 402, as quoted in Richard White, *The Republic for Which It Stands: The United States During Reconstruction and the Gilded Age, 1865-1896* (Oxford: Oxford University Press, 2017), 396-97.

40. New York City department of City Planning, Population Division, "1790–2000 NYC Historical and Foreign Born Population." Andrew Carnegie, "The Best Fields for Philanthropy," *North American Review* 149, no. 397 (December 1889): 686.

41. *Thirty-Second Annual Report of the New York Children's Aid Society, November, 1884* (New York, 1884): 4; Charles Loring Brace, *The Dangerous Classes of New York* (New York: Wynkoop & Hallenbeck, 1872), i-ii, 27, 29. See also "Certain Dangerous Tendencies in American Life," *The Atlantic Monthly* 42 (October 1878): 385-403.

42. *The Thirty-Seventh Annual Report of the Association for the Relief of Respectable Aged and Indigent Females* (New York, 1850): 2, 15-19; Pam Tice, "The Story of 891 Amsterdam Avenue and how it became a New York City Landmark," Bloomingdale History, https://bloomingdalehistory.com/2013/10/28/the-story-of-891-amsterdam-avenue-and-how-it-became-a-new-york-city-landmark/ (accessed January 15, 2020).

43. Richard Mayo Smith, *Emigration and Immigration: A Study in Social Science* (New York: Charles Scribner's Sons, 1890), 151-52; Samuel Osgood, *New York in the Nineteenth Century: A Discourse Delivered Before the New York Historical Society, on Its Sixty-Second Anniversary, November 20, 1866* (New York: New York Historical Society, 1867), 6; *Annual Report of the New England Society in the City of New York*, no. 76 (New York, 1881): np, 4, 92, 17, 21.

44. Russell Sturgis Jr., "The Work of J.Q.A. Ward," *Scribner's Magazine* 32, no. 4 (October 1902): 389.

45. Journal of Frédéric-Auguste Bartholdi, May 27–October 24, 1871, Manuscripts Collection 223, New York Public Library, New York; David Hackett Fischer, *Liberty and Freedom: A Visual History of America's Founding Ideas* (Oxford: Oxford University Press, 2005), 238-39; Marvin Trachtenberg, *The Statue of Liberty* (New York: Viking Press, 1976); June Hargrove and Pierre Provoyeur et al., *Liberty: The French-American Statue in Art and History* (New York: Harper

and Row, 1986), including Susan R. Stein, "Richard Morris Hunt and the Pedestal," 176–85; Bartholdi mounted the painting, reproduced here, at the base of the arm of the Statue of Liberty that he exhibited in Philadelphia to solicit funds. For the painting at the fair, see LC-DIG-ppmsca-02957; for early drawings by Hunt, see HLOC: LC-DIG-ppmsca-51637, -51638, -51639.

46. *Pedestal Art Fund Exhibition, at the National Academy of Design, December 1883* (New York, 1883): Introductory, 20, 141–42, 153.

47. Schuyler, "Works," 529.

48. Baker, 302–3.

49. "Yorktown Victory Monument 03," National Park Service, https://www.nps.gov/york/learn/historyculture/vicmon.htm (accessed June 23, 2021).

50. *Moniteur des Architectes* 15, no. 4 (1881): plates 7–8, 50. For stereocard of the Châtelet column, see HLOC: LC-DIG-ppmsca-71428.

51. Schuyler, "Works," 530. RMH to [Admiral Benjamin] Jaurès (1887), HLOC. Hunt mailed the admiral a photograph of the Yorktown monument, as he did with other projects throughout his career as a way to boast and insert American architecture into European thought.

52. RMH to Ward, March 3, 1886, and RMH to Alexander E. Orr, February 8, 1886, John Quincy Adams Ward Papers, New-York Historical Society, New York; see "Not Qualified for a Juror" [1873], Scrapbook, HLOC. For Hunt's criticism and suspicion of the press, see also CHHB, 257.

53. The Society raised money for John Ward as sculptor, and an Act of Congress in 1884 appropriated $30,000 for

Hunt's pedestal, see Sharp, *John Quincy Adams Ward*, 237–38, 69–70; "Garfield Monument," Architect of the Capitol, www.aoc.gov/explore-capitol-campus/art/garfield-monument.

54. Erastus B. Bigelow, "The Relations of Labor and Capital," *Atlantic Monthly* 42, no. 252 (October 1878): 475–78; Elliot F. Shepard, *Labor and Capital Are One*, 10th ed. (New York: American Bank Note, 1886), 8–11.

55. Sharp, *Ward*, 233–35. For Greeley statue, see LC-DIG-ggbain-19303.

56. The detailed account of the theft, with diagrams, "Ghouls in New-York City," *The New York Times*, November 8, 1878; Michael Caratzas, "Vanderbilt Mausoleum," New York City Landmarks Preservation Commission, April 12, 2016, Designation List 487, LP-1208, np; on this property, to the side of the Vanderbilt mausoleum, Hunt also designed the 1893 granite casket tomb for Elliott Shepard; and Hunt & Hunt (1897) built the Vanderbilt-Sloane crypt into the mausoleum hill.

57. William A. Croffut, *The Vanderbilts and the Story of Their Fortune* (Chicago and New York: Belford, Clarke, 1886), 214–15.

58. As quoted in Croffut, 213; Caratzas, "Vanderbilt Mausoleum." For the early rendering, see HLOC: LC-DIG-ppmsca-73171.

59. CHHB, 286–87.

60. CHHB, 287–88; banker Junius S. Morgan, Marquand collaborators Sir Lawrence Alma-Tadema and Sir Frederic Leighton, and American illustrator Edwin Austin Abbey were all dinner guests.

61. CHHB, 300, 289–90; A. Bartholdi to Richard Butler, July 21 and July 30, 1885, Correspondence of the American Committee of the Statue of Liberty, Manuscripts and Archives Committee, New York Public Library, as cited in Baker, 323n2, 519; other guests at the café on the Place de la Bourse included William-Adolphe Bouguereau, Jean-Léon Gérôme, and the Duc d'Aumale; CHHB, 293; 294-294a; 290-291.

62. CHHB, 26, 293; Butler's Diary, December 22, 1885, Archives, Chateau de Chantilly, Chantilly, France. Guests included the diplomat Joseph Alexander (Baron Hübner), Octave de Champeaux, landscape painter, and Émile Froment-Meurice, silversmith and collaborator with architect Félix Duban.

63. CHHB, 287, 297–301.

64. CHHB, 286, 315. See letters from RMH to William Hand, March 14, 1894, and CHH to Hand, May 1, 1894, regarding work for CHH at the Grace Episcopal Church Day Nursery (founded 1878), New York, William Hand Collection, Prints and Photographs Division, LOC.

65. *Annual Report of the Officers and Committees of the Architectural League of New York, 1909-1910*: 81. "The Architectural League of New York," *The Engineering and Building Record* 16, no. 24 (November 11, 1887): 684; photographs of the Marquand house were exhibited, see *Catalogue of the Third Annual Exhibition of the Architectural League of New York* (1887): 7, 19, 20, 26, 35. For an RMH Louvre drawing, see HLOC: LC-DIG-ppmsca-51626. Louise B. Bethune from Buffalo, New York was the

first woman to apply for AIA membership, see Tony Wrenn, "1887–1896: A Decade of Outreach, Inclusiveness, and Internationalism," *AIArchitect* (January 2006), https://info.aia.org/aiarchitect/thisweek06/0106/a150_tw010606.htm (accessed September 4, 2023).

66. Brimmer, *Address Delivered at Wellesley College*, 15.

67. Van Pelt, *Monograph*, 11.

Scrapbook Portfolio

1. Hunt's scrapbooks of printed materials survive, but the AIA dismantled most of the Hunt drawing folios and cataloged the drawings individually by project. A record of their original sequence in scrapbooks is at the LOC.

Chapter 5
Les Palais Hunt

1. "Personal," *Harper's Weekly* 31, no. 1579 (February 5, 1887): 91.

2. William H. Furness, "Closing Address," *Proceedings of the Fourth Annual Convention of the American Institute of Architects* (1870): 251, 248.

3. Bruce Price, *A Large Country House* (New York: William T. Comstock, 1887), preface, NA7610. P7, HLOC. The top one percent now owned forty percent of the nation's wealth; industrializing Europe tracked America, with the one percent at forty-nine percent in 1886 and over sixty percent by 1910, Piketty, *Capital*, 348–49.

4. For RMH Olana, see HLOC: LC-DIG-ppmsca-57952.

5. Letter from Morton to the director of the École, January 8, 1885, Archives of the École des Beaux-Arts, Paris; CHHB, 335. For Fairlawn's 1869 Neo-Grec interior, related to Griswold house and Chateau-sur-Mer rooms, see HLOC: LC-DIG-ppmsca-64871, -57614, -57615.

6. Josiah Granville Leach, *Memoranda Relating to the Ancestry and Family of Hon. Levi Parsons Morton* (Cambridge, MA: Riverside Press, 1894), 1.

7. CHHB, 162–63, also Baker, 234–35, 487, note 9, and Margery Deane scrapbook, clippings for June 21, 1870, and June 12, 1871, Newport Historical Society, as cited in Baker, 505n15.

8. Mary Murphy-Schlichting, "A Summer Salon: Literary and Cultural Circles in Newport, Rhode Island, 1850–1890" (PhD dissertation, New York University, 1992), 15, 26–27, 31; Frederick Law Olmsted, "Improvement of Easton's Beach," report to the Newport Improvement Association, March 13, 1883, 9.

9. Paul Bourget, *Outre-Mer, Notes sur l'Amérique* (Paris: Alphonse Lemerre, 1895), 1:60; CHHB, 368; Anthony to RMH, August 22, 1885, HLOC.

10. Schuyler, "Works," 168, 165. Construction drawings of Ochre Court in Prints & Photographs Division, Library of Congress. Unprocessed in PR 13 CN 2018:018.

11. CHHB, 370, cites Bowditch, confirmed by letters in the Goelet archives at Salva Regina University, Newport, RI, dating to 1896; Frederick Law Olmsted and Co. to C. Anthony Holland, April 11, 1893, Olmsted Archive, LOC. For an overall plan by Olmsted, see

HLOC: LC-DIG-ppmsca-58063. For unrealized flower parterre plans, possibly by Bowditch, see Ochre Court drawings file, HLOC. For period view from Cliff Walk with Ochre Court, see HLOC: LC-DIG-ppmsca-64853.

12. Clark, quoted in an unidentified Frank Leslie publication, mansions scrapbook, HLOC. The house decorators are noted in the second-floor plan reproduced here and in the Goelet Family Papers, Salva Regina University, Newport, RI, https://www.riamco.org/render?eadid=US-RNSRU-SP_02&view=inventory#c1 (accessed November 11, 2019). For period interior photographs, see HLOC: LC-DIG-ppmsca-64855 and -64865.

13. Marquand's glass dealer was Jules Charvet, see Esmée Quodbach, "Collecting Old Masters for New York: Henry Gurdon Marquand and the Metropolitan Museum of Art," *Journal of Historians of Netherlandish Art* 9, no. 1 (Winter 2017): 2; "Forging the Renaissance: On the Use of Glass Pieces in the (In)famous Spitzer's Collection," *Revista de História da Arte* 3, no. 94 (2015), https://www.academia.edu/12069574/Forging_the_Renaissance (accessed January 3, 2023); Jane Hayward, "Stained-Glass Windows from the Carmelite Church at Boppard-am-Rhein: A Reconstruction of the Glazing Program of the North Nave," *Metropolitan Museum Journal* 2 (1969): 75–114. The Ochre Court window is assembled from window segments, originally at Boppard, representing the Ten Commandments, donors, and saints.

14. Letter from Bert Lippincott to author, "Marble House," February 8, 2021, Newport Historical Society; Andrew Jackson Downing and Calvert Vaux, *Villas and Cottages* (New York: Harper & Brothers, 1857), v, 307–8.

15. CHHB, 366, 370. Another source of inspiration was the Chateau de Bizy, redesigned in 1740, Vernon, France, a photograph of which is in the HLOC, uncatalogued chateau photographs.

16. Alva Vanderbilt, admiring of Second Empire society, was referring to Empress Eugénie's escape to England after the Franco-Prussian War. She was in Paris at the time of the 1867 fair and no doubt saw the Empress' exhibition. Belmont, memoir, 63, 72. Jeanne Louise Henriette Campan, *The Private Life of Marie Antoinette, Queen of France and Navarre, with Sketches and Anecdotes of the Court of Louis XVI* (New York: Charles Scribner's Sons, 1887).

17. CHHB, 370; structure of Marble House per author correspondence, March 9, 2021, with Lauren Landi, Newport Society for Preservation; the entry drive was known as "the horseshoe," "Doors Fit for a Palace," *The New York Times*, April 26, 1892; CHHB, 364, 351; the capital cast was from L. Alexandre Desachy, a pioneer in the field, Hunt to Luigi di Cesnola, June 29, 1889, META; see Hunt's extensive cast purchases in 1867 RMHS, also CHHB, 212. For Hunt's sketch of the staircase at Fontainebleau, see 1856 RMHS; for period photographs of the front and back of Marble House, see HLOC: LC-DIG-ppmsca-53507 and HLOC: LC-DIG-ds-10772;

for the Petit Trianon photograph in the Hunt collection, see HLOC: LC-DIG-ppmsca-57028.

18. Price, *Country House*, preface. For Marble House and the Trianon, see Sam Watters, "Versailles Outre-Mer : Architecture et Décoration aux États-Unis," in *Versailles Revival, 1867–1937*, ed. Laurent Salomé and Claire Bonnotte (Paris: Chateau de Versailles, 2019), 316–23; Bourget, 65; for north portico, see Harry W. Desmond and Herbert Croly, *Stately Homes in America: From Colonial Times to the Present Day* (New York: D. Appleton, 1903), 426; also portico compared with south portico of the White House, "Doors Fit for a Palace," *The New York Times*, April 26, 1892; Belmont, memoir, 125.

19. Belmont, memoir, 9.

20. For the Gavet collection as it was originally displayed, see HLOC: LC-DIG-ppmsca-68591 and -68592, scanned from Hunt's copy of Émile Molinier, *Collection Émile Gavet : catalogue raisonné* (Paris: D. Jouaust, 1889), inscribed "*À mon très distingué confrère Monsieur Hunt, Architecte, Souvenir bien affectueux. Émile Gavet*" ("To my very distinguished colleague, Mr. Hunt, Architect, With warm regards..."), supporting that Hunt was engaged in the Vanderbilt purchase; HLOC: N5260. G3, fol. The Vanderbilts' purchase included metal work, ceramics, and furniture. Molinier was similary the editor of the multivolume 1891 catalogue for Gavet's competitor, Frédéric Spitzer. For Hunt's connections to Gavet, see Alan Chong, "Émile Gavet: Patron, Collector, Dealer," in *Gothic Art in

the Gilded Age*, ed. Virginia Brilliant (Sarasota, FL: The John and Mable Ringling Museum of Art, 2009), 2–10. The Gavet-Vanderbilt collection, substantially, was acquired in 1927 by John Ringling.

21. CHHB, 365; Belmont, memoir, 116. For Allard drawing of the stair landing, see HLOC: LC-DIG-ppmsca-52066.

22. 1867 RMHS; Hunt, "Paper on the Architectural Exhibit," 38; Garnier, *Théâtre*, 1–2.

23. Edwin P. Hoyt, *The Vanderbilts and Their Fortunes* (New York: Doubleday, 1962), 274; "The Breakers," National Historic Landmark Nomination, October 27, 1994, 1, https://npgallery.nps.gov/GetAsset/0d4671ef-bb62-485d-8168-e96a5bc97be5 (accessed March 15, 2022); "The Breakers," The Cultural Landscape Foundation https://www.tclf.org/landscapes/breakers (accessed June 2, 2023).

24. Marble House is on 5.36 acres and is 28,800 square feet, email to author from Bert Lippincott, May 31, 2022, Newport Historical Society. The Breakers is on 13.1 acres and is 126,000 square feet, email to author from Katherine Garrett-Cox, March 12, 2019, Preservation Society of Newport County. For Breakers exterior photographs, see HLOC: LC-DIG-ppmsca-53514 and HLOC: LC-DIG-ds-04988. Schuyler, "Works," 174.

25. The French architect Richard Bouwens van der Boijen (1863-1939) worked for Allard on the music room, see drawings, dated November 11, 1895, the Breakers file, Newport Historical Society. For a period photograph of

Allard's salon/music room, see HLOC: LC-DIG-ppmsca-64852; for library, - 58053; for billiard room, -53509; for the Pythia fountain, see HLOC: LC-DIG-ppmsca-74931 and Hunt's version at the Breakers, LC-DIG-ppbd-01332.

26. *The Diary of George A. Lucas: An American Art Agent in Paris, 1857-1909* (Princeton, NJ: Princeton University Press, 1979), 2:514, 516, 542.

27. As quoted in Eleanor Dwight, *Edith Wharton: An Extraordinary Life* (Los Angeles: University of California Press, 1992), 52, the letter was written in the same year as the publication of Wharton and Codman's *The Decoration of Houses* (1897). RMH to Codman, May 2, 1894, August 13, 1894, and September 25, 1894, Papers of Ogden Codman Jr., Codman Family Papers, Box 99, Library and Archives, Historic New England, Boston, Massachusetts.

28. Sara Eve Wermiel, "Nothing Succeeds like Failure: The Development of the Fireproof Building in the United States, 1790-1911" (PhD dissertation, MIT, 1966), introduction and passim; Eric P. Lints, "The Breakers, a Technologies and Construction Report," Educational Department, February 1992, Preservation Society of Newport County; "The Breakers," National Historic Landmark Nomination, 4; for contractors consistently employed by Hunt, see letter from RHH to Cornelius Vanderbilt II, June 26, 1896, Newport Historical Society.

29. S.C. de Soissons [Guy Jean Raoul Eugène Charles Emmanuel de Savoie-Carignan, comte de Soissons], *A Parisian in America* (Boston: Estes and Lauriat, 1896), 167-68, 170; for Hunt's copy, dedicated by the author, see HLOC: Hunt N6535.B5757.

30. Belmont, memoir, 111; David Sadighian, "The Renaissance Inside and Out: Historical Reference and Financial Modernity in the 'Rothschild Style' Interior, c. 1820-1860," in *The Italian Renaissance in the 19th Century*, ed. Lina Bolzoni and Alina Payne (Florence: Villa I Tatti, 2018), 157-88. The differences and implications of what might be called "aesthetic branding" by the rich are beyond the present scope, but worth pursuit; the second-floor Winthrop and Bronson reception rooms opened to one another, *The American Architect and Building News* 4, no. 140 (August 31, 1878): 77; "The Case of Wonderful Wainscotings and Furniture Liable to Confiscation," *San Francisco Examiner*, ca. 1895, Astor and Vanderbilt house scrapbook HLOC. Early color renderings of exterior elevations show that Hunt initially proposed a French Renaissance, limestone and brick mansion, see HLOC: LC-DIG-ppmsca-56356, -56357, -56358.

31. Jules Verchère, *L'art du mobilier. Traité graphique d'ameublements des styles. Renaissance, Louis XIII, Louis XIV, Louis XV & Louis XVI avec coupes & plans de constructions à l'échelle de 0m 10 cent. pour 1 mètre accompagné de tous les éléments d'ornamentation et motifs d'architecture pour servir à la composition ou à la décoration du meuble. Composé & gravé à l'eau forte par J. Verchère, sculpteur, architecte d'ameublement* (Paris: J. Verchère, 1879), "Cheminée style Renaissance," pl. 11, WK2260.V4 XX in HLOC. For the illustration, see HLOC: LC-DIG-74934. Frank A. Lesley launched his society pictorial with "The New Astor Mansion," *The Puritan* 1, no. 1 (January 1897): 188. For the stairs in the Caroline Astor wing, see HLOC: LC-DIG-ppmsca-58056; for a view of the ballroom from the fireplace to Caroline Astor's dais, see HLOC: LC-DIG-ppmsca-64869.

32. Belmont, memoir, 92; CHHB, 422; as quoted in B.H. Friedman, *Gertrude Vanderbilt Whitney* (New York: Doubleday, 1978), 55–56; also, for letters exchanged and depth of the relationship, see Clarice Stasz, *The Vanderbilt Women: Dynasty of Wealth, Glamour, and Tragedy* (San Jose, CA: Excel, 1990), 110-13.

33. John Gilmore Speed, "A Recent Glimpse of Biltmore," *New York Herald*, May 29, 1898, the quote being from 1890-91.

34. William Deverell, "Conquest to Convalescence: Nature and Nation in United States History," in *The Oxford Handbook of Environmental History*, ed. Andrew C. Isenberg (New York: Oxford University Press, 2014), 657; Hoyt, *Vanderbilts*, 274; John M. Bryan, *Biltmore Estate: The Most Distinguished Private Place* (New York: Rizzoli, 1994), 31; Cathleen Henshaw, *The Furniture of Biltmore House* (Asheville, NC: Biltmore Company, 1990), 6.

35. Olmsted to Frederick J. Kinsbury, January 20, 1891, Frederick Law Olmsted Papers, LOC; for friendships, see letters between the parties in

the Biltmore Estate Archives, Asheville, NC. Letter from Monet to George Vanderbilt, March 11, 1904, Edith Vanderbilt Correspondence, 3.9/6.1, Box 1 Folder 11, Biltmore Estate Archives; Stapleton Dabney Gooch IV, "The Art and Architectural Library at Biltmore," in *The American Association of Architectural Bibliographers, Papers*, ed. William B. O'Neal (1967), 4:19–46, estimating that Vanderbilt's library had 25,000 volumes.

36. Bryan, *Biltmore Estate*, 38–40; R. Chad Stewart, "Blue Ridge Chateau: The Conceptual Design Evolution of Biltmore House" (Master's thesis, Clemson University, South Carolina, 2020), 34, https://tigerprints.clemson.edu/all_theses/3468 (accessed May 23, 2023), revises the architectural evolution of Biltmore. For some early plans, see HLOC: LC-DIG-ppmsca-54504 through -54510. For the Georgian house, see HLOC: LC-DIG-ds-09292.

37. For unknown reasons, except rest, Hunt also traveled to Mexico with Henry Marquand in the latter's private rail car, CHHB, 280; CHHB, 336–38; Jules Allard Fils to RMH, November 10, 1894, for staining of paneling, Superintendent's incoming correspondence, Box 38 Folder 26, Biltmore Estate Archives; American firms were William Baumgarten; A. Feron; and George Tolmie; the library paneling was by Asheville Woodworking Company, and a London source was Morant, Henshaw, *Furniture*, 23–28, 35. *Hertford House Visitors' Book*, Wallace Collection Archive, London; CHHB, 337; Howard E. Covington Jr., *Lady on the Hill: How Biltmore*

Estate Became an American Icon, introduction by Lord Rothschild (New York: John Wiley and Sons, 2006), x.

38. Michael Hall, *Waddesdon Manor: The Heritage of a Rothschild House* (New York: Harry N. Abrams, 2002), 38–40, 67; "Visitors' Book," June 26, 1886, the Waddesdon Archive at Windmill Hill, Oxfordshire, England; Stewart, "Blue Ridge," 104; Ferdinand de Rothschild, *Waddesden* (London: privately printed, 1897).

39. Rothschild, *Waddesdon*, 3–4, 9.

40. CHHB, 338, 340–43; HLOC Mansion scrapbook, with schedule for the Congress, June 21, 1889; letter from RMH to George Vanderbilt [1889], Incoming Correspondence, 3.9/6.1, Box 1 Folder 7, Biltmore Estate Archives; Butler's Diary, June 21, 1889, Archives, Domaine de Chantilly; CHHB, 308; unidentified clipping, house scrapbook, HLOC.

41. For Biltmore interiors, see https://www.Biltmore.com

42. Schuyler, "Works," 170. Hunt's interest in spiraling staircases at Blois and Chambord was evident in his École-period drawings; see HLOC: LC-DIG-ppmsca-57953 and -59724.

43. CHHB, 425; as quoted in *American Architecture and Other Writings*, ed. William H. Jordy and Ralph Coe (Cambridge, MA: Belknap Press of Harvard University Press, 1961), 2: 544–45. A chateau on a small piece of land, wrote Schuyler, was a "water-place villa."

44. For example, see St. Michael and All Angels, Berwick, East Sussex, near Knole, a house visited by the Hunts and Vanderbilt, heavily restored

in 1856 by Henry Woodyer, student of William Butterfield.

45. CHHB, 382; Olmsted to Eliot, May 5, 1895, Olmsted Papers, LOC. RMH submitted in 1893 a design for a Roman arch flanked by colonnades, with sculpture by Karl Bitter, in the competition for a Soldiers and Sailors monument at Fifty-Ninth Street and Fifth Avenue, see *Catalogue of the Thirteenth Annual Exhibition of New York* (1898): 96, and miscellaneous 1890s clippings scrapbook, HLOC. For rendering, see HLOC: LC-DIG-ds-09314.

46. "A Useful Legacy," *New York Journal*, March 17, 1890; "Biltmore," *The Turf, Field and Farm* 63, no. 3 (March 3, 1896).

47. For published press responses, see Vanderbilt houses scrapbook, HLOC; "fury," James to George Vanderbilt, from Philadelphia, February 1905, Incoming Correspondence, 3.9/6.1, Box 1 Folder 8, Biltmore Estate Archives; James to Wharton, February 8, 1905; James to Gosse, February 16, 1905, *Henry James Letters*, ed. Leon Edel (Cambridge, MA: Belknap Press of Harvard University Press, 1984), 4:346–47, 350–51.

48. For Buberl, see Van Pelt, *Monograph*, 15, the statue is at Eagles Nest, Centerport, New York. For its photograph on the Vanderbilt roof, see Fig. 4.9.

49. Two modest mansions were Archibald Rogers, Crumwold Hall (1889) in New York, and Grey Towers (1886) in Pennsylvania for Huguenot descendant and wall-paper manufacturer James Pinchot, inspired by the Marquis de Lafayette's La Grange castle in France; Pinchot's son

Gifford oversaw forestry at Biltmore; CHHB, 350. For Rogers, see HLOC: LC-DIG-ppmsca-64866; for Pinchot, -55248. Bert Lippincott, "325 Ocean Avenue," July 14, 2020, Newport Historical Society. For views of the Busk house and the singular extant period interior view, see HLOC: LC-DIG-ppmsca-64867 and -64868; and -58055; for an early sketch by Hunt, -57179; for first-floor plan, see -58357.

50. Schuyler in *American Architecture and Other Writings*, 2:536, possibly written with the 1886 Robert Treat Paine house in mind, a Richardson and Olmsted collaboration outside Boston.

51. Baker, 437–38; Woods, "From Craft to Profession," 42–43; see letters from Hunt to AIA chapters, with newspaper clippings, in March 1893, Misc. Letters, HLOC.

52. Baker, 381–91. For a colored postcard of the gym, see LOC: PR 13. CN2019.004. no. 3. For Central Barracks, see Historic American Building Survey, US Military Academy, West Point, https://tile.loc.gov/storage-services/master/pnp/habshaer/ny/ny1400/ny1422/data/ny1422data.pdf (accessed March 7, 2019).

53. Steven J. Dick, *Sky and Ocean Joined: The U.S. Naval Observatory 1830–2000* (Cambridge: Cambridge University Press, 2003), 112.

54. United States Census records, https://www.census.gov/history/www/through_the_decades/fast_facts/1900_fast_facts.html (accessed January 14, 2017).

55. Benjamin Harrison, *Proclamation 335—400th Anniversary of the Discovery of America by Columbus*, June 29, 1892, https://www.presidency.ucsb.edu/documents/proclamation-335-400th-anniversary-the-discovery-america-columbus (accessed May 13, 2023); Baker, 392–94.

56. CHHB, 364; Hunt, "President Richard M. Hunt's Address," at the Twenty-Fifth Annual Convention of the AIA, Boston (October 29, 1891), revised by Hunt, *The Inland Architect and News Record* 18, no. 5 (November 1891): 40.

57. As quoted by CHH, who wrote that Hunt "was largely responsible for carrying [the review] through its first year." CHHB, 318–19.

58. Sara Dodge Kimbrough, *Drawn from Life: The Story of Four American Artists Whose Friendship & Work Began in Paris during the 1880s* (Jackson: University of Mississippi Press, 1976), 42–44. For additional images in the HLOC, see LC-DIG-ppmsca-57186, -53813; and for rare photograph of scale model, see -74915.

59. Charles Eugene Banks, *The Artistic Guide to Chicago and the World's Columbian Exposition* (Chicago: Columbian Art, 1892), 225; Soissons, *Parisian*, 134–35; Alfred J. Bloor, *A Letter on Current American Architecture (Including the "Skyscraper") and Architects* (New York: A.J. Bloor, November 20, 1906), 11; Schuyler in *American Architecture and Other Writings*, 2:546–47.

60. CHHB, 388–89; regarding travel arrangements, McKim to Hon. Henry E. Howland, September 15, 1893, Charles Follen McKim Papers, Manuscript Division, LOC; significantly, architecture was exhibited with the fine and decorative arts. *World's Columbian Exposition, 1893: Official Catalogue, Part X, Department K, Fine Arts* (Chicago: W.B. Conkey, 1893); World's Columbian Exhibition [*sic*], *Catalogue of New York State Loan Exhibit of Embroideries, Miniatures, Watches, Snuff-boxes, Fans and Laces* (New York: Knickerbocker Press, 1893), 2–3, 6, 21.

61. Charles Mulford Robinson, *Modern Civic Art, or the City Made Beautiful* (New York: G.P. Putnam's Sons, 1903), 306.

62. CHHB, 395–404, 300; "Presentation of the Royal Gold Medal," *The American Architect and Building News* 41, no. 916 (July 15, 1893): 40.

63. "Presentation," 40.

64. Ibid., 40–41.

65. CHHB, 404–5; as quoted in *R.I.B.A Journal*, June 22, 1893: 327, RMH Biographical File, RIBA.

66. McKim to RMH, March 8, 1895; also for CHH recommending people for founding the academy in Rome, see McKim to CHH, March 15, 1895, McKim to RMH, April 29, 1895, McKim Papers, LOC; Andrew S. Dolkart, *Morningside Heights: A History of Its Architecture and Development* (New York: Columbia University Press, 1998), 29–31, 367n63; for the Columbia plan, see 117–21.

67. "The Municipal Art Society of New York" (New York, 1893), pamphlet, scrapbook, HLOC.

68. CHH, 385; "Harvard Alumni," *Boston Daily Advertiser*, June 30, 1892.

69. *Boston Daily Advertiser*, September 25, 1894.

70. "The Choicest Art Objects," *Boston Daily Advertiser*, March 8, 1895; and "The Fogg

Museum," March 18, 1896. Norton chaired the University's 1906 Committee on Fine Arts and Architecture to restore a consistent architecture to the college's by then much-admired colonial campus.

71. Morrison H. Heckscher, "An Edifice for Art," in *Making the Met, 1870–2020*, eds. Andrea Bayer and Laura D. Corey (New York: Metropolitan Museum of Art, 2020), 21. Funding was secured in April 1895, three months before Hunt's death.

72. Pencil note by RMH on a report of the much-publicized trial when Cesnola was accused of stealing Cyprian art, see Metropolitan Museum scrapbook, HLOC; "Cesnola," *The New York Times*, October 24, 1899; RMH to Johnston, July 10, 1884, Hunt file, Institutional Archives, META.

73. Domenico Palombi, *Rodolfo Lanciani: l'archeologia a Roma tra Ottocento e Novecento* (Rome: L'Erma di Bretschneider, 2006), 115; also CHHB, 240, 311, suggesting that Hunt met the Roman archeologist in 1875. Karl Friedrich Schinkel, *Sammlung architektonischer Entwürfe* [1820–27] (Berlin: Ernst & Korn, 1858), pl. 58, could have been known to Hunt. For Hunt sketch of library wing of his Metropolitan wing, see HLOC: LC-DIG-ppmsca-58354.

74. The niece was Florence Adele Sloane; CHHB, 432; 434–37; "Death of Richard M. Hunt," *The New York Times*, August 1, 1895.

75. "Funeral of Mr. Hunt," *Boston Tribune*, August 4, 1895.

Afterword

1. "*Neue Welt*," unidentified clipping, obituary scrapbook, HLOC: "L'Influence de l'art français à l'étranger," *La Construction moderne* 49 (September 7, 1895): 577; "Richard Morris Hunt," *The New York Times*, August 1, 1895.

2. Barr Ferree, "Richard Morris Hunt: His Art and Work," *Architecture and Building* 23, no. 23 (December 7, 1895): 271; Wight, *Richard Morris Hunt*, 3.

3. Herbert Croly [and Henry W. Desmond], "The Work of Messrs. McKim, Mead & White," *The Architectural Record* 20, no. 3 (September 1906): 182, as first cited in David Van Zanten, "What American Architects Learned in Paris, 1845-1914," in *Nineteenth-Century Architecture*, ed. Martin Bressani and Christina Contandriopoulos, vol. 3, part V (Chichester: Wiley-Blackwell, 2017), section 26, 518; D.F. Hamlin, "The Battle of the Styles," *The Architectural Record* 1, no. 3 (January–March 1892): 275.

4. Wight, *Richard Morris Hunt*, 2.

5. "'In Memory,' to Mrs. Hunt," August 1, 1895, HLOC; also *Proceedings of the Twenty-Ninth Annual Convention of the American Institute of Architects* (1895): 83.

6. Her divorce, wrote Alva, was a "glaring defiance of custom," Belmont, memoir, 151.

7. Catharine's only mention of her early education is an "old school mate of mine at Germantown," possibly the "dame" school associated with the Germantown Friends School, Philadelphia, founded 1845, CHHB, 315A.

8. "Choate Pays Tribute"; CHHB, 228.

9. "Death of Richard M. Hunt."

10. CHH to Marquand, February 6, 1896, File: Building 1896, Institutional Archives, META; CHHB, 431.

11. "New Art Museum Wing" and "Museum's Wing Opened," *The New York Times*, December 22 and 23, 1902. For RMH pencil sketches of the entrance wing, see HLOC: LC-DIG-ppmsca-57597 and -58354; for published architectural section of the wing, see HLOC: LC-DIG-ppmsca-56361.

12. For instance, see exhibition in *Catalogue of the Eleventh Annual Exhibition at The Architectural League of New York* (New York: Architectural League of New York, 1896), 42, a photo of which is HLOC: LC-DIG-ppmsca-57963. Also Pennsylvania Academy of Fine Arts, "The Life and Works of the Late Richard Morris Hunt" (Philadelphia: American Institute of Architects, Philadelphia Chapter, 1896).

13. A photograph of a model for one of the Rossini submissions is in the Hunt collection, see HLOC: LC-DIG-ppmsca-57620; the bust was cast by the Bonnard Company, which collaborated with Hunt and John Ward. CHHB, 417. Hunt's birth year on the monument is 1828. Hunt consistently asserted 1827 as the correct year, though CHH had her doubts and clearly authorized the later year for the Central Park memorial. The birth year on his Newport gravestone (installation date unknown) is 1827. See Baker, chapter 1, note 1, 462–63.

14. Bell to Marquand, December 20, 1895, H9131, File: Central Park, Institutional Archives, META.

Central Park, Institutional Archives, META.

15. Diary of RMH daughter "Kitty," Catharine Howland Hunt, as quoted in Baker, 455; not in the HFP; CHHB, 416; CHH to Vanderbilt, October 31, 1898, and nd (1898), Incoming Correspondence, 3.9/6.1, Box 1 Folder 7, Biltmore Estate Archives; for Hunt window, by Helen and D. Maitland Armstrong, see LC-DIG-ppbd-01284; and for its iconography, see CHHB, 430–31.

16. Henry-Russell Hitchcock Jr., *Rhode Island Architecture* (Providence: Rhode Island Museum Press, 1939), 61.

17. T.J. Jackson Lears, *No Place of Grace: Antimodernism and the Transformation of American Culture, 1880-1920* (Chicago and London: University of Chicago Press, 1981), xvii, 4, and passim; Thorstein Veblen, *The Theory of the Leisure Class: An Economic Study in the Evolution of Institutions* (New York: Macmillan, 1899), 68; "Certain Dangerous Tendencies in American Life," *Atlantic Monthly* 62, no. 152 (October 1878): 393.

18. RMH personally lobbied the governor of New York, Howe, *Metropolitan*, 240, 244–45; for tensions on the board around this opening and Cesnola on securing funding, see CHHB, 313; George Frederick Kunz, "Heber Reginald Bishop and His Jade Collection," *American Anthropologist* New Series 5, no. 1 (January–March 1903): 111–17. For a photograph of the Bishop room after installation, see LC-DIG-det-4a22224.

19. For merger negotiations of the Lenox and Astor libraries, see Lenox Library Records, 1866–1915, corporate minutes, Boxes 1 and 2, LXNY; CHHB, 423.

20. Heather Mac Donald, "The Guardians in Retreat," *City Journal* (Winter 2022), https://www.city-journal.org/art-institute-of-chicago-redefines-its-purpose-as-antiracism (accessed February 8, 2022).

21. "Manifesting Statement of the Black Reconstruction Collective," for *Reconstructions: Architecture and Blackness in America* exhibition, Museum of Modern Art, February 24, 2021, https://www.moma.org/magazine/articles/510 (accessed March 3, 2021).

22. Van Brunt, "Richard Morris Hunt," 79.

23. As quoted in CHHB, 410–11.

Captions

1. CHHB, 292.

2. "Porteur de lettres, femme de la haute Egypte, Dais Tunisien"; with gratitude to Marie-Emmanuelle de La Broïse for translation.

3. CHHB, 423.

4. In the rear right is a plaster cast of William Hunt's "The Horses of Anahita or The Flight of Night," sculpted ca. 1858-60, likely the casting RMH donated to the Metropolitan Museum of Art in 1880.

5. For views of dining room, see page 10 and LC-DIG-ppbd-01310.

6. Likely cartoons for windows at the Basilique Notre-Dame de Bonsecours (1844), Rouen, France.

7. For a view of the library looking southeast, see photograph HLOC: LC-DIG-ppmsca-57608.

8. CHHB, 169–70. For the portrait in the collection of RHH, see 2.3.

9. *The American Architect and Building News* 9, no. 278 (April 23, 1881): 196.

10. Napoléon III reserved the first *La Marguerite* at the 1852 Paris Salon, today at the Musée d'Orsay; a second version, seen here, is in Boston's Museum of Fine Arts, from the estate of Martin Brimmer. For this history, see https://www.musee-orsay.fr/fr/collections/catalogue-des-oeuvres/notice.html?no_cache=1&nnumid=000820&cHash=7d45580b86 (accessed October 11, 2014), and Knowlton, *Art-Life*, 26-27.

11. For MacKaye as model, see Sharp, *Ward*, 52; for photograph of 1869 Ward house exterior, see HLOC: LC-DIG-ppmsca-58064; for Dodge statue, see HLOC: LC-DIG-ppmsca-58060.

12. For period view, see HLOC: LC-DIG-ppmsca-58058.

13. For plan and interior of chapel, see HLOC: LC-DIG-ppmsca-74001.

14. For period view of Second Academic Hall, by Frances Benjamin Johnston, see LC-DIG-ppmsca-17491.

15. From Osgood's speech at the AIA annual dinner, *Proceedings of the Eighth Annual Convention of the American Institute of Architects* (October 1874): 40.

16. For exterior of music pavilion, see Michael Froio's LC-DIG-ppbd-01327.

17. For plan of The Corners, see HLOC: LC-DIG-ppmsca-73173.

18. For a view of the chapel altar, see HLOC: LC-DIG-ppmsca-57044.

19. Sheldon, *Artistic Houses*, vol. 1, part 2: 135.

20. Croffut, *Vanderbilts*, 183-84.

21. For ca. 1890 long view of church exterior, see LC-DIG-ppmsca-68586.

22. For James Garrison basement and

third-floor plans, see LC-DIG-ppbd-01358 and -01361.

23. Per the will of William K. Vanderbilt, the portraits, *Mrs. Grace Dalrymple Elliott*, 1778, by Thomas Gainsborough (left, in dining hall) and *Captain George K.H. Coussmaker*, 1782, by Sir Joshua Reynolds (right), were bequeathed to the Metropolitan Museum of Art in 1920.

24. The inscription reads: "*Souvenir d'aimité, et de sympathique--admiration à mon cher ami R.M. Hunt, Eug Oudinot, New York 17 May-82*." ("Souvenir of friendship, and sympathetic admiration for my dear friend R.M. Hunt....").

25. For Alhambra, see CHHB, 311; though the house was largely completed by 1884, the décor of this room was later, as suggested by a letter from Hunt to Luigi Cesnola, Metropolitan Museum of Art, October 1, 1886, advising the director that he was sending Marcotte for "some casting from Moorish work," likely from the Alhambra casts Hunt donated to the museum, acquired on his trip to Spain in 1886; the room was possibly created specifically for the Iberian ware Marquand collected and donated to the Metropolitan Museum; for cast collection, see here chapter 5.

26. Stereograph card, LC-DIG-ppmsca-02957, shows Bartholdi's painting mounted on the pedestal for the arm of Liberty, exhibited at the 1876 Philadelphia exhibition.

27. For period photograph, see HLOC: LC-DIG-ppmsca-58059.

28. Montgomery Schuyler to John Ward, March 29, 1910, Albany Institute of History and Art, Albany, New York, as quoted in Sharp, *Ward*, 276.

29. For second variant, see HLOC: LC-DIG-ppmsca-65168 and -51627.

30. For photograph of Indian Spring main hall, see HLOC: LC-DIG-ppmsca-58055.

31. RMH to George W. Vanderbilt, from 2 Washington Square, nd (1889), Incoming Correspondence, 3.9/Box 1 Folder 7, Biltmore Estate Archives, Asheville, NC. Hunt refers to another version of the bust, once in the collection of RHH, and today at the National Portrait Gallery, Washington, DC; CHHB, 297, an uncharacteristically sharp opinion that CHH excised in her editing.

32. For this view in the period, see HLOC: LC-DIG-ppmsca-64853.

33. For additional views of Ochre Court stairs, main hall, and second-floor hall, see LC-DIG-ppbd-01297, -01299, -01300, -01302, -01304, and for library, -01303. For period view of main hall, see HLOC: LC-DIG-ppmsca-64855 and -64865.

34. The portrait is a period copy, like so many "old masters" of the time, now in the German Historical Museum, Berlin; "'Marie und Marie,' Der Weg eines Gemäldes durch 250 Jahre europäischer und amerikanischer Geschichte," *DHM-Magazin* 25, no. 10 (Fall 2000): 24-49.

35. For the Breakers ocean façade, see HLOC: LC-DIG-ppmsca-53508.

36. For contemporary view of hall as seen from stairs by Michael Froio, see LC-DIG-ppbd-01333.

37. Henry James, *The American Scene* (London: Chapman and Hall, 1907), 224-25.

38. For grand salon looking toward the windows, see LC-DIG-ppmsca-94076.

39. Ouradou and Jean J.G. Lisch, a student of Henri Labrouste and Léon Vaudoyer, completed Pierrefonds by 1885, six years after Eugène Viollet-le-Duc's death; RMH and George Vanderbilt could have visited the castle on their 1889 tour.

40. For first-floor plan of Indian Spring, see HLOC: LC-DIG-ppmsca-58357. For cut, see SC.9.

41. For close-up view and lecture hall exterior, see HLOC: LC-DIG-ppmsca-57035 and -57036.

Image Credits

Library of Congress image identification numbers are given below. The online images can be located by searching for those numbers at www.loc.gov/pictures. HLOC indicates that an image is in the Richard Morris Hunt Collection at the Library of Congress, but those letters are not part of the online call number. LC is part of the online call number and indicates that an image is in the collection of the Library of Congress. For instance, search LC-DIG-ppmsca-58362 for the image ID "HLOC: LC-DIG-ppmsca-58362".

Cover:
The National Portrait Gallery, Smithsonian Institution, Washington, DC

Front End Paper:
HLOC: LC-DIG-ppmsca-85632

Back End Paper:
HLOC: LC-DIG-ppmsca-89713

Frontispiece:
HLOC: LC-DIG-ppmsca-57183

Page 4:
Watercolor and graphite on paper, Brooklyn Museum, Brooklyn, NY, accession number 31.194

Page 8:
HLOC: LC-DIG-ppmsca-57985

Page 10:
LC-DIG-ppbd-01308

The Players

P.1 William H. Aspinwall, holding a lithograph of his painting of the Virgin attributed to Bartolomé E. Murillo that he exhibited in his residential gallery; Daniel Huntington, oil on canvas, 1871, The National Portrait Gallery, Smithsonian Institution, Washington, DC

P.2 Jane M.L. Hunt, Richard M. Hunt, ca. 1850; HLOC: LC-DIG-ppmsca-89700

P.3 HLOC: LC-DIG-ppmsca-56366

P.4 Jules C. A. Allard, Fernand Cormon, oil on canvas, 1889, Preservation Society of Newport County, Newport, RI

P.5 Martin Brimmer, Sarah Wyman Whitman, oil on canvas, 1892, Gift of Mrs. Richard Morris Hunt and Mrs. Sarah Wyman Whitman, 19.143, Photograph ©2024, Museum of Fine Arts, Boston, MA

P.6 Joseph H. Choate, John Singer Sargent, oil on canvas, 1899, Harvard Club of New York City

P.7 Charlotte Cushman, William Page, oil on canvas, 1853, The National Portrait Gallery, Smithsonian Institution, Washington, DC

P.8 Duc d'Aumale, Victor-Louis Mottez, oil on canvas, 1853, Musée Condé, Chateau de Chantilly/Art Resource, NY

P.9 J.-L. Charles Garnier, Paul-J.A.-Baudry, oil on canvas, 1868, ©RMN Grand Palais/Art Resource, NY

P.10 Ogden Goelet, Léon Bonat, oil on canvas, 1891, photograph: Michael Froio, courtesy of Salva Regina University, Newport, RI

P.11 James Lenox, Sir Francis Grant, oil on canvas, 1848, The New York Public Library Digital Collections, NYC

P.12 Charles F. McKim, Frances B. Johnston, photograph, ca. 1890–1909, LC-DIG-ds-04713

P.13 Levi P. Morton, George Hughes after Léon Bonat, oil on canvas, 1896, formerly in the collection of the Chamber of Commerce, Albany, NY, courtesy of Nadeau's Auction Gallery, Windsor, CT

P.14 Dr. Eleazer Parmly, DDS (1797–1874), Thomas Pritchard Rossiter, oil on canvas, ca. 1850–55, Gift of William F. Ward, through Mrs. Richard Billings, ©New-York Historical Society

P.15 George Ticknor, Thomas Sully, oil on canvas, 1831, Hood Museum of Art, Dartmouth, NH, Gift of Constance V.R. White, Nathaniel T. Dexter, Philip Dexter, and Mary Ann Streeter

P.16 Eugène E. Viollet-le-Duc, holding a model of his Notre-Dame de Paris restoration, Eugène Giraud, watercolor, 1860, Bridgeman Images

P.17 Daniel Webster, Frances Alexander, oil painting, 1835, The National Portrait Gallery, Smithsonian Institution, Washington, DC

Introduction

Légion d'Honneur medal, HLOC: LC-DIG-ppmsca-73366

Business cards, HLOC: LC-DIG-ppmsca-57939 and -57940

Chapter 1

1.1a Vermont Historical Society Library, Barre, VT

1.1b HLOC: LC-DIG-ppmsca-74918

1.2 Bennington Museum, Bennington, VT

1.3a Oil on canvas, private collection, courtesy of Clars Auction House, Oakland, CA

1.3b Oil on canvas, Bennington Museum, Bennington, VT

1.3c Oil on canvas, ca. 1845, Gift of Susan W. and Stephen D. Paine, Photograph © 2024, Museum of Fine Arts, Boston, MA

1.4 Bennington Museum, Bennington, VT

1.5 HLOC: LC-DIG-ppmsca-64859

1.6 Private Collection, New York

1.7 HLOC: LC-DIG-ppmsca-57942

1.8 HLOC: LC-DIG-ppmsca-73172

1.9 Henri Deverin, Honoré Daumet, *Petite histoire d'un atelier* (1862–1911): *accompagnée d'une lettre autographe de Monsieur Daumet* (Paris: Association Amicale, Atelier Daumet, 1910), HLOC: LC-DIG-ppmsca-57960

1.10a HLOC: LC-DIG-ppmsca-74208

1.10b HLOC: LC-DIG-ppmsca-74905

1.11a HLOC: LC-DIG-ppmsca-57935

1.11b HLOC: LC-DIG-ppmsca-57943

1.12 HLOC: LC-DIG-ppmsca-57599

1.13 HLOC: LC-DIG-ppmsca-89718

1.14 HLOC: LC-DIG-ppmsca-64861

1.15 HLOC: LC-DIG-ppmsca-57984

1.16 Oil on canvas, © RMN-Grand Palais, Image source, Art Resource, NY: ART544543

1.17 The Metropolitan Museum of Art, NYC

Chapter 2

2.1 LC-DIG-pga-03183

2.2 Oil on canvas, Metropolitan Museum of Art, NYC/Art Resource, NY

2.3: LC-DIG-ppmsca-56270

2.4 HLOC: LC-DIG-ppmsca-73357

2.5 Oil on canvas, © RMN-Grand Palais/Art Resource, NY

2.6 X2010.11.4450, Museum of the City of New York, NY

2.7 HLOC: LC-DIG-ppmsca-74906

2.8 HLOC: LC-DIG-ppmsca-56282

2.9 HLOC: LC-DIG-ppmsca-56363

2.10 HLOC: LC-DIG-ds-04961

2.11 HLOC: LC-DIG-ppmsca-57039

2.12 Boston Public Library

2.13 HLOC: LC-DIG-ppmsca-74922

2.14a Newport Historical Society, Newport, RI

2.14b Vermont Historical Society Library, Barr, VT

2.15 HLOC: LC-DIG-ppmsca-73364

2.16 HLOC: LC-DIG-ppmsca-57034

2.17 HLOC: LC-DIG-ppmsca-74923

2.18 Richard Morris Hunt, *Designs for the Gateways of the Southern Entrances to the Central Park* (New York: D. Van Nostrand, 1866). LOC call number: SB483.N55 H8, https://catalog.hathitrust.org/Record/008587413

2.19 LC-DIG-ppbd-01306

2.20 LC-DIG-ppbd-01351

2.21a LC-DIG-ppbd-01307

2.21b LC-DIG-ppbd-01311

Sketchbook Portfolio

SK.1a
HLOC: LC-DIG-ppmsca-89698

SK.1b
HLOC: LC-DIG-ppmsca-57969

SK.2 HLOC: LC-DIG-ppmsca-89712

SK.3 HLOC: LC-DIG-ppmsca-57989

SK.4 HLOC: LC-DIG-ppmsca-57966

SK.5 HLOC: LC-DIG-ppmsca-89697

SK.6 HLOC: LC-DIG-ppmsca-89719

SK.7 HLOC: LC-DIG-ppmsca-89705

SK.8 HLOC: LC-DIG-ppmsca-74908

SK.9 & back cover
HLOC: LC-DIG-ppmsca-89706

SK.10
HLOC: LC-DIG-ppmsca-89704

SK.11 HLOC: LC-DIG-ppmsca-74907

SK.12
HLOC: LC-DIG-ppmsca-89703

Chapter 3

3.1 HLOC: LC-DIG-ppmsca-57595

3.2 Royal Institute of British Architects (RIBA), London

3.3 LC-DIG-ppbd-01353

3.4 HLOC: LC-DIG-ppmsca-74924

3.5 LC-DIG-ppbd-01355

3.6 HLOC: LC-DIG-ppmsca-64845

3.7 LC-DIG-det-4a31802

3.8 Historic Architecture and Landscape Images Collection, Ryerson and Burnham Archives, The Art Institute of Chicago, digital file #2310

3.9a LC-DIG-ppbd-01356

3.9b LC-DIG-ppbd-01357

3.10a LC-DIG-ppmsca-15416

3.10b LC-DIG-ppmsca-15415

3.11 & back cover Oil on canvas, photograph © 2024, Museum of Fine Arts, Boston, MA

3.12 HLOC: LC-DIG-ppmsca-74926

3.13 HLOC: LC-DIG-ppmsca-53803

3.14 HLOC: LC-DIG-ppmsca-74927

3.15 Chicago History Museum, Chicago, Illinois

3.16a George Sheldon, *Artistic Houses*, vol. 2, Part 1, (New York: D. Appleton, 1884), 43, photograph courtesy of Historic Architecture and Landscape Images Collection, Ryerson and Burnham Archives, The Art Institute of Chicago, digital file #62771; also available as LC-DIG-ppmsca-56274

3.16b
HLOC: LC-DIG-ppmsca-58353

3.17a HLOC: LC-DIG-ppmsca-57957

3.17b HLOC: LC-DIG-ppmsca-59727

3.18 HLOC: LC-DIG-ppmsca-55259

3.19 LC-DIG-ppbd-01309

3.20 LC-DIG-ppbd-01317

3.21 LC-DIG-ppbd-01346

3.22 Collection of James Madden

3.23 LC-DIG-ppbd-01281

3.24a Courtesy of Hampton University Archives, Hampton, VA

3.24b LC-DIG-ppbd-01282

3.25a
HLOC: LC-DIG-ppmsca-58057

3.25b LC-DIG-ppbd-01328

3.26a LC-DIG-ppbd-01324

3.26b LC-DIG-ppbd-01325

3.27 Newport Historical Society, Newport, RI

3.28a Manuscripts and Archives Division, The New York Public Library, NYC

3.28b LC-DIG-ppbd-01337

3.29 LC-DIG-ppbd-01340

3.30a George Sheldon, *Artistic Houses* (New York: D, Appleton, 1884), vol. 2, part 1, 83, also available as LC-DIG-ppmsca-56276

3.30b LC-DIG-ppbd-11515

3.31 Newport Historical Society, Newport, RI

3.32 Musée de la Ville de Paris, Musée Carnavalet, Paris, photo credit, Eric Lessing. Image source: Art Resource, NY

3.33 HLOC: LC-DIG-ppmsca-74909

3.34 Oil on canvas, Musée d'Orsay, © RMN-Grand Palais/Art Resource, NY

Chapter 4

4.1 LC-DIG-ppmsca-74917

4.2a HLOC: LC-DIG-ppmsca-57043

4.2b Princeton University Archives, Mudd Library, Grounds & Buildings, Box 23, public domain

4.3 HLOC: LC-DIG-ppmsca-64864

4.4a LC-DIG-ppbd-01347

4.4b LC-DIG-ppbd-01349

4.5 George Sheldon, *Artistic Houses* (New York: D. Appleton, 1883), vol. 1, part 2, 135, also available as LC-DIG-ppmsca-56272

4.6a-b Oil on canvas, Historic Mobile Preservation Society, Mobile, Alabama, from the estate of Consuelo Vanderbilt Balsan

4.7 LC-DIG-ppbd-01322

4.8 LC-DIG-ppbd-01323

4.9 HLOC: LC-DIG-ds-10771

4.10a LC-DIG-ppbd-01359

4.10b LC-DIG-ppbd-01360

4.11a Consuelo Vanderbilt Balsan, *The Glitter and the Gold* (New York: Harper & Brothers, 1952), 16–17

4.11b HLOC: LC-DIG-ppmsca-55917

4.12 HLOC: LC-DIG-ppmsca-64851

4.13a HLOC: LC-DIG-ppmsca-56284

4.13b Uffizi, Florence, Scala/Art Resource, NY

4.13c HLOC: LC-DIG-ppmsca-53801

4.13d Uffizi, Florence, Scala/Art Resource, NY

4.14 Oil on canvas, Princeton University Art Museum, Princeton, NJ

4.15 HLOC: LC-DIG-ppmsca-57042

4.16a LC-DIG-ppbd-01362

4.16b LC-DIG-ppbd-01363

4.17 *The American Architect and Building News* (1894), International Edition, Courtesy of The Clark Art Institute, Williamstown, MA

4.18a Musée Carnavalet, Paris

4.18b LC-DIG-ppmsca-94075

4.19 LC-DIG-ppbd-01318

4.20 LC-DIG-ppbd-01316

4.21 Musée Bartholdi, Colmar, France, photographer Christian Kempf

4.22 Lithograph from *Universal Atlas of the World* (New York: Rand, McNally, 1896), LOC call number: G1019 .R482 1896, also available as LC-DIG-ppmsca-56805

4.23 LC-DIG-ppbd-01290

4.24 Collection of the United States House of the Representatives, Washington, DC

4.25 HLOC: LC-DIG-ppmsca-51821

4.26 LC-DIG-ppbd-01312

4.27 HLOC: LC-DIG-ds-10691

4.28 Olmsted Archives, Brookline, MA: photo album 00218-01-p001

Scrapbook Portfolio

SC.1 HLOC: LC-DIG-ppmsca-89714

SC.2 HLOC: LC-DIG-ppmsca-74986

SC.3 HLOC: LC-DIG-ppmsca-51640

SC.4 HLOC: LC-DIG-ppmsca-53474

SC.5 HLOC: LC-DIG-ds-03945

SC.6 HLOC: LC-DIG-ppmsca-73182

SC.7 HLOC: LC-DIG-ppmsca-59723

SC.8 HLOC: LC-DIG-ppmsca-65167

SC.9 HLOC: LC-DIG-ds-15241

SC.10 HLOC: LC-DIG-ppmsca-57180

SC.11 HLOC: LC-DIG-ppmsca-89716

SC.12 HLOC: LC-DIG-ppmsca-89717

Chapter 5

5.1 HLOC: LC-DIG-ppmsca-73367

5.2 HLOC: LC-DIG-ppmsca-74929

5.3a-b and 5.4a Manuscripts and Archives Division, The New York Public Library, NYC

5.4b HLOC: LC-DIG-ppmsca-57184

5.5 HLOC: LC-DIG-ppmsca-57182

5.6a HLOC: LC-DIG-ppmsca-57988

5.6b HLOC: LC-DIG-ppmsca-57023

5.7a HLOC: LC-DIG-ppmsca-57181

5.7b HLOC: LC-DIG-ds-10183

5.8 HLOC: LC-DIG-ppmsca-74930

5.9 LC-DIG-ppbd-01295

5.10 HLOC: LC-DIG-ppmsca-74913

5.11a LC-DIG-ppbd-01305

5.11b LC-DIG-ppbd-01301

5.12a HLOC: LC-DIG-ppmsca-57607

5.12b LC-DIG-ppbd-01293

5.13 HLOC: LC-DIG-ppmsca-52064

5.14 HLOC: LC-DIG-ppmsca-58362

5.15 Oil on canvas, Private Collection, Paris

5.16 HLOC: LC-DIG-ds-10851

5.17a LC-DIG-ppbd-01342

5.17b HLOC: LC-DIG-ppmsca-89699

5.18a HLOC: LC-DIG-ppmsca-53468

5.18b HLOC: LC-DIG-ppmsca-52067

5.19 LC-DIG-ppbd-01344

5.20a RHiX3 1298, Lot 100, Hewitt, Mattie Edwards [Interior view of "Marble House" residence of H.P Belmont]. Newport, RI, 1926. Silver gelatin print. Photograph. Graphics Collection, Courtesy the Rhode Island Historical Society, Providence, RI

5.20b LC-DIG-ppbd-01343

5.21 LC-DIG-ppmsc-05178

5.22 Oil on canvas, presented by Alice Vanderbilt to the New York Chamber of Commerce, in honor of her husband's presidency, 1894–95, Courtesy Nadeau Auctions, Windsor, CT

5.23 LC-DIG-ppbd-01331

5.24a-d Ogden Codman architectural drawings and papers, 1793–1936, Avery Architectural & Fine Arts Library, Columbia University, New York, NY

5.25 HLOC: LC-DIG-ppmsca-53506

5.26a LC-DIG-ppbd-01329

5.26b LC-DIG-ppbd-01336

5.27 LC-DIG-ppbd-01334

5.28 LC-DIG-det-4a31825

5.29 LC-DIG-ppbd-01364

5.30a&b Museum of the City of New York, NYC

5.31 Biltmore Estate Collection, Asheville, NC, BH8-00129

5.32 Baron Ferdinand de Rothschild, *Waddesdon,* "the Red Book," privately printed, November 1897, ink in red leather, Waddesdon (National Trust), Bequest of Dorothy de Rothschild, acc. No. 54; Waddesdon Image Library, Capita Document & Information Services

5.33 Biltmore Estate Archives, Asheville, NC, BHA4-02057

5.34 HLOC: LC-DIG-ppmsca-55250

5.35 Ink, pencil, and wash on paper, Drawings Collection, Biltmore Estate Archives, Asheville, NC, BHA1-01005

5.36 LC-DIG-ppbd-01319

5.37a HLOC: LC-DIG-ds-09771

5.37b LC-DIG-ppbd-01320

5.38a Colombe Clier, CMN Dist. Art Resource, NY

5.38b LC-DIG- ppbd-01321

5.39 LC-DIG-ppbd-01286

5.40 LC-DIG-ds-11680

5.41a LC-DIG-ppbd-01283

5.41b LC-DIG-ppbd-01285

5.42 LC-DIG-ppbd-01341

5.43 LC-DIG-ppbd-01326

5.44 HLOC: LC-DIG-ppmsca-74932

5.45 & back cover HLOC: LC-DIG-ppmsca-70892

5.46a LC-DIG-ppbd-01365

5.46b Courtesy of Allen & Judy Koessel

5.47 HLOC: LC-DIG-ppmsca-57037

5.48 Postcard, collection of Kent Lydecker/Art Resource, NY

5.49a HLOC: LC-DIG-ppmsca-64857

5.49b ©Metropolitan Museum of Art, NY/Art Resource, NY

Afterword

6.1 Oil on canvas, Biltmore Estate Collection, Asheville, NC, BH8-01595

6.2 HLOC: LC-DIG-ppmsca-53505

6.3 HLOC: LC-DIG-ppmsca-57610

6.4 Biltmore Estate Archives, Asheville, NC: 3.9/6/1 B1 F7 – 31 Oct 1898: CHH to GWV

Back Matter

Page 274: LC-DIG-ppbd-01289

Pages 305: HLOC: LC-DIG-ppmsca-52068

Page 312: Bettman/Getty Images

Proposed north wall, dining room (detail), Alice and Cornelius Vanderbilt II house, the Breakers, Newport, Rhode Island; signed, "New York, December 28, 1893, E.L.M" [Emmanuel L. Masqueray]

Index

Page numbers in *italics* refer to the illustrations and their captions

Acropolis, Athens *46*

Adler and Sullivan 105

AIA (American Institute of Architects) 13, 15, 17, 57, 68, 69, 70–72, 88, 115, 147, 149, 152, 172, 174, 192, 247, 267, 270, 272, 282n.17, 283n.34, 293n.65

Albert, Prince, consort of Queen Victoria 43, 77

Allard, Jules C.A. 13, *13*, 169 *see also* Jules Allard Fils

Alma-Tadema, Sir Lawrence 170, 293n.60

American Institute of Architects *see* AIA

American Museum of Natural History 115, 116, 287n.38

Appleton, Thomas G. 13, 100

    cottage, Newport (RMH) 138, 204

Architectural League of New York 192, 255, 267, 273

Armstrong, Samuel C. 131, 133, 288n.59

Aspinwall, William H. (cousin of Catharine Howland Hunt) 12, *12*, 75, 76, 115, 153, 283n.34, 287n.32

Association for the Relief of Respectable Aged and Indigent Females: residence, Amsterdam Avenue, New York (RMH) 177, *178*

Astor, Charlotte Augusta Gibbes (wife of John J. Astor III) 81, 190

Astor, John Jacob, IV 231

    Astor house on Fifth Avenue *see under* Astor, William B. and Caroline S.

Astor, William B. and Caroline S. 13, 57, 115, 159, 166, 200, 231, 291n.24

    Astor double house (Caroline with John Jacob Astor IV), Fifth Avenue, New York (RMH) 268

        exterior *232*, 296n.30

        interior 231, 232, *234*

        plan of first floor *233*

    Beechwood, Newport (Downing and Vaux) 211, 217, 225

    Ferncliff Farm, Rhinecliff 200

    house on Thirty-Fourth Street and Fifth Avenue, New York (Thomas) *60*, 61, 81, 231

Bancroft, George 13, 28, 30, 35, 57, 83, 91, 206, 249

Barbedienne, Ferdinand: portrait bust of RMH (with Gautherin) *200*, 301n.31

Bartholdi, Frédéric-Auguste 180–81, 191

    Liberty Enlightening the World (Statue of Liberty) *146*, *180–81*, 181, 292n.45, 301n.26

Barye, Antoine-Louis 13, *79*, 80

Bayard, Émile-Antoine: Field of the Cloth of Gold window for William K. Vanderbilt New York house (with Oudinot) 166, *167*, 301n.24

Beecher, Catherine E.: *The American Woman's Home* (with H.B. Stowe) 158–59

Beecher, Henry Ward 13, 64, 142, 145, 153, 158

    memorial (RMH and Ward) 186, *186*, 187

Beechwood, Newport (Downing and Vaux) *see under* Astor, William B. and Caroline S.

Belmont, August and Catherine P. 68, 125, 153

    exedra and tomb, Island Cemetery, Newport (RMH and Ward) *187*

Bibliothèque Sainte-Geneviève, Paris (Labrouste) 39, 42, 100, 111, 260

Biltmore, Asheville, North Carolina *see under* Vanderbilt, George W.

Bitter, Karl F. *187*, *196*, 222, 231, *240*, 251, 260, 297n.45

Blondel, Jacques-François: *Architecture française* 57, *58*

Bloor, Alfred J. 13, 68, 71, 251

Blouet, Guillaume-Abel 13, 42, 88

Bonaiuto, Andrea di: *Church Militant and Triumphant 169*, 291n.32

Bonat, Léon J.-F. *14*, 304

Borden, William 98, 169, 291n.34

Boston

    Great Boston Fire (1872) 108, 142, *152*

    Museum of Fine Arts (Sturgis and Brigham) 13, 116, 256

Bourget, Paul 206, 218

Bowditch, Ernest W. 211, 218, 224, *225*, 294n.11

Brattleboro, Vermont 24, *25*, 153, 278n.4

the Breakers, Newport *see under* Vanderbilt, Cornelius, II

Brimmer, Martin and Marianne T. 13, *13*, 45, 118, 119–20, 121, 193, 256, 261, 290n.16

    house on Beacon Hill, Boston (RMH) 119, *120*, 120–21, *121*, 122–23

Briquet, Rev. Matthias-Alphonse 33, 34

    school in Geneva 33–34, *34*, 37, 279n.24

Bronson, Frederic, Jr. and Sara G. King 154, 159, 291n.24

    Winthrop-Bronson house, Murray Hill, New York (RMH) 154–55, *155*, 231

    interiors *156*, *157*, 157–58, 296n.30

Brooklyn Bridge 106, 107, *107*, 181, *196*

Bruen, Mary A.D.: rubble stone house, Newport (remodeled by RMH) 138, *139*

Bryant, William Cullen 13, 31, 84, 85, 115

Buberl, Caspar: statue of RMH as a stone mason *206*, *207*, 246, 297n.48

Busk, Joseph R. and Mary L. 246–47

    Indian Spring house (RMH and Olmsted) 246, 247, *247*

    interior *197*

Campan, Madame Louise Henriette (lady-in-waiting to Marie Antoinette) 217, *217*

Carnegie, Andrew 110, 154, 176, 290n.18

Catherine de' Medici (unknown artist) *168*

Centennial International Exhibition (1876), Philadelphia 17, 117, 147, 148, *148*, 176, 177

Central Park, New York 84–86, 102, 109, 114, 115, *126*, *170*, *179*, *232*

    gates 84, 244, 284n.61, 297n.45

    RMH's rejected designs 83, 84–86, *85*, 105, 126–27, 270

    landscaping (Olmsted and Vaux) 83, 84, 86

    memorial to RMH (French and Price) 268–69, *269*, 270–71

Century Association, New York 14, 15, 68, 76, 103

Chateau de Blois 44, *44*, 236, 240, *274*, 297n.42

Chateau de Chambord 224, 240, 297n.42

Chateau de Chantilly 13, 191, 238

Chateau de Chenonceau 43, 193

Chateau de Fontainebleau 14, 42, 43, 80, *94*, 218

    Hermitage de la Madeleine 218, *220*

    Horseshoe Staircase *80*, 218

Chateau de Petit-Val, Sucy-en-Brie 32, *32*, 57

Chateau de Pierrefonds 144, 145, *145*, 156, 164, 240, 301n.39

    Knights of the Round Table fireplace (Ouradou) *242*

Chauncey, Henry C. (brother-in-law of Catharine Howland Hunt) 12, 52, 279n.24

Chicago 121, *122*, 163–64, 192, 193, 249

    Great Chicago Fire (1871) 108, 121, 142

    see also World's Columbian Exposition

Choate, Joseph H. 13, 81, 105, 115, 116, *179*, 181, 261, 266, 286n.21

    portrait (Sargent) *13*

Church, Frederic E. 67, 82, 200

Church, Simeon E. 109, 153–54

City Beautiful movement 249, 253–54, 255, 269, 273

Civil War (1861–65) 17, 20, 25, 35, 38, 53, 76, 80, 82–83, 87, 98, 131, 174, 235, 283n.48

Civil War memorials (RMH and Ward) *125*, *126*, 126–27

classicism 38, 39, 43, 48, 71, 86, 91, 100, 109, 218, 230, 240, 256, 266, 273 *see also* neoclassicism

Coal and Iron Exchange building, New York (RMH) 108

Codman, Ogden, Jr. 230

The Decoration of Houses (with Wharton) 158, 296n.27
Columbia College (later University) 14, 15, 23, 28, 69, 70, 110,
    154, 174
    campus (RMH) 255
Commune uprising, Paris 142, *143*
The Corners, Newport *see under* Cushman, Charlotte S.
Couture, Thomas 13, 48
    portrait of RMH *6*, 21, 278n.6
Crawford, Thomas G. 13, 33, 65
The Crayon journal 51, 68, 71
Crystal Palace, London (Paxton) 43, 72, 147
Cushman, Charlotte S. 13, *13*, 136, *138*
    The Corners, Newport (RMH) 136, *138*, 204

Daly, César 119
Dana, William P.W. 77, *78*
Darier, Samuel 13, 35, 37, 38, 71
d'Aumale, Henri d'Orléans, Duc (son of Louis-Philippe) 13,
    191–92, 238
Daumet, P.-J. Honoré 13, *38*, 238, 254
Delaware and Hudson Canal Co. building, Courtland Street
    (RMH) 106
Destailleur, Hippolyte-A.-G.-W. 236, 237, *237*
Dodge, William de Leftwich: *Glorification of the Arts and Sciences*
    251, *253*
Downing, Andrew Jackson 84, 134
    Beechwood, Newport (with Vaux) 211, 217
Draft Riots, New York (1863) 174, *175*
Drayton, Colonel Percival: memorial, Trinity Church, New York
    (RMH and Larmande) 126
Duban, Félix-L.-J. 44, 77, 89, 100, 293n.62
Duc, Joseph-Louis 100, 286n.10

École des Beaux-Arts, Paris 13, 14, 15, 19, 31, 35, 37–39, *38*, 42, 48,
    81, 100, 191, 201, 237, 280n.37 *see also under* Hunt, Richard
    Morris
Eidlitz, Leopold 13, 71, 88, 108, 152
Eiffel, A. Gustave 181
Eliot, Charles W. 14, 149, 244, 256
Emerson, Ralph Waldo 14, 24, 29, 30, 60, 69, 97, 254
Episcopal Church of the Ascension Fifth Avenue, New York
    (Upjohn) 76
Equitable Life Assurance tower, New York (Gilman, Kendall and
    Post) 105–6
Eugénie, Empress of France 14, *49*, 51, 89, 295n.16
Everett, Edward 14, 24, 28, 279n.14
Exposition Universelle (1855), Paris 51, 52, 61
Exposition Universelle (1867), Paris 17, 89, 100, 139, 176, 217,
    295n.16
Exposition Universelle (1889), Paris 237

Fichot, Michel-Charles: *Paris Incendie 96*, *143*
Field, Marshall and Nannie D. Scott 121, 122
    house on Prairie Avenue, Chicago (RMH) 121–23, *122*
        interiors 122, *123*, 158
        plan of first floor *123*
fireproofing 106, 108, 132, 138, 230
Fornachon, Maurice 98, 110, 192, 249, 261
French, Daniel Chester: memorial to RMH (with Price) 268–69,
    269, 270–71
French Revolution (1848) 47, 48, 174
Fuller, Margaret 30–31, 32, 53, 191
Furness, Frank H. 14, 69, 75, 79, 126, 140, 282n.24
Furness, Rev. William H. 14, 69, 70–71, 199

Gambardella, Spiridione 28
    portrait of Jane M. Hunt *27*
    portrait of Jane M.L. Hunt *26*
Gambrill, Charles D. 69, 119, 147
Gambrill & Richardson 147

Garfield, James A.: memorial (RMH and Ward) 185, *185*, 293n.53
Garnier, J.-L. Charles 14, *14*, 39, 71, 144, 222, 224, 251, 254,
    286n.10
Gautherin, Jean: portrait bust of RMH (with Barbedienne) *200*,
    301n.31
Gavet, Émile 59, 222, 237, 295n.20
Germany 45, 46, 48, 89, 91, *95*
Gilded Age 17, 21, 98, 119, 145, 152, 157, 174, 195, 201, 222, 255,
    261, 264, 271
Gilman, Arthur D. 72–73, 106, 122
Goelet, Ogden and Mary Wilson 14, *14*, 208, 211, 232, 255
    Ochre Court, Newport (RMH and Olmsted) 14, *197*, *208–9*,
        208–11, 225, 231, 233
        façade 208, *208–9*
        interior *197*, 211, *212–15*, 294n.12
        plan of second floor *210*
Gosse, Sir Edmund G. 246
Grace Episcopal Church, University Place, New York (Renwick)
    192, 267
Great Exhibition, London (1851) 43
Great Panic (1873) 142, 153
Greeley, Horace 30, 107, 186
    memorial (RMH and Ward) 186, 187
Green, Andrew H. 84, 115
Griswold, John N. A. and Jane Emmet 77
    Newport summer cottage (RMH) 77, 87, *87*, 88, *90*, *91*, 125,
        136, 263, 284n.63
        interior *10*, *11*, 88, *90–91*
        plans *87*

Hampton Normal and Agricultural Institute 131
    Academic Halls (RMH) *130*, 131, 132
    Virginia Hall (RMH) *132–33*, 133
Harper's Weekly 185, 199
Harvard University 14, 15, 17, 24, 28, 29, 48, 102, 149, 256
    William Hayes Fogg Museum (RMH) 256–57, *257*, 267
Haussmann, Baron Georges-Eugène 49, 191
Herter Brothers 108, 164
Hill-Top Cottage, Newport *74*, 75, 81, 131, 204, *204*, 206
    carriage house studio (William Hunt) 75
        RMH's office atelier *206*, 207
        interior 204, *205*, *206*, 260
historicism 88, 154, 155–56, 164, 247, 271
Hitchcock, Henry-Russell, Jr. 271
Holland, C. Anthony 207
Hoppin, William J. ("Civis") 14, 85, 86, 88–89, 115
Hôtel de Cluny, Paris 59, *59*, 155, 164, 174, 211
Howe, Julia Ward 204
    "Battle Hymn of the Republic" 206
Howland, Eliza N.Woolsey (wife of Joseph Howland) 12, 133,
    134, *134*
Howland, Joanna E. Hone (mother of Catharine Howland Hunt) 12,
    57, 75
Howland, Joseph (brother of Catharine Howland Hunt) 12, 82, 133,
    134, *134*, 192
Howland, Samuel S. (father of Catharine Clinton Howland Hunt)
    12, 57, 75, 283n.39
Hunt, Catharine Clinton Howland ("Kate," wife of RMH) 12, 75–76,
    78, *116*, 147, 191, 192, 232–33, 256, 260, 266–67, 299n.7
    assembles scrapbooks of RMH 195, 267, 285n.7
    biography of RMH 20, 76–77, 80, 81, 82, 131, 267, 285n.69
    character 75–76, 153, 266, 267
    death 266
    decorative arts involvement 117, 147, 151, 155, 164, 253, 267
    dressed as Catherine de' Medici for Vanderbilt costume ball
        166, *168*
    ill health 143, 152, 192
    lends items to exhibitions and museums 117, 181
    marriage to RMH and birth of children 76, 77, 80, 81, 266
    travels and tours *see under* Hunt, Richard Morris

Hunt, Catharine Howland ("Kitty," daughter of RMH) 12, 81, 190, 191, 246, 260, 266, 267, 283n.47

Hunt, Esther Morris, later Woolsey (daughter of RMH) 12, 81, 191, 232–33, 260, 266, 267, 283n.47

Hunt, Henry Leavitt ("Leav," brother of RMH) 12, 24, *27*, 28, *29*, 33, 37, 44, 48, 77, 82, 131, 153, 290n.16
    photograph of Temple of Olympian Zeus and the Acropolis *46*

Hunt, Herbert Leavitt (son of RMH) 12, 81, 191, 192, 260, 266, 267, 283n.47

Hunt, Jane M. ("Jennie" or "Jenney," sister of RMH) 12, *12*, 24, *27*, *29*, 37, 46, 48, 75–76, 77, 153, 278n.4

Hunt, Jane Maria Leavitt (mother of RMH) 12, *12*, 20, 23, 24, 27, 28–29, *29*, 34–35, 46, 48, 76, 152, 265
    portrait (probably by Gambardella) *26*
    portraits of children *27*

Hunt, Jonathan ("John" or "Jack," brother of RMH) 12, 24, 28, *47*, 47–48, 77, 142, 143, 279n.14, 289n.68

Hunt, Jonathan (grandfather of RMH) 12, 23

Hunt, Jonathan, Jr. (father of RMH) 12, 23, 24, 27, 55, 102, 281n.3

Hunt, Joseph Howland ("Dody" or "Joe," son of RMH) 12, 13, 57, 81, *95*, 192, 238, 260, 266, 267, 283n.47

Hunt, Katherine L. Jarvis (wife of Leavitt Hunt) 12, 77

Hunt, Louisa D. Perkins (wife of William M. Hunt) 74, 75, 152, 153

Hunt, Richard Howland ("Dickie" or "Dick," son of RMH) 12, 13, *56*, 57, 77, 80, 81, 88–89, 91, 98, *116*, 191, 201, 238, *238*, 260, 266, 267, 283n.47, 287n.37

Hunt, Richard Morris ("Dick")
    architectural career 19, 28, 49, 51, 81–82, 98–99, 249
        AIA co-founder and later President 17, 70, 71, 72, 192
        art collecting on commission 19, 169–70, 204, 211, 292n.35
        ateliers 67, *67*, 69, 70, 75, *207 see also* studios *below*
        awards and prizes *16*
            honorary LL.D, Harvard University 17, 256
            Légion d'Honneur *16*, 17, 184
            Royal Gold Medal, RIBA 17, 232, 254–55
        business cards *16*
        clubs 68, 76, 83, 181, 190, 206
        criticism 102–3, 111, 114, *118*, 119, 184, 208, 246, 256, 264, 282n.12
        École des Beaux-Arts 19, 37, 38, 39, 42–43, 44, 46, 53, 69, 84, 93, 280n.37 *see also under* "drawings" *under* " works" *below*
        influences
            Egyptian and Moorish architecture 97, 105, *106*, 127, *128*, 129, 147, 170, *173*, 181, 249, 301n.25
            French architecture 32, 43–44, 51, 60, 67, 69–70, *80*, 102, 108, 110, 119, 136, 160, 264, 280n.39
            Romanesque architecture 149, *150*, 151, 246, 247
        interior decoration 19, 53, 64, 88, 122, 124, 139, 157, 158, 163, 166, 192
        joint founder and member of Board of Trustees, Metropolitan Museum of Art 115, 259
        juror to architecture section, Exposition Universelle (1867) 89
        landscape architecture 19, 133, 211
        Louvre building inspector *16*, 49, 51, 52
        member of societies and academies 17, 68, 117–18, 177–79, 192, 237–38, 255–56 *see also* AIA *above*
        praise 103, 111, 163, 170, 187, 208, 230–31, 232, 246, 247, 254, 263–64, 268
        president of Board of Architects, World's Columbian Exposition (1893) 17, 249–50
        rejected designs 83, 84–86, 87, 98, 102, 105, 109, 115, 116, 147, 148, 151, 177, 200, 270
        reputation 19, 69, 151, 230–31, 246, 263–64, 268, 270, 272–73
        studio staff and assistants 98, 100, 110, 192, 207, 208, 249, 261, 287n.42
        studios 55, *56*, 69, 75, 100, 108, 142–43, 204, *204, 206 see also* Tenth Street Studio

teaches architecture 14, 15, 44, 69–70, 119, 127, 264, 285n.69
tradesmen and workers, relationship with 230, 264–65, *265*
views on compensation for creative input 64–65 *see also under* Parmly, Dr. Eleazer

biographical details
    appearance 31, 99–100, *200*
    birth and early life 17, 19, 21, 23, 270, 299n.13
    burial and memorial service 260–61, 264, 299n.13
    character 28, 52, 53, 76, 97, 100, *200*, 232, 266
    collections 21, 45, 47, *47*, 52, *56*, 57–58, *58*, 58–60, *59*, *81*, 89, 91, 99, 266, 267
    death 244, 260–61
    diaries 20, 33, *79*
    dressed as Cimabue for Vanderbilt costume ball 166, 168, *169*
    education 27, 28, 33, 34–35
    family 12, 23, 24
    homes 24, *25*, 27, 46, 69, *74*, 81, 192, 278n.4
    marriage and birth of children 76, 77, 80, 81, 266
    memorial in Central Park (French and Price) 268–69, *269*, *270*, 270–71
    obituaries 263
    poor health 31–32, 45, 75, 76, 77, 142–43, 192, 249, 250, 253, 255, 260
    travels and tours
        America 43, 76, 260
        England 43, 77, *78*, 190, 236, 244, 254, 297n.44
        Europe 20, 29, *29*, 30–35, 43–44, 45–46, 89, 91, 98, 143–44, 189–91
        Middle East 45, 119–20
        Norway 89, *95*, 97, 159, 242
        Paris 31–32, 35, 37, 77, 80, 88–89, 91, 102, 189, 236–37, 255 *see also* École des Beaux-Arts *above*

portraits, photographs and sculptures *29*, *66*, *78*, *238*
    Couture 21, 278n.6
    portrait bust (Gautherin and Barbedienne) *200*, 301n.31
    Sargent 246, 260, *262*
    sculpture as a stone mason (Buberl) *207*, 246, 297n.48

scrapbooks 21, 99, *194–97*, 267, 285n.7, 294n.1
    architects *197*
    candelabra designs for Breakers *194–95*
    capitals *197*
    country house planning schema *196*
    dining room chandelier for Breakers *196*
    Marble House stair landing *196*
    profile of hammer beam for Lawrence house *197*
    rendering for Ochre Court's Pompeian-style bathroom *197*
    sketch for New-York Historical Society museum *197*
    stained-glass cartoons (poss. Oudinot) *99*, 300n.6
    stained-glass window and dado for Vanderbilt house *196*

sketchbooks 45, *92–95*, 93, 285n.1
    Beau Séjour hotel, Lausanne *95*
    "Dody in paper cap" *95*
    family dogs in Paris *94*
    Fontainebleau *94*
    Hermitage de Madeleine, Fontainebleau *220*
    list of books purchased from Lenoir-Rapilly, Paris *95*
    measured drawing, Protestant Great Church, The Hague *95*, 135
    notes on Egypt *45*, *94*
    Palazzo Cavalli-Franchetti, Venice *94*
    patriotic banner *8*
    polychrome details (Rome) *93*
    Romanesque apse, Basilika St. Aposteln, Cologne *95*
    Tyristrand Kirke, Norway *95*, 159–60
    William "admiring Rubens picture Antwerp" *94*

works
    architecture *see under* clients; named architectural works
    bookplates *2*

drawings
  Bay of Angels, Nice *144–45*
  Briquet's school in Geneva 34
  entablature for Darier *36*
  from sketchbooks 45, *45*, *47*, *93-95*, *205*
drawings, École des Beaux-Arts *40–41*, 93
  Algerian series *22*, *41*, *42*, 192, 280n.35
  Archives of the National Audit Office *41*, 42
  iron bridge 39, *40*
  theater *40*
sculpture 80
  model of an ocelot *79*, *206*
  tomb memorials for father and brother 153, 261, 290n.15
watercolors 98, 192, 207
  École des Beaux-Arts assignments *40–41*, 42
writing 100
  Designs for the Gateways ... to the Central Park. 85, *85*, 86
  "History of Architecture" talk to AIA and essay 71–72, 100
see also architectural career *above*
Hunt, Samuel (great-grandfather of RMH) 24
Hunt, William Morris ("Bill," brother of RMH) 12, 13, 24, *27*, 28, 29, *29*, 34, 46, 117
  artistic career 35, 45, 48, 52, 69, 116–17, 119, 152
  art education 80
  painting 73–74
    La Marguerite 89, *121*, 300n.10
    Mother and Child 116, 117
  murals 152
  sculpture 300n.4
  studio at Hill-Top Cottage 75
  Talks on Art 117
  death and burial 152–53, 290n.15
  drawing of (RMH) *94*
  marriage 74, 75, 152
Hunt & Hunt 12, 267
Huntington, Collis P. and Arabella D. 98, 192
Huntington, Daniel
  portrait of Cornelius Vanderbilt II *224*
  portrait of William H. Aspinwall *12*

immigration, effects of 72, 98, 103, 177, 184, 193, 249, 273

Jacques Coeur house, Bourges, France 164, *223*
James, Henry 75, 91, 235, 246, 301n.37
Jenney, James Le Baron 193
Johnston, James B. 67, 68 *see also* Tenth Street Studio Building
Johnston, John T. 68, 115, 153, 259
Jules Allard Fils 13, 164, 166, *196*, 211, *214*, *222*, 225, 228, 231, 253, 291n.30

Kellum, John 163
Kendall, Edward H. 106
Klenze, Leo von 100, 102

La Farge, John 67, 75
Laboulaye, Édouard René Lefèbvre de 180, 181
Labrouste, P.-F. Henri 14, 39, 44, 61, 88, 100, 139, 260
Lawrence, Warrington G. 236
Leavitt family 12, 23, 24
Lefuel, Hector-Martin 14, 38, 43, 44, 49, *49*, 52, 64, 71, 77, 89, 100, 111, 156, 170, 193, 199, 222, 254, 255, 292n.36
Leighton, Sir Frederic 170, 293n.60
Lenoir, G. Félix 164, 291n.30
Lenox, James 14, *14*, 68, 101, 102, 110, 114, 119, 149, 286n.24
Lenox Library (RMH) 42, 100, *101*, 110–11, *111*, *113*, 114, 145, 147, 254, 260, 263, 268, 270, 272
  plans *112*
Leutze, Emanuel G. 45, 82
  portrait of William M. Hunt *27*
Lienau, Detlef 61, 156–57
Lincoln, Abraham 17, 83, *116*

Little Moreton Hall, Cheshire, England 201, *201*
Louis XIV, king of France 33, 34
  bust of *196*, 222
Louis-Napoléon Bonaparte *see* Napoléon III
Louis-Philippe, king of France 13, 30, 37, 48, 156
Louvre, Paris 14, *16*, 49, *49*, *50*, 51, 64, 77, 156, 292n.36

Marble House, Newport *see under* Vanderbilt, Alva Erskine Smith
Marcotte, Léon A. (L. Marcotte & Co., New York) 14, 61, 122, *122*, 154, *156*, 156–57, *157*, 211, 290n.21, 301n.25
Marie Antoinette, queen of France 37, 158, *164*, 166, 217, *217*, 228, 232, 236, 253
Marquand, Frederick 130–31, 149
Marquand, Henry G. and Elizabeth A. 14, 89, 119, 130, 138, 149, 169, *170*, 181, 211, 257, 268, 283n.34, 294n.13, 297n.37
  Linden Gate, Newport (RMH) 14, 138
  Madison Avenue house (RMH) 170, *170–71*, 174
    interiors 170, 172, *173*, 292n.36, 301n.25
    plans *172*
Mason, George C. 14, 33, 140
Masqueray, Emmanuel L. *194–95*, 208, 224, 267, 305
Massachusetts Institute of Technology (MIT) 15, 70, 174, 251
Matteawan (Beacon), New York
  Howland Circulating Library (RMH) 133, 134–35, *136*, *137*
  Presbyterian Church (RMH) 133, 134
  see also Tioronda
McCosh, James 149, 151
McKim, Charles F. 14, *14*, 255, 260, 261
McKim, Mead & White 14, 142, 170, 208, 236
Metropolitan Fair, New York (1864) 82, 131
  patriotic banners (RMH) *8*, 82
Metropolitan Museum of Art, New York (Vaux and Mould) 14, 15, 20, 68, 102, 103, 114, 115–17, 119, 166, 169, 211, 218, 224, 225, 268, 271–73, 300n.18, 301n.23
  Fifth Avenue entrance (RMH) 257, *257*, *258–59*, 259–60, 264, 267–68
Millet, Jean-François 48, 80, 117
Mills, Ogden 191, 207
Minturn, Robert B. and Anna M. Wendell 84
Morland, Dr. William W. 14
  houses in Back Bay, Boston (RMH) 73, *73*, 75, 103, 120
Morris, Gouverneur 23, 30
Morton, Levi P. and Anna L.R. 14, *14*, 201, 246, 257, 287n.32
  Ellerslie, Rhinecliff (RMH) 200, 201, *201*, *202*
    interior *203*, 204
    plan of first floor *203*
Mould, Jacob Wrey 65, 84, 102, 115–16, 186
  Metropolitan Museum of Art 115
Municipal Art Society, New York 255, 267, 268–70, 272

Napoléon I, Emperor of France 30, 33, 37, 42
Napoleon III, Emperor of France 14, 30, 48–49, 51, 86, 89, 144, 176, 180, 292n.36
National Academy of Design, New York 51, 67, 83, 84, 117, 123, 151, 181
New York Central Railroad 15, 55
New York City 19, 28, 37, 51, *54*, 55, 60, 61, 64, 65, 67, 69, 72, 81, 83, 86, 98, 108–9, 153
  lack of museums and libraries 68, 82, 98, 109–10, 114–15
  public library (RMH) 57, 236, 272
  see also Central Park; Metropolitan Museum; Statue of Liberty
New York Times 114, 185, 260, 263, 266, 267
New York Times tower (Post) *107*
New York World tower (Post) *107*
Newport, Rhode Island 14, 33, 68, 74–75, 81, 110, 204, 206
  artist colonies 75
  Bellevue Avenue 75, 138, 211, 217
    Travers block 140, 142, *142*
  The Casino (McKim, Mead & White) 142
  houses designed and remodeled by RMH 32, 73, 87–88, 140
    see also named houses

Island Cemetery *187*, 261, 267
  Ochre Point 140, 224
  Town and Country Club 204, 206
  Trinity Church 260–61
New-York Evening Post 13, 57, 85
New-York Historical Society 83
  Museum 115, *197*
New-York Sun building *107*
New-York Tribune 30, 85, 86, 107, 108, 125–26, 186
New-York Tribune building (RMH) *54*, 106, 107, *107*, 108–9, 147,
  263, 268, 272, 286n.21
Norton, Charles Eliot 14, 256, 299n.70

Ochre Court, Newport *see under* Goelet, Ogden
Olmsted, Frederick Law 14, 15, 68, 83–84, 86, 115, 127, 134, 152,
  206, 235, *238*, 249, 271
  Biltmore, Asheville, North Carolina *see under* Vanderbilt,
    George W.
  Busk House, Indian Spring *see under* Busk, Joseph
  Ochre Court, Newport *see under* Goelet, Ogden
  see also Central Park; Vanderbilt family mausoleum
Osborn, William H. and Virginia S. 89, 118–19, 287n.38
  house on Fourth (Park) Avenue (RMH) *118*, 119, 154
Oudinot de la Faverie, Eugène-Stanislas 14, *99*, 166, 170, 191,
  291n.31, 300n.6
  Field of the Cloth of Gold window for Vanderbilt house (with
    Bayard) 166, *167*, 301n.24
Ouradou, Maurice-A.-G. *242*, 301n.39

Paris *31*, 31–32, 33, 37, 46–49, 51–52, 77, 80, 84, 89, 91,
  143–44, 147
  Commune riots *96*, 142, 143, *143*, 174
  see also Expositions Universelles
Paris Opera House (Garnier) 14, 39, 144, 222, 224, *224*, 225, 251,
  253, 286n.10
Parmly, Dr. Eleazer 15, *15*, 61, 64
  sued by Hunt for architect's fees 64–65, 282n.12, 282n.13
Pavillon de la Bibliothèque, Louvre (Lefuel with Hunt) *50*, 51, 77,
  192, 255, 281n.48
Paxton, Joseph 43
Peabody & Stearns 140, 224
Perry, Commodore Matthew 125
  memorial, Touro Park, Newport (RMH and Ward) 125–26, *126*,
    288n.47
Philadelphia 14, 15, 43, 55, 65, 69, 102, 140, *260 see also*
  Centennial International Exhibition
Pilgrim memorial, Central Park (RMH and Ward) *179*, 179–80
Pinchot, James W. 89, 287n.32, 297n.49
Porter, Benjamin: portraits of William K. and Alva Vanderbilt *158*
Post, George B. 15, 69, 86, 98, 100, 102, 106, *107*, 108, 109, 145,
  147, 248, 249, 261, 270, 286n.11
poverty, violence and 19, 49, 174, *175*, 176, 217, 253, 271, 272
Presbyterian Hospital, Madison and Fourth (Park) Avenue, New
  York (RMH) *101*, 102–3, 109, 110, 111, *111*, 286n.11
Price, Bruce 199–200, 218
  memorial to RMH (with French) 268–69, *269*, 270–71
Princeton Theological Seminary: faculty houses and Lenox Library
  (RMH) 149
Princeton University 102, 149, 151
  Marquand Chapel (RMH) 149, *150*, 151
Protestant Great Church, The Hague *95*, 135
Protestantism and Protestant values 33, 48, 61, 151, 168, 177,
  179, *179*
Providence, Rhode Island 75
  office building (RMH) 103

race and racism 19, 82, 131, 136, 174, 273
Reiber, Émile-Auguste 59, 166
Reid, Whitelaw 107, 108, 286n.18, 286n.21
Renwick, James, Jr. 76, 192

Richardson, Henry H. 15, 73, 105, 119, 121–22, 139, 143, 147, 151–52,
  166, 246, 263, 264, 290n.12
"Richardsonian Romanesque" 15, 151, 246
Roosevelt family 68, 83, 153
Rossiter, Thomas P. 33, 51–52, 61, 69, 98
  New York home and studio (RMH) 52, 61, *61*, *62–63*, 64, 65, 102
Rothschild, Baron Ferdinand de 236–37
  Waddesdon, Buckinghamshire, England 236, *237*, 240
Royal Institute of British Architects (RIBA): Royal Gold Medal
  awarded to RMH 17, 232, 254–55
Ruskin, John 60, 61, 73, 86, 88, 116, 129, 256
  The Stones of Venice 83
Russell, Charles H. (brother-in-law of Catharine Howland Hunt) 12,
  77, 84, 177, 247

Sandier, Alexandre 164, 166, 291n.30
Sargent, John Singer 235
  portrait of George W. Vanderbilt *235*
  portrait of Joseph H. Choate *13*
  portrait of Olmsted 246
  portrait of RMH 246, 260, *262*
Schinkel, Karl Friedrich 89, 91, 100, 102, 260
Schuyler, Montgomery 15, 64, 88, 98, 103, 114, 119, 132, 164, 182,
  184, 208, 225, 242, 251, 297n.43
Sedgwick, Catharine M. 27–28
Seventh Regiment, New York Militia *56*, 76
  monument in Central Park (RMH and Ward) 125, *125*, *126*,
    126–27
Shepard, Elliott F. 186
  casket tomb, Staten Island (RMH) 293n.56
Skull and Bones society, Yale University 127, 138
skyscrapers 19, 106
Society of Decorative Art, New York 117, 151, 164, 267, 287n.37
Soissons, Count S.C. de 230–31, 251
Sommerard, Alexandre du and Edmond du 59, 60, 89, 155–56
South Kensington Museum, London (later Victoria and Albert
  Museum) 43, 68–69, 115, 117, 228
Spitzer, Frédéric 211
St. Mark's Episcopal Church, Islip, New York (RMH) 159, 160
  interior *160*, *161*
Statue of Liberty (Bartholdi, Eiffel and Viollet-le-Duc) *54*, *146*,
  180, 180–82, *182*, 189, *196*, 261
  pedestal (RMH) 181–83, 254, 264
Stevens, Paran and Marietta R. 103, 105
Stevens House apartment building, New York (RMH) 103, 105, 114
Stewart, Alexander T. 15, 188
  department store, Broadway, New York (Trench & Snook)
    60–61
  house, Thirty-Fourth Street, Fifth Avenue, New York *60*,
    163, 168
Stillman, William J. 68, 281n.50
Stowe, Harriet Beecher 13
  The American Woman's Home (with C.E. Beecher) 158–59
Sturges, Jonathan 118–19
Sturgis, Russell, Jr. 15, *15*, 68, 129, 174, 180
Stuyvesant, Rutherfurd 103, 108
Stuyvesant Apartments, New York (RMH) 103, *104*, 263, 272
Sullivan, Louis 70, 100, 163–64, 254

Tenth Street Studio building, New York (RMH) 65, *66*, 67–68, 69,
  70, 75, 76, 145, 263, 272, 282n.19
Thomas, Griffith *60*, 61
Ticknor, George 15, *15*, 28–29, 30, 35, 52, 119
Tiffany, Charles L.: house on Madison Avenue (McKim, Mead &
  White) 170
Tioronda, Matteawan, New York 134
  music pavilion (RMH) with organ by Johnson & Son 134, *134*,
    135, 136
Travers, William R. 139–40
  commercial block, Bellevue Avenue, Newport (RMH) 140,
    142, *142*

house at Ochre Point, Newport (remodeled by Hunt) 140
Trinity Church, Boston (Richardson) 151, 166
Trinity Church, Broadway, New York (Upjohn) 60, 75, 126
Tuckerman, Henry T. 15, 68, 82
Tudor Revival 170, 204, *241*
Tuileries, Paris 49, 51, 89, 156

Union League Club, New York City 83, 114–15, 117, 147, 181
Unitarianism 14, 25, 27, 28, 52, 68, 69, 151
United States Military Academy, West Point *see* West Point
University Building (Town, Davis & Dakin), Washington Square,
    New York (RMH's studio) 55, *56*, 60, 69, 75, 192
University Club, New York City 190
Upjohn, Richard 15, 53, 60, 65, 69, 70, 76, 88, 147
US Capitol, Washington, DC (RMH and Walter) 65, 185, *185*

Van Brunt, Henry 15, 44, 69, 76, 144, 256, 285n.69
Van Rensselaer, Mariana A. Griswold 77, 168, 240
Van Rensselaer Building, Broadway, New York City (RMH) *106*, 147
Vanderbilt, Alva Erskine Smith (wife of William K. Vanderbilt) 15,
    105, 117, 159, 162, 164, 174, 193, *196*, 217, 222, 231, 232, 236,
    246, 260, 261, 266, 271, 295n.16, 299n.6
  house on Fifth Avenue (RMH) 162, *162*, 164, *165*, 166, 168,
      230–31, 238, 246, 263, 266, 268, 271, 272
    costume ball (1883) 166, *168*, *169*
    exterior 208
    Field of the Cloth of Gold window (Oudinot and Bayard) 166,
        167, 301n.24
    interiors *18*, 164, *165*, 166, *167*, *196*, 291n.31, 301n.24
    plans *163*
  Idle Hour, Islip, New York (RMH) 159
  Marble House, Newport (RMH) 15, *196*, 217, 218–24, *222*, *223*,
      230–31, 233, 237, 246, 266, 295n.24
    elevations *216–17*
    exterior 218, *220*
    interior 218
    plans *221*
      landscape plan *219*
  portrait (Porter) *158*, 222
Vanderbilt, Consuelo (Duchess of Marlborough, later Balsan) 15,
    266, 291n.24
Vanderbilt, Cornelius 15, 24, 55, 57, 159, 162
Vanderbilt, Cornelius, II and Alice C. Gwynne 15, 68, 77, 86, 166,
    181, *224*, 224–25, 232, 255, 261
  the Breakers, Newport (RMH) 15, 17, 77, 224–31, 246, 271,
      295n.24
    exterior 225, *225*
    interior *194–95*, *196*, 225, 228, *228*, *229–30*, 232, 295n.25,
        302–3
    plans *226–27*
  house on Fifth Avenue (RMH) 162
  portrait (Huntington) *224*
Vanderbilt, George W. 15, 99, 189, *200*, 233, 235–36, 246, 261,
    264, *270*, 271
  Biltmore estate, Asheville, North Carolina (RMH and Olmsted)
      15, *44*, 86, 189, 233, 235–45, 246, 267
    Biltmore Village 242, *244*
      All Souls Episcopal Church 242, *245*, 271
    exterior *239*, *243*, *261*
    interior *198*, 240, *240*, *241–42*, *274*
    park and nature preserve with lagoon 238, *238*, 242, *243*
    plan of first floor *239*
  portrait (Sargent) *235*
  travels to Europe with RMH 236–37, 244, 297n.44
Vanderbilt, William H. 15, 159, 162, 188–89
  house, Fifth Avenue (RMH) 162
Vanderbilt, William K. 15, 159, 163, 166, 191
  house, Fifth Avenue *see under* Vanderbilt, Alva Erskine Smith
  Marble House *see under* Vanderbilt, Alva Erskine Smith
  portrait (Porter) *158*
Vanderbilt family mausoleum, Staten Island, New York (RMH and
    Olmsted) *188*, 188–89, *189*

"Vanderbilt Style" 231
Vaux, Calvert 15, 68, 83, 84, 86, 103, 115, 127
  Beechwood, Newport (with Downing) 211, 217
  Metropolitan Museum of Art 115, 259
  see also Central Park
Venice 33, 45, 46, *94*, 126, 251
Vermont 12, 14, 21, 23–24, 77, 110, 152, 153, 201
Versailles 37, 166, 184, 218, *222*, 231, 272
  Petit Trianon 217, 231, 266
Viollet-le-Duc, Eugène E. 15, *15*, 37, 39, 42, 71, 102, 135, 144, *145*,
    148, 156, 181, 240, 301n.39
  Entretiens sur l'architecture 144, 151
Visconti, Louis T.J. 37, 49, *49*, 156

Walter, Thomas U. 15, 43, 69, 172, 174
  US Capitol, Washington, DC 65
Ward, John Q.A. 15, 115, 118, 123, *125*, 184, 186, 256, 268
  collaboration with Hunt on public monuments 17, 74, 100,
      124–27, *126*, *179*, 179–80, *183*, 183–84
  house-studios (RMH) 124, *125*
    elevation *6*, *124*
Ware, William R. 15, 69, 70, 256, 282n.25
Washington, Booker T. 131, 264
Washington, DC 27, 76, 185, 260
  US Capitol, Washington, DC (RMH and Walter) 65, 185, *185*
  US Naval Observatory (RMH) 249, *250*, 256–57
Washington Square, New York 55, *56*, 57, 69, 75, 192
Webster, Daniel 15, *15*, 20, 24–25, 27, 28, 29, 53, 278n.6
Weehawken gallery, New Jersey (RMH) 67
Wells, Joseph 64, 65
Wells, William 25, 27
West Point (United States Military Academy) 35, 102
  Academic Hall (RMH) 247, *248*, 248–49
  gym (RMH) 248
  library renovation and guardhouse (RMH and RHH) 249
Western Association of Architects (WAA) 70, 192
Western Union Telegraph Building (Post) 109, 147
Wetmore, George P. and Edith K.: Chateau-sur-Mer, Newport
    (remodeled by Hunt) 139, *140*, *141*, 208, 289n.65
Wetmore, William S.: Chateau-sur-Mer, Newport (Bradford) 138
Wharton, Edith J. 105, 155, 228, 230, 235, 246
  The Age of Innocence 153
  The Decoration of Houses (with Codman) 158, 296n.27
Wheeler, Candace T. 117
Whigs 19, 24, 25, 52, 82, 281n.2
Whitney, Gertrude Vanderbilt 232–33
Wight, Peter B. 15, 19, 83, 264
Winckelmann, Johann J. 88, 97
Winthrop, Egerton L. 154–55
  Winthrop-Bronson house, Murray Hill, New York (RMH) 154–55,
      155, 231
    interiors *156*, *157*, 157–58, 296n.30
Winthrop, Theodore W. 15, 46, 51, 57, 68, 76, 82, 98
  Cecil Dreeme (novel) 57, 68
Withers, Frederick C. 134
Wooster Street apartment building (RMH) 103
World's Columbian Exposition (1893), Chicago *4*, 17, 152, 249–50,
    251, 253, 255, 256, 273
  Administration Building *4*, 246, 251, *252–53*, 257, 259
Wright, William 67, 68, 282n.22
Wynne, Dr. James 57, 58

Yale College (later University) 27, 138
  Marquand Chapel (RMH) *129*, 130
  Scroll and Key Hall (RMH) 127, *128*, 129
Yorktown, Virginia, battle of 37, 74
  Yorktown column (Hunt, Ward and Van Brunt) 74, 100, *183*,
      183–84, 264, 293n.51
    Légion d'Honneur awarded to Hunt for *16*, 17, 184

About the Author

Sam Watters writes about cultural movements that shaped American art, architecture, and landscape before World War II. His first book in association with the Library of Congress, *Gardens for a Beautiful America 1895–1935: Photographs by Frances Benjamin Johnston* (2012), won the Botanical and Horticultural Libraries Annual Literature Award. He studied at Yale University and the University of Marseilles.

Lunch at Alva Vanderbilt's
1882 dining hall, New York City,
during its 1927 demolition